Human Reproduction, Emerging Technologies, and Conflicting Rights

Human Reproduction, Emerging Technologies, and Conflicting Rights

Robert Blank
University of Canterbury

Janna C. Merrick
University of South Florida

A Division of Congressional Quarterly Inc.
Washington, D.C.

Library of Congress Cataloging-in-Publication Data

Blank, Robert H.
   Human reproduction, emerging technologies, and conflicting rights
/ Robert H. Blank, Janna C. Merrick.
     p.   cm.
   Includes bibliographical references and index.
   ISBN 0-87187-938-7 (pbk. : alk. paper)
   1. Human reproductive technology--Moral and ethical aspects.
2. Human reproductive technology--Government policy.   I. Merrick,
Janna C.   II. Title.
RG133.5.B576   1995
176--dc20   95-10455
                                                        CIP

For Bill and Carla Merrick

Contents

Tables, Figures, and Box

Tables

Figures

Box

Foreword

The media are full of reports about scientific breakthroughs in the technology associated with human reproduction. Creating a human life *in vitro* is no longer front page news; newer technologies such as fetal surgery now grab the headlines. The secrets of the womb are secrets no more, and the fetus is now widely recognized as having patient status separate from its mother. Newspaper columnists and talk show hosts marvel at the great benefits such technology brings to society, and for the most part the results of emerging reproductive technology have been positive.

Like political revolutions,scientific revolutions, however, are not without negative side effects as well. Our society is being thrust into new conceptualizations of when and how we reproduce as a species, and this revolution has entered a political arena that is ill-equipped to deal with it.

The revolution in human reproduction is not one just of changing technology. Rather it is a mechanism by which we define ourselves as human beings—as parents, children, brothers, and sisters. And these definitions are no longer clear. In cases of surrogate motherhood, for example, who is the mother? The surrogate who provides one-half the genetic makeup of the child and who gestates the fetus, or the biological father's wife who is the anticipated social mother? Who are the siblings? We will get differing answers from persons such as William Stern and Mary Beth Whitehead, the biological parents of Baby M, the most publicized surrogacy case of what seems to be an unending series.

The massive social and scientific changes in human reproduction have in many instances introduced third parties into what was originally an act of sexual intimacy, usually between married partners. As we redefine human reproduction, we simultaneously redefine the family and parenthood, and as such redefinition occurs, third party actors come to perceive that they, too, have decision-making rights. Such actors include government agencies; health care providers; business ventures, such as in vitro clinics or surrogacy brokerage firms; and family members. Such a diversity of actors leads invariably to conflict, and the American political system has not responded adequately to these conflicts.

In the area of reproductive policy, the political agenda is in great flux. New issues arise quickly with each emerging technology, and legislative bodies do not deal adequately with the situation because change rather than stability is the norm. When conflicts arise in this vacuum of statutory policy, issues and actors are thrust into the courts—the only policy-making institution available to resolve disputes in the absence of statutory law. This has led to a quagmire of diverse and often contradictory public policy.

Blank and Merrick address the issues in emerging reproductive policy in a direct and forceful way. Chapter one provides an indepth analysis of the nature of rights—both negative and positive. Individual chapters are devoted to abortion, sterilization, assisted reproduction, surrogate motherhood, prenatal interventions, conflict in the maternal-fetal relationship, fetal and embryo research, and care of critically ill newborns. In each chapter, the authors provide a sophisticated synthesis of clinical and policy analysis, focusing on the speed at which the clinical procedures have changed and on how such change has created conflict among individuals, families, and institutions.

Arthur L. Caplan

Acknowledgments

The authors owe numerous debts to numerous people. Brenda Carter and Ann O'Malley at CQ Press provided excellent editorial guidance. Henry Glick (Florida State University), Joel Grossman (University of Wisconsin), and Deborah McFarlane (University of New Mexico) made very helpful suggestions after reviewing the first draft of the book. Lainie Sue Ross (University of Chicago) and Dana Johnson (University of Minnesota) handled a number of clinical questions. Any errors, however, belong to the authors.

Bob would like to thank Jill Dolby and Philippa Greenman at the University of Canterbury for their excellent work in typing and processing his chapters, and Janna owes the same gratitude to Lynn Gilmore at the University of South Florida. Janna would also like to thank Greg and Brenda Geoghagen who served as "surrogate parents" for her son during the last few weeks of writing as well as Dean David Schenck, her mentor and friend, who provided both university and moral support for this project. Finally, Bob and Janna would like to thank their families, Mallory, Jeremy, Mai-Ling, and Maigin Blank and Christopher Merrick for their patience and cooperation.

Reproductive Rights: Ethical and Policy Context

In Australia, a 16-month-old girl is introduced to her baby sister, who was conceived through in vitro fertilization at the same time as she but had been frozen as an embryo and stored for two years. In South Africa and also in South Dakota, grandmothers serve as surrogate mothers and give birth to their daughters' children. In Italy postmenopausal women become pregnant in their late fifties. In Tennessee, a divorced couple fights over custody of seven frozen embryos, in a case that ultimately is decided by the state Supreme Court, and in France a widow goes to court to obtain the right to have a child using the embryo that had been fertilized, frozen, and stored before her husband died. In the United States, a prisoner demands that he be allowed, as a matter of right, to have a child with his partner on the outside, using artificial insemination.

Seldom does a day pass that there are not news reports focusing on complex events in the area of human reproduction. In the Baby M case, the New Jersey Supreme Court rules that commercial surrogacy contracts are unenforceable. Michigan passes legislation prohibiting such contracts. In California, a lesbian who is breaking up with her lover sues for ''paternity'' rights to the child produced by insemination of the lover with donor sperm. In Florida, a woman who admits to having used cocaine during her pregnancies is convicted of delivering a controlled substance to her children through the umbilical cord. In Bloomington, Indiana, a newborn with Down's syndrome dies after his parents refuse surgery to correct a defective esophagus. In Washington, D.C., a court approves an order requiring that a cesarean section be performed on an unwilling cancer patient who is twenty-six weeks pregnant and near death. Both mother and daughter die before the order is overturned.

Such events have created important ethical and public policy dilemmas, most of which have not been adequately addressed by policy makers. They also challenge conventional notions of reproductive rights because increasingly complicated technologies of reproduction have brought many third parties into the procreative process. There is no doubt that a dynamic transformation of biomedical capabilities is under way, especially in the areas of genetics and reproduction. Rapid advances in prenatal diagnosis and therapy are now joined with reproduction-assisting technologies such as in vitro fertilization and increasingly precise genetic tests. These technologies, combined with the expanding knowledge of fetal development and the causes of congenital illness, are altering society's perception of the relationships between parents and children. The challenge to prevailing values posed by the new biology has created novel policy issues that are the subject of frequently acrimonious debates.

The purpose of this chapter is to provide a framework for studying reproductive rights in this rapidly changing social and technological environment. An examination of the concept of reproductive rights includes a discussion of the problems created by using a rights approach in a pluralistic society. The progressive expansion of reproductive rights in the United States is also traced. A discussion of the constitutional protections afforded individuals in matters of procreation and childrearing is followed by an examination of the social, legal, and technological forces that challenge parental choice. This is followed by an analysis of the policy process, with an emphasis on policy formulation. Although reproduction has until recent decades been largely a private matter, it has always had clear public implications. Recent developments in a variety of areas have put reproductive issues on the public agenda, thus requiring responses by political institutions. The chapter ends with a brief discussion of the future role of government in clarifying reproductive rights.

The Concept of Reproductive Rights

An emphasis on individual rights is central to liberal democratic theories which have at their base a concern for the individual in society. Rights are "valuable commodities" (Wasserstrom 1964, 629) because to claim that one has a right is to demand or to insist that one's claim be recognized. In philosopher Joel Feinberg's view, the rightsholder is not dependent on beneficent treatment by others, or on "gifts and services and favors motivated by love or pity or mercy for which gratitude is the sole fitting response" (1980, 142). To the contrary, a claim of rights calls for dutiful actions by others that the rightsholder can demand without shame or embarrassment and without the constant expression of gratitude.

Rights are thus entitlements both to do, have, omit, or be something and to demand that others act or refrain from acting in certain ways. These entitlements, or claims, impose correlative duties on others in society, thus increasing the potential for conflict. The translation and application of moral principles of rights to legally articulated and binding rights involves problems of interpretation, consistency, and authority that in large part must be resolved within a specific constitutional or legal system that itself is in a constant state of development.

From the earliest attempts to lay the foundations of natural rights theory to current attempts to apply the language of rights to reproductive issues, rights have been problematic. Essentially, a rights approach raises three questions pertaining to its ultimate value in resolving conflicts: (1) What constitutes a right? (2) Who has rights? and (3) How should conflicts among rightsholders over rights be resolved?

What Constitutes a Right?

Many of the most volatile political issues are raised by differing interpretations of rights and the relative weights accorded them. Although natural rights theorists attempted to enumerate immutable rights, and some contemporary observers assert the existence of absolute rights that all persons share by virtue of being human, rights are primarily legal constructs that exist within a particular constitutional or legal framework. The language of rights, therefore, must be interpreted according to a complex set of social values and institutions existing in a specific time and place. Although there is no such thing as an absolute, unchangeable natural right, this definition of rights is the basis of the American governmental system.

One basic distinction to be made is that between negative rights and positive rights. Negative rights impose obligations on others to refrain from interfering with the rights bearer. The seventeenth-century English philosopher John Locke placed almost exclusive emphasis on the obligation of government to refrain from interfering with an individual's life, liberty, or property. Each person thus has a sphere of autonomy that others cannot violate, but no one is further obliged to take positive action to provide that person with life, liberty, or property. In other words, a person is entitled to protection of certain rights but has no claims on others.

Positive rights impose an obligation on others (such as society) to provide the goods and services necessary for each individual to have at least a minimally decent level of existence.

A positive right is a right to other persons' positive actions; a negative right is a right to other persons' omissions or forebearances. For every positive right I have, someone else has a duty to do something;

for every negative right I have, someone else has a duty to refrain from doing something. (Feinberg 1973, 59)

Although the necessary level of positive rights is not clearly defined, this additional dimension requires the existence of institutions that guarantee a certain level of material well-being, through the redistribution of goods and services if necessary. Tom Beauchamp and James Childress (1979, 51) suggest that "much confusion in moral discourse about public policies governing biomedicine" can be traced to the failure to distinguish positive rights from negative rights. The negative rights approach suggests that the state is a referee among competing interests whose duty is to ensure that the natural rights of all are protected, whereas the positive rights approach implies the need for positive action by the state to provide for the welfare of its citizens. Those who focus exclusively on negative rights attack positive rights as being an unjustified restriction on the liberty of those asked to take positive action to protect the rights of others.

Reproductive rights can have many aspects (see Figure 1-1); thus, there is the potential for even more disagreement as to what limits, if any, should be set and where. In general, reproductive rights can include: (1) a right not to have children; (2) a right to have children; and (3) a right to make decisions concerning the quality and quantity of children. Because each category has many manifestations and variations, there is a need for clarification and, to some degree, the setting of boundaries. People's opinions regarding the technological and policy developments discussed in this book depend in large part on how they view these categories of rights and how broadly they are willing to define reproductive rights.

Some observers link the right not to have children with the right to have children (Brodribb 1984; Robertson 1983); others argue that we should not assume that there is any "ethical, political, or logical symmetry" between the two (Overall 1987, 168). Christine Overall contends that the right not to reproduce is a legitimate one and that a woman has no moral obligation to have a child against her will. Women who do not have access to contraceptive devices and abortion services are, as a result of "biological 'destiny'," victims "of a sort of reproductive slavery" (1987, 167). Although a woman, therefore, cannot legitimately be required to procreate, this right not to reproduce neither implies a right to reproduce nor follows from a right to reproduce, according to Overall. According to Sara Ann Ketchum, the asymmetry between the right not to reproduce and the right to reproduce is that the decision to reproduce involves other persons—at a minimum the person to be produced and the other biological parent. "Thus, the claim of a privacy right to reproduce is a claim to the right to make decisions about

Figure 1-1 Defining Reproductive Rights

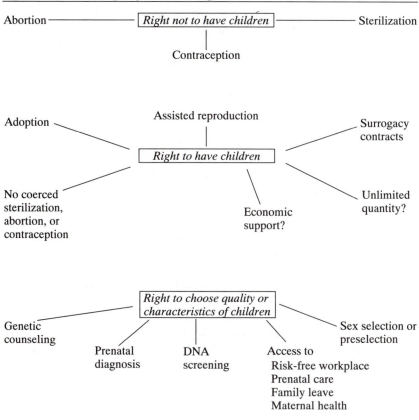

other people's lives, and those people's rights and interests must be weighed on the balance'' (1992, 292). On similar grounds, Sarah Boone rejects the argument that women have a right to enter into surrogacy contracts (1992, 349).

Overall argues that if there is a right to reproduce, then such a right is necessarily limited, if for no other reason than to protect innocent people (1987, 168). Whereas the right not to have children is absolute, the right to have children, if it exists, is necessarily ''hedged with qualifications,'' just as other rights are. Overall also makes a distinction between weak (negative) rights and strong (positive) rights and is concerned that acceptance of the right to reproduce as an entitlement allowing women to be given all necessary assistance to reproduce, using any technique of reproduction, may contribute to the ''commodication of children and to the misappropriation of women's reproductive capacities'' (1987, 170).

Who Has Rights?

The second question raised by a rights approach is, who qualifies as a person with moral and legal claims on others in society? In other words, what characteristics are necessary to achieve personhood? If, as Norman Bowie and Robert Simon (1977) contend, rights give us basic human dignity and allow us to respect persons, then the definition of "person" is crucial. Society has always set arbitrary requirements, such as age or socioeconomic status, for rights that are considered basic. Voting is considered a citizen's fundamental right and necessary to protect one's interests, yet there is a lack of universal agreement concerning the criteria necessary for the exercise of this "fundamental" right.

Although problems have always been encountered in attempts to define the qualifications necessary to claim certain rights, in the context of biomedical technology it is becoming increasingly difficult to define human life. At what stage does the developing human organism become a person for the purpose of being afforded rights? Is it conception, or viability, or birth, or some point after birth? Furthermore, are certain characteristics (such as a "near normal" genetic profile or an average IQ) considered the minimum requirement for achieving personhood? The decisions made concerning these questions go far to explain how individuals approach a broad range of reproductive issues. Someone who believes that an eight-cell human embryo has rights has little in common, from a rights perspective, with an individual who believes that personhood, and thus possession of rights, begins only with the live birth of the infant.

Resolving Conflicts over Rights

The language of rights is often presented as straightforward, thus allowing choices. Unfortunately, the converse is more accurate: because of the questions of how rights should be defined and who should have them, the rights discourse always produces conflict. First, the lack of clear hierarchies or priorities of rights results in a conflict between the rights themselves (freedom of the press versus the right of the accused to a fair trial).

A second, often overlapping conflict can arise between the rights of two individuals. (Who has the valid claim to parenthood—the genetic father or the surrogate mother who decides to keep her baby?) As discussed earlier, this conflict is complicated with regard to many reproductive issues by the lack of consensus as to what the right to reproduction includes and whether a fetus has rights that might contradict the right to privacy of a pregnant woman. As rights have expanded from the right not to have children to the right to have children and to control their characteristics, the concept of rights has become more problematic and therefore possibly impractical as the basis for reproductive policy. Moreover, the introduction of third parties to the procreative process has multiplied areas of potential conflict. Because reproduction is so basic to human existence and so relevant to family structure, the status of women, and the common perception of others in society, the inevitable conflicts tend to be volatile. An emphasis on rights naturally leads to conflict among various groups that, perceiving themselves as having rights, intensify their demands for public action to protect them. This conflict explains why reproductive issues are so complex, volatile, and politically sensitive in contemporary American society.

Because of these problems, a number of observers reject reproductive rights as the framework for making policy in the area of human reproduction. Helen Holmes criticizes the "unfortunate use" of reproductive rights because "when everyone claims rights for one or another entity, a nonproductive competition between rights arises" (1992, xi). Sheryl Ruzek concurs, asserting that we must move beyond the individual rights model because it is bound to be divisive and unproductive in the attempts of society to resolve the issues raised by reproductive technologies (1991, 83). Gena Corea attacks the use of "reproductive rights" by "antifeminist reproductive engineers" to obscure the impact of new technologies on women as a class (1985a, 313).

Thomas Shevory uses a custody case that concerned seven frozen embryos to show how easy it is to manipulate the emphasis on reproductive rights in the legal context and expresses grave reservations about the utility of the rights argument in deciding reproductive matters (1992, 239). Furthermore, rights are particularly indeterminate and unsettled in the context of rapid technological change (240). Similarly, Mark Tushnet contends that the rights approach is indeterminate in that it does not provide an established standard for the equitable allocation of claims in the legal and political contexts in which it is often advanced (1984, 1371).

Despite genuine concern over the "rhetoric of rights" in framing reproductive policy issues, they will continue to be fought in a legal, if not moral, context in which the rights argument will be invoked. The imprecision and inconsistency inherent in the rights argument notwithstanding, its terms have become part of the public debate over reproduction. The rights approach will no doubt continue to influence public opinion on reproductive issues and public policy in the United States. Nevertheless, its predominance must not exclude consideration of other frameworks.

Reproductive Rights in the United States

All societies place some limits on reproductive rights; in most western countries, however, procreation is viewed as a fundamental right necessary for the survival of the individual. The United Nation's Universal Declaration of Human Rights (1948) emphasizes the right to marry and to found a family "without limitation due to race, nationality or religion" (Article 16); it states that mothers and children are entitled to special care and assistance (Article 25). Article 16 states that the family is the natural and fundamental group unit of society and is entitled to protection by society and the state. Moreover, the United Nation's Declaration of the Rights of the Child, adopted in 1959, states:

> The child shall enjoy the benefits of social security. He shall be entitled to grow and develop in health; to this end, special care and protection shall be provided both to him and his mother, including adequate pre-natal and post-natal care. The child shall have the right to adequate nutrition, housing, recreation and medical services.

In the United States, reproductive rights are considered as fundamental human rights. In the decision in *Skinner v. Oklahoma* (1942), Justice William O. Douglas asserted that procreation is an "important area of human rights" (at 536) and that compulsory sterilization is not allowable under the equal protection clause of the Fourteenth Amendment: "We are dealing here with legislation which involves one of the basic civil rights of man. Marriage and procreation are fundamental to the very existence and survival of the race" (at 541). Since *Skinner,* the interpretation of reproductive choice by the Supreme Court has been considerably broadened. Justice Arthur Goldberg, in a concurring opinion in *Griswold v. Connecticut* (1965), said the marital relationship is a fundamental area of privacy protected by the Ninth Amendment. Citing *Bates v. Little Rock* (1960), he held that the state can interfere with marriage and procreation only upon proof of a "subordinating interest which is compelling" (at 497).

Reiterating this philosophy, the Supreme Court ruled in *Roe v. Wade* (1973) that the right of privacy protects a woman's right to decide whether to terminate a pregnancy. Similarly, in *Eisenstadt v. Baird* (1972), the Court recognized "the right of the *individual,* married or single, to be free from unwarranted governmental intrusion into matters so fundamentally affecting a person as the decision whether to bear or beget a child" (at 453; emphasis in original). The Court restated this interpretation in *Thornburgh v. American College of Obstetricians and Gynecologists* (1986); it held that the right of privacy is a "central part of the sphere of liberty" (at 772).

The Aspects of Reproduction

In discussing reproductive rights, there is a danger of vastly oversimplifying what procreation entails. Contemporary debate has focused largely on the right of a woman to control her body and to terminate an unwanted pregnancy through abortion, or on the right of individuals not to be sterilized against their will. Reproduction, however, is a complex process that develops over time and involves a series of different though interrelated decisions. Its importance stems from its genetic and biological implications as well as from the fact that it is a social experience.

Claims of reproductive freedom logically extend to four aspects of reproduction: conception, gestation, labor, and childrearing. Although these aspects "combine to create a powerful experience," each of them has an independent personal value and meaning (Robertson 1983, 408). Only recently has attention focused on the biological experience of giving birth as an aspect of procreative freedom. Childrearing is a fulfilling experience deserving of respect, whether or not the person who raises the child also provided the genes or bore it. There is a tendency today to concentrate almost exclusively on reproductive choices about who may conceive, bear, and rear a child—again with a clear emphasis on the woman's rights to avoid or to terminate a pregnancy. These choices, however, are distinct from choices about the conduct that occurs in the process of conceiving, bearing, and rearing. John Robertson distinguishes between "freedom to procreate" and "freedom in procreation."

> Freedom to control every activity related to procreation—to determine how conception will occur, to manage the pregnancy, decide how, when, where, and with whom parturition occurs, or how the neonatal period will be managed—may be of great significance to individuals and may also deserve protection. Although these activities may be lumped under the broad rubric of procreative freedom, analytically they involve choices distinct from the decision to procreate, which is the decision to conceive, gestate, or rear another person. (1983, 410)

Considerable effort is required to clarify this important broadening of the notion of reproductive rights, especially in light of recent advances in genetics and medicine. No longer is the genetic linkage unambiguous, for many novel combinations of germ material are now possible. Artificial insemination, in vitro fertilization, and various embryo transfer techniques are also making outdated the traditional premise that the woman who conceives the child is the woman who bears it and usually raises it. It is dangerous, therefore, to focus solely on one aspect of reproductive rights. The more inclusive reproductive rights agenda for the 1990s recommended by Kathryn Kolbert (1990), head of the Reproductive Freedom Project of the American Civil Liberties Union, includes a range of factors that are often ignored, such as access to quality health care and human services, life skill education, freedom from violence, economic equity, freedom from reproductive hazards, and equitable family law and services. "Reproductive freedom means the ability to choose whether, when, how, and with whom one will have children. Choice means not only having a legal option, but also the economic means and social conditions that make it possible to effectuate one's choice" (1990, 298).

Constraints on State Intervention in Defining Responsible Parenthood

Reproductive freedom is highly valued in the United States, but it is not absolute. The state does have an interest in intervening and limiting this freedom—most often, when parents inadequately care for their children, either deliberately or through ignorance. The important issue is: Under what circumstances is the state justified in intervening in the reproductive process by imposing restrictions or requirements on parents or potential parents? Three rights are generally presented as legally limiting the power of the state to intervene in the health care decisions of a pregnant woman: the right to control one's person, the right to make intimate family decisions, and the right to parental autonomy in childrearing. These rights are subject to different interpretations over time and across jurisdictions.

The Right to Control One's Own Person

In *Union Pacific Railway v. Botsford* (1891), the Supreme Court held that "[n]o right is held more sacred, or is more carefully guarded, . . . than the right of every individual to the possession and control of his own person, free from all restraint or interference of others, unless by clear and unquestionable authority of law" (at 251). This right derives from the Fourth Amendment "right of the people to be secure in their persons, houses, papers, and effects, against unreasonable searches and seizures" and from that amendment's due process clause. This right to self-possession and to control of one's own person has long been applied to decisions concerning medical treatment: in *Schloendorff v. Society of New York Hospitals* (1914), the court held that a doctor who does not obtain the patient's consent before treatment can be charged with battery. Since that time consent has come to be interpreted by the courts as informed, thus allowing the individual to weigh the risks and benefits of a proposed treatment *(Canterbury v. Spence,* 1972). Implicit in the concept of informed consent is the right to refuse treatment, even if it might lead to the death of a patient who does so *(Bouvia v. Superior Court,* 1986).

Although the right to control one's own person is a fundamental right, it is a qualified one. The courts have not prohibited all state action that interferes with that right, but they have applied a balancing test that weighs its infringement against the legitimate state interest in taking such an action. In fact, much of modern constitutional jurisprudence focuses on determining the acceptable balance between private rights and public good. The interest of the state in countering a fundamental right must be necessary and compelling. If the right is not fundamental or if the encroachment on individual liberty is insignificant, then the state must show only some legitimate state purpose and a rational relationship of the action to the achievement of that purpose. In cases where less intrusive means have not accomplished the state's goal, the courts have upheld more extreme intrusions. (Examples include compulsory vaccination and premarital blood tests.) When state action has been found to invade an individual's personal privacy, however, the courts have required safeguards of procedural rights.

The Right to Make Intimate Family Decisions

In *Griswold v. Connecticut,* the Supreme Court enunciated a right to marital privacy that protects couples from governmental efforts to prevent their use of contraceptives. The Court struck down a Connecticut statute proscribing all individuals and couples from using birth control and held that the Ninth Amendment implicitly protects a "zone of privacy" (at 484). There is no explicit mention in the Constitution of the word "privacy"; the Court forged this right from the penumbras surrounding the First Amendment right of association, the Third Amendment prohibition against quartering soldiers in peacetime, the Fourth Amendment prohibition against unreasonable searches and seizures, the Fifth Amendment protection against self-incrimination, and the Ninth Amendment, which vests in the people those rights not enumerated in the Constitution (at 484).

In *Eisenstadt v. Baird,* the Court extended the right to use contraceptives to nonmarried couples, basing its decision on the equal protection clause of the Fourteenth Amendment. The right to autonomy in intimate decision making rests on two principles: a person should be free from governmental intrusion into his or her home or family, and a person should be free to make certain personal decisions. In its decision in *Roe v. Wade,* which invalidated a Texas statute prohibiting abortion, the Court elaborated on the second principle, holding that it prevents a state from interfering in the making of fundamental intimate decisions in the absence of a compelling state interest. The right to decide to terminate a pregnancy is a personal right deemed "implicit in the concept of ordered liberty" (at 152) and therefore falls within the zone of privacy protected by the Constitution. To deny a woman the right to make this decision would cause distress and would risk the harm resulting from the imposition of an unwanted child on the woman. Only after the fetus is viable can the state demonstrate a compelling interest allowing it to intervene.

As pointed out in a *Virginia Law Review* Note ("Constitutional Limitations" 1981), the *Roe* decision is interesting in that the Court accepts state authority to regulate abortion procedures after the first trimester. The disparity between the Court's treatment of state prohibition of abortion and its treatment of state regulation of abortion procedures implies that the Court is willing to be less demanding in its scrutiny of state actions that do not go so far as to deny the woman the right to decide.

> It appears, therefore, that a less demanding form of scrutiny, such as a "balancing test," is appropriate when a state action restricts or burdens a protected individual decision but does not completely remove individual autonomy. The slighter the impact of a state action, the less compelling the state interest necessary to justify it; thus, state actions carefully tailored to serve their purposes would seem likely to survive the Court's scrutiny. (Note 1981, 1059)

In *Harris v. McRae* (1980), for example, the Court held that the denial of Medicaid funding, even for medically indicated abortions, does not unduly interfere with the freedom of choice protected in *Roe,* even though it makes "childbirth a more attractive alternative than abortion" (at 325). The *Harris* decision also established that freedom of choice does not impose an obligation on the state to subsidize all alternatives equally.

Although the Court has been adamant in prohibiting absolute denial of the constitutional right to make autonomous procreative decisions, for lesser intrusions it is willing to apply a balancing analysis that varies in rigor according to the means employed and the extent of intrusion on privacy rights. Considerable care is required on the part of the state in framing any regulations that affect childbearing decisions. Where there is a compelling state interest, the Court is willing to permit lesser forms of interference with procreative rights *(Webster v. Reproductive Health Services,* 1989).

The Right to Parental Autonomy in Childrearing

American society has traditionally shown a preference for minimal state intervention in childrearing decisions. It is based on the assumption that parents are able to determine and will pursue the course of action that is in their child's best interest. In its decision in *Parham v. J. R.* (1979), the Supreme Court explained that

> [t]he law's concept of the family rests on a presumption that parents possess what a child lacks in maturity, experience, and capacity for judgment required for making life's difficult decisions. More important, historically it has recognized that natural bonds of affection lead parents to act in the best interests of their children. (at 602)

The parent-child relationship is special, for it comprises deep psychological and social bonds as well as physical and material dependence. When in doubt, the courts have chosen to err on the side of nonintervention in order to preserve the stability of the parent-child relationship: "[S]ince the state should usually defer to the wishes of the parents, it has a serious burden of justification before abridging parental authority by substituting its judgment for that of the parents" (*In re Phillip B.*, 1979, at 51).

In *Bowen v. American Hospital Association* (1986), the Supreme Court challenged a law that mandated aggressive treatment of ill newborns despite parents' refusal to consent to treatment. The Court held that the state should intervene only in "exceptional" cases: "In broad outline, state law vests decisional responsibility in the parents, in the first instance, subject to review in exceptional cases by the State acting as *parens patriae*" (at 2112-2113). The courts have also been disinclined to allow state intervention in childrearing decisions because such action might undermine the diversity of views and life-styles that is promoted by allowing children to be raised in a wide variety of living situations. There is an implicit grounding of this right to autonomy of parents' decisions in the First Amendment freedom of religion, which has figured prominently in many cases that have concerned medical decisions (for example, *Jehovah's Witnesses in the State of Washington v. King's County Hosp.*, 1967). In 1989 and 1990, at least five Christian Science couples were convicted for causing the death of their children by withholding medical care. In June 1990, a jury found David and Ginger Twitchell guilty of negligent homicide in the death of their 2½-year-old son, Robyn. They were sentenced to ten years' probation for their failure to provide medical care that, by eliminating a bowel obstruction, could have saved his life. Trial testimony revealed that although Robyn suffered excrutiating pain in the last days of his life, he received no care other than "heartfelt yet disciplined prayer" from a Christian Science nurse and a practitioner (Skolnick 1990, 1226).

Limitations on Parental Choice in Procreation

In the United States there have generally been few restrictions on the right to reproduce; it is considered so fundamental that the state should not interfere without demonstrating a compelling interest. As a result of recent technological advances (described in subsequent chapters), however, there has been a gradual lessening of the emphasis on the stability and inviolability of the parent-child relationship, especially the assumption that parents will make good-faith efforts to act in the best interests of their children. Cases of child abuse, state support of dependent children, decision making by medical practitioners, and lack of fertility control by those who are often least able to raise their children have heightened this concern.

In both case law and literature, there is an increased emphasis on the parental duty to provide a stable environment so that children have at least a minimal chance to succeed, for they have a right to be allowed to develop as sound a body and mind as possible. New pressures for setting limits when the exercise of reproductive rights conflicts with what is in the best interest of children, including the unborn, are increasingly evident.

Emerging technologies that increase procreative control are lending support to the view that society has not only the authority but the duty to intervene in reproductive decision making. Whether out of concern for the affected children, future generations, the health of the gene pool, or some other good, there is evidence of a gradual shift to the viewpoint that some constraints ought to be placed on human reproduction when individuals abuse those rights. Even though procreation is an inalienable right, it can be regulated by a society that is concerned with the existence of each child and with its own survival. Reproduction, according to this view, is a right shared with society as a whole and is part of a larger complex of rights, responsibilities, and obligations. State intervention might be justified under certain circumstances; each case must be analyzed carefully.

In the mid-1970s, Bentley Glass correctly predicted that advances in human genetics would result in a reordered priority of rights. The right of individuals to procreate would be superseded by "the right of every child to enter life with an adequate physical and mental endowment" (1975, 56-57). For Michael Bayles, it is justifiable to limit the procreative liberty of some individuals if that action would increase the quality of life for the rest of society: "If it could be shown, for example, that most persons with a certain genetic defect such as Tay-Sachs [a degenerative disease that causes death by age 3 or 4] did not have a quality of life of level 'n', then there would be sufficient grounds for the principle to support a law to prevent their birth" (1976, 301).

The Changing Relationship between Parents and Children

The importance of children as a link to the future and the perpetuation of individual identity have led to "an extraordinary heightening of emotional expectations of children" (Fletcher 1983, 297). Parents' longing for emotional fulfillment is frequently projected onto their children—in many ways, they live through their children. With the trend toward smaller families, parental expectations for each newborn have increased. Parents who have only one or two children want them to be as "healthy" as possible—that is, consistent with their own value system.

The state, too, has a profound interest in maximizing the aggregate quality of progeny, especially when the prevailing preference is for small families. There has been a predisposition in western society to be wary of, or even prejudiced against, those who are different—the mentally ill and, to a lesser extent, the physically disabled. Despite passage of the Americans with Disabilities Act in 1990, and an increased acceptance of persons with disabilities, in many cases they are still targets of prejudice. The availability of technologies to treat or to prevent the birth of persons with "defects" is bound to increase the emphasis on quality of progeny.

The Expanded Role of Medicine in Reproduction

The issues of reproductive rights and responsibilities are influenced by prevailing social values in the United States. Americans' increasing reliance on medical technology has not only increased medical intervention in pregnancy but encouraged the view that the probability of bearing a healthy child can be increased. This is clearly reflected in the acceptance by some courts of medical "fact" in cases concerning coerced cesarean sections, even when data are uncertain and conclusions are probabilistic. Laura Woliver contends that reproductive technologies often have hidden policy implications—"they increase medical intervention in women's lives, diminishing women's power over their bodies and babies" (1989, 43). Significantly, the public's notion of what constitutes responsible maternal behavior is being shaped by the rapidly changing technology.

Pressures on pregnant women to utilize available fetal therapies will increase as techniques that are now experimental become routine therapeutic procedures. Although fetal surgery and therapy are still in a primitive stage and immediate concern still focuses on possible harm to the fetus and the mother, rapid advances in instrumentation, technique, and skills will soon lower the risk to both fetus and mother and substantially increase the options available for intervening in utero to correct fetal problems surgically. Many women are then likely to accept or even demand therapy for their unborn child. Policy dilemmas will arise, however, when a pregnant woman, for whatever reason, does not consent and third parties apply pressure on her to comply with their demands for intervention.

One result of Americans' increasing reliance on medical technology has been that when new "choices" become available to women, many of them feel obligated to make the "right" choice by "choosing" the socially approved alternative (Hubbard 1990, 156). Because they necessitate third-party involvement and dependence on medical expertise, these technologies may threaten the freedom and dignity of women in general, by forcing them to surrender their control over procreation.

Ruth Hubbard decries the practice of making every pregnancy a medical event; she sees it as a result of physicians' economic incentive to create the perception of a need for their services during pregnancy, in light of declining birth rates and the increasing interest in midwifery and home birth (1985, 567). Barbara Rothman observes that the new images of the fetus made possible by prenatal technologies are making everyone aware of the "unborn" as people, "but they do so at the cost of making transparent the mother" (1986, 114). Furthermore, prenatal diagnostic technologies that enable judgments to be made halfway through the pregnancy make extraordinary demands on a woman to separate herself emotionally from the fetus she is carrying.

One problem with these trends is the danger, in such a medicalized society, that new technologies might be offered to, or even forced on, pregnant women without adequate proof of benefit. The dependence on technological solutions, reinforced by a medical community trained in the technological imperative, can engender a false degree of security as to what medicine can accomplish (Blank 1988, 35). Moreover, many therapies come into widespread use before a thorough assessment has been made as to their risks and benefits (Blank 1992a). As demand for medical answers escalates, and as women are encouraged to make more routine use of the technologies discussed in Chapter 4, the line between experimentation and therapy becomes increasingly more tenuous. Arguments that a pregnant woman has a legally enforceable responsibility to use "established" medical procedures must therefore be viewed critically. It cannot be assumed that the benefit to the fetus of a procedure, simply because it has been accepted as routine, warrants state intervention under force of law.

The status of women is clearly affected by reproductive technologies. Technology both reflects and influences social values. Because of women's important biological role as the bearers of children, any technologies that are concerned with reproduction have a direct effect on their societal role. Moreover, because these technologies focus on the role of women as mothers, they could lead to a diminution of their other roles. Some feminists argue that society is already placing too much emphasis on the role of motherhood, to the exclusion of women's other roles. Robin Rowland insists that women must evaluate this societal overstatement: "The catchcry 'but women want it' has been sounded over and over again by the medical profession to justify continuing medical advances in their field. Women need to reevaluate just what it is they want and question this justification for turning women into living laboratories" (1985, 39).

Intervention of Third Parties in Matters of Reproduction

Reproductive technologies introduce third parties into what traditionally has been a private matter between the parents. The more complex the intervention, the more mediators are necessary. Embryologists, geneticists, and a range of other medical specialists, and sometimes lawyers, are key players. The desire of these specialists to help their clients may be genuine, but their very presence takes control of procreation away from the parents.

> The perceived need for massive technological intervention in conception, pregnancy, and childbirth is bolstered by the conviction that women's bodies are incompetent and inadequate, in need of a "technological fix" in order to function adequately. (Overall 1987, 201)

Perhaps more disquieting is that many of these third parties represent commercial interests. The shift of fertility research and services from the public sector to the private, profit-making sector has heightened concern about the rights of women to privacy in matters relating to conception. The introduction of economic relationships thus transforms men and women into consumers of reproductive services and products. The commercialization of procreation poses the danger that both women and children will be treated as commodities because it leads to specialization, with each aspect of reproduction being controlled by a different agent. Under these conditions, women become the suppliers of children, who in effect become consumer goods to be purchased on the open market; the result is to encourage "an emphasis on acquiring one's own children as property" (Overall 1987, 200).

Reproductive Rights and the Policy Process

Reproductive policy making can be better understood if analyzed as part of the broader policy process.* There have been many useful analyses of this process by political scientists. James Anderson (1990) views the process as consisting of five stages:

1. Problem identification and agenda setting
2. Policy formulation
3. Policy adoption
4. Policy implementation
5. Policy evaluation

Problem identification and agenda setting is the stage in which issues become matters of public concern. Of the multitude of problems faced by society, only a small proportion receive public recognition and not all of

---

* *Policy* is a term that is used in many ways. It can be a label for a field of government activity, a statement that expresses broad purposes or goals of governments or political parties, a formal authorization, a specific proposal, a governmental decision, an output, or an outcome. It is often confused with the term *program,* which refers to a relatively specific sphere of government activity that usually includes a package of specific authorizations and governmental decisions. Although reproductive policy can encompass all of these meanings, as used here it usually denotes specific governmental proposals or decisions.

them result in governmental action. Issues that are currently matters of public debate are considered possible agenda items. Roger Cobb and Charles Elder identify two agendas. The systemic agenda consists of "all issues that are commonly perceived by members of the political community as meriting public attention and as involving matters within the legitimate jurisdiction of existing government authority." The institutional or formal agenda is "that set of items explicitly up for active and serious consideration of authoritative decision makers" (1972, 85-86). The systemic agenda consists of general categories that define which legitimate priorities may be considered by government; the institutional or formal agenda consists of those problems perceived by decision makers as warranting serious attention and effort to develop a course of action.

Once an issue has been placed on the government's formal agenda, policy formulation begins. This is a complex process involving a range of actors inside and outside government. Interest groups push for particular policies and attempt to influence priorities. Formulation usually includes analysis of various policy options, including inaction. Although policy adoption, which typically includes a legislative enactment or an executive directive, is usually the most salient stage of policy making, policy formulation is the stage where the boundaries of government action are defined.

After a policy is adopted, the focus shifts to the executive branch, which is responsible for implementation. Agencies make rules (which explain how the legislation is to be applied), adjudicate (apply the rules to specific situations and settle disputes), use their discretion to enforce the rules and laws, and maintain program operations (Anderson, 1990). Policy formulation, adoption, and implementation are often closely related, since the policy process is generally one of continual, incremental change.

Once a policy has been implemented, it is important to evaluate its impact. What change, if any, has taken place, and has that change been positive or negative? Evaluation consists of the comparison of the expected and the actual performance levels to determine whether the goals have been met as well as to assign responsibility for discrepancies in performance. Anderson advises evaluators to distinguish between policy outputs and policy outcomes. Outputs "are the things actually done by agencies in pursuance of policy decisions and statements." Outcomes "are the consequences, for society, intended and unintended, that stem from governmental action or inaction" (1990, 223).

Setting the Reproductive Policy Agenda

To be effective, a reproductive policy should have progressed through all five stages. But the newness of many reproductive issues means that most attention should be paid to the initial stage. Although some issues routinely make their way through the stages of the policy process, many have yet to be placed on the formal agenda. It can be argued that reproductive issues have always had a policy aspect and that it has been broadened and made more important by changes in technology and social values.

Simply because an issue is a matter of public concern, however, does not guarantee that policy makers will recognize it and consider it a legitimate priority and put it on the formal agenda. Dorothy Nelkin points out that the policy importance of a technological innovation depends on both the degree to which it provokes a public response and how it is perceived by organized economic and political interests (1977, 413). Only those issues that are "commonly perceived by members of the political community as meriting public attention and involving matters within the legitimate jurisdiction of existing government authority" are placed on the systemic agenda (Cobb and Elder 1972, 85).

Agenda setting is complicated because reproductive policy making takes place at the federal, state, and local levels of government, and multiple agendas may exist in various institutions at each level. A particular problem might be perceived and acted on by decision makers in one institution at one level of government in one state but not be perceived at all (or be perceived differently) in another. The developments that would cause a particular issue to be placed on the government agenda (technological change, interest group demands, a widely publicized event) might take place only in certain geographical areas (Jones and Matthes 1983, 125).

Another complicating factor is the constant interaction of the myriad professional associations, business enterprises, and individual practitioners in the private sector that are active in the area of human reproduction and can influence reproductive policy. The agendas of the wide range of institutions and organizations in the public and private sectors may be parallel or even overlap.

Andrea Bonnicksen presents a private-sector policy model that defines "regularized rules and procedures in the medical setting as the desired end of decision-making" (1992, 54). She favors increased emphasis on this model because she believes that governmental action is "unlikely, premature, and unwise" in many areas of biomedicine.

> Private policies have weaknesses, but these can be partly remedied by political strategies. Public policies, in contrast, are difficult to refine or revamp if found to be erroneous or misguided. Traditional values of self-determination are perhaps more easily protected in the medical than in the political setting. At the very least, a private policy alternative warrants consideration for contentious biomedical issues. (1992, 55)

It is important that private-sector solutions be pursued; however, the scope of reproductive issues and their broad implications for many societal groups make them a matter of public concern.

Reproductive Rights in Perspective

Individual rights are only one of the societal values that can influence reproductive policy (see Figure 1-2). Other values (community, privacy, intellectual freedom, justice, and health) can either conflict with or strengthen perceptions of individual rights. Technology can have an independent effect on the perceived need for public policy. Furthermore, technology and societal values have a reciprocal relationship: new technologies challenge societal values, and values influence the direction of technological development.

Reproductive innovations, taken cumulatively, are encroaching on many traditional values, particularly the concept of individual rights. The issues that are raised present policy dilemmas because of the conflicting interests. Whether these dilemmas, in combination, constitute a crisis or a chronically existing condition depends on the viewpoint of the observer. Many pro-life groups perceive the situation created by the social and scientific trends as a crisis, as do many feminists and civil libertarians. This perception has led to calls for public action.

Reproductive policy can be affirmative, prohibitive, or regulatory (see Figure 1-2). Affirmative policies promote or encourage certain activities— for example, government funding of research or services to facilitate more widespread use of a particular technique or application. Whether the government ought to be providing such encouragement and if so, by what means, is a subject of debate. Should Medicaid funds be used to pay for expensive reproduction-assisting technologies when couples cannot afford them? Or should private insurers be required by law to cover these expenses? Affirmative policies are often redistributive; thus there is a potential for conflict between the negative rights of taxpayers to expend their resources as they see fit and the positive rights of recipients of government support who require it to maintain a decent level of existence.

Prohibitive policies can be used to determine the options available in reproductive matters. For example, the government has prohibited funding of specific areas of research and development (human embryo research) or specific reproductive services (abortion, sterilization). Such policies often reflect political motives or are a response to interest groups' demands. A prohibitory policy whose enforcement is problematic in a liberal society focuses on the use of certain reproductive applications. Laws banning surrogate mother contracts, fetal research, and nonconsensual sterilizations, for example, arouse concern about the restriction of private choices and individual rights.

Figure 1-2   The Formulation of Reproductive Policy

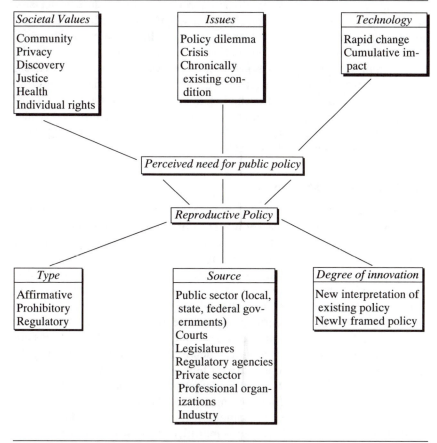

Source: Adapted from Blank and Bonnicksen 1993, xiii.

Although regulatory policy can be framed to apply only to government-supported activities, it usually consists of sweeping rules governing all activities, in both the public and private sectors. States have regulated medical care by establishing licensing criteria, standards of care, and a tort system for the resolution of conflicts. Regulation can be used to ensure that standards of safety, efficacy, and liability are adhered to. Unlike professional association guidelines, which also set minimum standards, regulations have the force of law; they usually include legal sanctions for violations. In most areas of medicine, private guidelines and public regulations operate simultaneously. Many of the new reproductive services are largely unregulated, however.

Reproductive policy can have a variety of sources (see Figure 1-2). The American political system is characterized by fragmentation. The federal system (the sharing of power between the national government and the fifty state governments) has resulted in decentralized reproductive decision making; responsibility for public health rests primarily with the states, despite the increase in federal power in the area of health care since the mid-1930s. The framers of the Constitution also ensured division of power by establishing the principle of separation of powers and the various checks and balances between the executive, legislative, and judicial branches. As a result, it has been difficult to establish a consistent national policy, especially in such controversial areas as reproductive and family matters, where the strategies of bargaining and compromise that are central to legislative policy making often prove ineffective.

The Central Role of the Courts

The textbook model of the policy process suggests that the early stages are dominated by legislatures; however, court decisions often arouse public concern and trigger legislative action. Furthermore, because reproduction often raises emotional issues that are readily manipulated by interest groups, many elected officials view them as no-win issues to be avoided, and have often deferred difficult decisions concerning them to the courts, which are, in effect, forced to make policy.

Because decisions concerning so many reproductive issues turn on the notion of individual rights, it is to be expected that the courts would assume a central role in reproductive policy making. The courts, not the legislatures, have the prime responsibility for interpreting the constitutional bases of rights, setting the limits of government intervention in the exercise of rights, and resolving conflicts among parties claiming rights.

The constantly changing technological context of reproduction, the hesitancy of legislators to become embroiled in controversies over reproductive issues, and the significant rights component of these issues also explain why much of the public-sector activity is judicial—even though other branches of government, both state and federal, have been involved in policy making in areas such as sterilization, fetal research, and the treatment of disabled newborns. To the extent that the government has a reproductive policy, then, it is more a product of court action than of the policy process as it is generally assumed to operate in the United States. (Table 1-1 shows the magnitude of judicial involvement in making reproductive policy.)

Largely because of the scope and degree of judicial activity and its significant policy implications, there has been a continuing debate as to whether courts are the most appropriate agency for making reproductive policy. Critics charge that there are inherent limitations on judicial policy making. Because the judicial process is passive and retrospective, the

Table 1-1   Judicial Involvement in the Making of Reproductive Policy

Preconception torts
  Sterilization (consent questions)
  Contraception (accessibility)
  Medical malpractice
  Product liability
  Radiation injuries
  Workplace hazards
  Agent Orange cases

Wrongful conception or wrongful pregnancy
  Failed sterilization
  Failed contraception
  Misdiagnosis or failure to diagnose pregnancy
  Unsuccessful abortion

Assisted reproduction
  Legal status of donor insemination children
  Legal status of frozen embryos (custody)
  Surrogacy contracts
  Access to reproductive services
  Use of genetic materials (ownership)

Prenatal issues
  Abortion (accessibility, age, other qualifications)
  Injury torts (mother, third parties)
  Substance abuse
  Fetus as patient
  Forced cesarean sections
  Workplace exclusionary policies
  Fetus as organ or tissue supply

Neonatal issues
  Treatment issues (Baby Jane Doe)
  Euthanasia
  Torts for wrongful birth
  Torts for wrongful life

courts are slow to react to rapid technological progress.

Also, because the primary function of the courts is to resolve conflicts concerning the rights and obligations of the parties to an action, each case is supposedly decided on the basis of evidence produced by those parties, not public policy considerations. Although decisions in some cases might yield implicit principles with important policy implications, the courts "generally refrain from deciding individual cases on the basis of deliberately establishing public-policy controls" (Green 1976, 171). In instances where judicial decisions have consequences for groups or individuals other than the immediate parties to a case, there are often "serious difficulties in communicating new legal requirements to populations that are not yet within the jurisdiction of courts" (Nakamura and Smallwood 1980, 107).

Moreover, decisions are episodic, unpredictable, and often inconsistent. Case-by-case adjudication by a wide variety of state and federal courts adds to the confusion.

The Role of Government in Redefining Reproductive Rights

The future role of the government in defining reproductive rights will depend to a large extent on prevailing values and how they influence the accepted definition of those rights. Because tradition supports the right of married couples to have children, there is general agreement that few, if any, restraints ought to be placed on them. Even the use of new reproduction-aiding technologies by infertile couples appears to have widespread popular support. There is less support for the right of singles and unmarried couples to procreate, although opposition has lessened since the 1980s.

Social policies that focus on the education of potential parents are likely to be more successful than coercive policies. For instance, voluntary, not mandatory, genetic screening and prenatal diagnostic programs are compatible with prevailing values concerning procreative rights in the United States. Tax incentives might be used to supplement education efforts, but they result in inequities based on wealth. The elimination or reduction of public support for the indigent, combined with the provision of family planning services, might encourage some couples not to have children, but again the economic impact on various groups would not be equitable. In the past, more explicit policies to limit procreative choice focused on sterilization. They failed to reach even their most modest objectives, however, and to many people they represent state intrusion at its extreme.

Certainly, the licensing of potential parents would conflict with prevailing values in American political culture. Even if it could be demonstrated that requiring a couple to undergo a series of genetic, medical, social, and personality examinations would ensure that a child born to them would have a chance to compete in this complex world, any policy of this type would understandably be widely attacked. From a practical standpoint, it would be politically unfeasible in such a pluralistic society. No public officeholder in command of his or her senses would be likely to propose a policy that would determine who should be allowed to have children.

Nevertheless, the pressures for legal acknowledgment of fetal rights, of a tort classification for wrongful life and prenatal damage, and of the criminal liability of parents for abuse of their unborn children reflect support for placing limits on the reproductive choice of individuals. Moreover, with the increase in knowledge about fetal development and the continuing development of intervention technologies, reproduction has come to be viewed less as an unmitigated right than a right that includes a responsibility to produce healthy children. Those who knowingly produce unhealthy children are increasingly likely to be subject to social pressure to conform to standards of "responsible" procreative behavior.

Certainly, these issues are not politically attractive in a society with a tradition of individual autonomy and privacy in parenting. It is difficult to revise the prevailing notion of parenting so that responsibility to progeny takes precedence over the right to have progeny. The easiest response by society is to rationalize the tradition of parental autonomy; a more prudent response would be to reevaluate the notion of parenthood in the new technological, social, and legal contexts.

Conclusion

Reproductive rights are currently undergoing strong pressures from many directions. New technologies and increased knowledge are raising novel and challenging policy issues regarding a full range of reproductive rights. Abortion and sterilization, which have always been areas of conflict, have been complicated by assisted reproduction techniques, surrogate motherhood, genetic technologies, fetal research, and aggressive treatment possibilities for critically ill newborns. Moreover, the active intervention of courts and other parties in matters affecting the lives of pregnant women has challenged conventional definitions of rights.

Reproductive innovations and the increasing range of intervention capabilities promise significant benefits for many individuals, but they also create ethical and policy dilemmas. Problems are inevitable in such a dynamic environment; they require thoughtful and objective analysis. There is also a need for public debate about society's goals and priorities.

Abortion: Private Choices, Public Actions

Norma McCorvey had had an unstable childhood; she dropped out of high school, married, and became pregnant while a teenager. In 1969, her young daughter was living with relatives and McCorvey, who had held a series of unskilled jobs, was unemployed and living alone in Texas. Upon learning that she was pregnant again, she sought an abortion. But Texas, like most other states at that time, prohibited abortion except to save the mother's life. McCorvey's physician had told her that she could seek an abortion in California or Colorado, but she could not afford to travel. She contacted an unlicensed abortionist who offered to perform an illegal abortion for $500 (Faux 1989, 10-11). McCorvey decided not to risk her life; she carried the pregnancy to term and gave up her son for adoption.

McCorvey's pregnancy might have gone unnoticed had it happened at another point in time. But in 1969, the social structure of the United States was undergoing dramatic change. The civil rights movement had awakened—or perhaps re-awakened—Americans to the harsh reality that racial discrimination was widespread in a nation that prided itself on upholding the principles of democracy and equality. Furthermore, U.S. troops were engaged in what would be a long and controversial war. Americans were reexamining their culture, their personal values, and the role that government should play in their lives.

The development of a reliable, low-cost method of birth control had prepared the way for the women's movement for equal rights. As Rosalind Petchesky has pointed out, in the early 1970s there was a marked change in women's roles, in both the family and the economy. Women delayed marriage and childbearing. Their level of college attendance increased, as did their participation in the labor force (although most women held low-paying jobs). The divorce rate and the number of families headed by women also increased (Petchesky 1990, 103-104). American women were choosing to alter their life-styles and their goals. They would also attempt to change some of the laws that defined their rights.

Midway through her pregnancy, McCorvey was approached by attorneys Sarah Weddington and Lynda Coffee, both recent law school graduates, who asked if she would be the complainant in a lawsuit challenging the Texas abortion statute. She agreed, taking the pseudonym Jane Roe. Together, Weddington, Coffee, and McCorvey would change some of the fundamental principles of abortion law.

This chapter begins with an analysis of abortion in the United States today and of the various actors in the abortion debate. A brief review of abortion policy in the nineteenth century is followed by an analysis of the agenda-setting events that led to the 1973 decisions in *Roe v. Wade* and *Doe v. Bolton,* and a discussion of the subsequent policy battle between pro-life and pro-choice interest groups. The chapter concludes with a review of other major abortion court cases and an analysis of public opinion concerning abortion.

Abortion in the United States Today

Abortion is the most commonly performed surgical procedure in the United States. Approximately 28 percent of all pregnancies—about 1.6 million—are terminated annually. Abortion rates have declined modestly since 1976. Henshaw and Van Vort conclude that the possible causes of this decline are an increase in the number of women using contraception, an increase in public acceptance of nonmarital childbearing, a decrease in the number of abortion providers, and vacillation in public opinion regarding abortion (1994, 101). The typical abortion patient is young (57 percent are 24 years of age or younger), single (63 percent), and has a family income of less than $25,000 (68 percent). Minority-group women are almost twice as likely as white women to have an abortion (Gold 1990, 14-22). The overwhelming majority of abortions (91 percent) are performed prior to the thirteenth week of pregnancy; less than .05 percent are performed after twenty weeks. In fact, 75 percent of the providers do not perform abortions after the sixteenth week (Gold 1990, 23).

Women give a variety of reasons for seeking an abortion (see Figure 2-1). Nearly 80 percent say that they are not ready to have a child, and 68 percent say they cannot afford to have a child. Most abortions (69 percent) are performed in freestanding abortion clinics; however, the availability of

Figure 2-1   Reasons for Seeking an Abortion

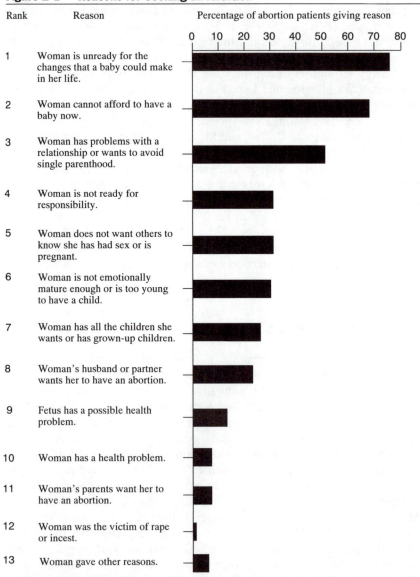

Rank	Reason	Percentage of abortion patients giving reason

0 10 20 30 40 50 60 70 80

1   Woman is unready for the changes that a baby could make in her life.

2   Woman cannot afford to have a baby now.

3   Woman has problems with a relationship or wants to avoid single parenthood.

4   Woman is not ready for responsibility.

5   Woman does not want others to know she has had sex or is pregnant.

6   Woman is not emotionally mature enough or is too young to have a child.

7   Woman has all the children she wants or has grown-up children.

8   Woman's husband or partner wants her to have an abortion.

9   Fetus has a possible health problem.

10   Woman has a health problem.

11   Woman's parents want her to have an abortion.

12   Woman was the victim of rape or incest.

13   Woman gave other reasons.

Source: Adapted from Gold 1990.

abortion providers is limited geographically. In 1992, 84 percent of U.S. counties had no identified abortion provider, 94 percent of nonmetropolitan counties had no abortion services, and 51 percent of metropolitan areas had no such services. Moreover, the number of abortion providers declined, from 2,908 facilities in 1982 to 2,380 in 1992 (Henshaw and Van

Vort 1994, 103-105). It is important to note that more than half of the pregnancies in the United States are unintentional, and at least two-thirds of all U.S. women have at least one unintended pregnancy during their lifetime. Approximately 43 percent of all unintended pregnancies occur despite the use of a contraceptive (Gold 1990, 11-12).

Three methods of abortion are commonly used. Early abortions are usually performed by dilation of the cervix and removal of the fetus by suction, using a process of vacuum aspiration (Gold 1990, 24). Use of prostaglandin—administered as a vaginal suppository, through a catheter to the uterus, or by injection into the amniotic sac—causes the fetus to be expelled; this procedure is widely used during the second trimester (Pritchard, McDonald, and Gant 1985, 479). Injection of saline solution into the amniotic sac is common in performing late abortions. The risk of maternal death from a legal abortion is estimated to be no more than one-seventh of the risk of maternal death from childbirth (Pritchard, McDonald, and Gant 1985, 483). The abortion pill RU-486, an antiprogestin, causes the fetus to abort when used in conjunction with prostaglandin. It was developed in France and is widely used there. It has not been approved for use in the United States.

Abortion: Whose Rights and Whose Responsibilities?

The abortion issue has been a subject of controversy in the United States for more than twenty years; it is so complex that it is not likely to be resolved in the near future. Abortion is a matter of personal and societal concern, for it raises questions about how personhood should be defined and about the proper roles and rights of women, men, parents, and children. It is also a primary focus of the women's movement.

The abortion debate has led to a virtual collision of rights—those of the fetus, the pregnant woman, the woman's partner, other family members (particularly grandparents), health care providers, taxpayers, and the state. The debate centers largely on the potential for conflict between the rights of the fetus and the rights of the pregnant woman. The pro-life movement is fetus-oriented; that is, it holds to the principle that life begins at conception, and therefore abortion constitutes the murder of a vulnerable, helpless fetus—the taking of an innocent life.

The pro-life personification of the fetus has been emphasized in court actions, made more vivid by the media, and given credibility by developments in the field of medicine (Petchesky 1990, xiii). In recent years, the fetus has in effect become a litigant in civil actions involving fetal injury, fetal rights in inheritance, and so forth. Fetal rights have also been at issue in criminal cases, most notably those in which an attempt was made to prosecute a woman for substance abuse during pregnancy. The fetus has become a "media star" as a result of the publication of still photographs and video images of its life in utero. Petchesky points to the impact that the televised ultrasound video "Silent Scream" had on viewers in 1984 (1990, xiv). The video (whose authenticity she questions) depicts a fetus "screaming" with pain as it is aborted.

But perhaps the most important factor in the increased attribution of personhood to the fetus has been recent advances in prenatal technology that make possible visualization and treatment of the fetus in utero, thereby granting it "patient" status. Improvements in neonatal care and technology have reduced the gestational age of viability (the point at which the fetus is capable of independent survival outside the womb) to twenty-three to twenty-four weeks (Allen, Donohue, and Dusman 1993), thus making late abortion more controversial. The more that physicians and the public have learned about the fetus, the greater has been the tendency to protect its rights.

The pro-choice movement is woman-oriented; it supports the principle that women have the right to control their bodies and their lives. To claim otherwise disempowers them and defines them by virtue of their reproductive capacities. The philosophical differences between the pro-choice and pro-life positions are evidenced by the artwork at the organizations' headquarters. At the headquarters of the National Abortion and Reproductive Rights Action League (NARAL), there are prints and posters of women. In the head office of the National Right to Life Committee (NRLC), there are pictures of babies (National Issues Forum Staff 1990, 28).

But the battle between pro-choice and pro-life activists is more than a battle about abortion. It is a battle about the role of women in society. Kristin Luker's classic study of pro-life and pro-choice activists in California in the mid- to late 1970s revealed the demographic differences between the two sides at that time:

The average pro-choice activist is a forty-four-year-old married woman who grew up in a large metropolitan area and whose father was a college graduate. She was married at age twenty-two, has one or two children, and has had some graduate or professional training beyond the B.A. degree. She is married to a professional man, is herself employed in a regular job, and her family income is more than $50,000 a year. She is not religiously active, feels that religion is not important to her, and attends church very rarely if at all.

The average pro-life [activist] is also a forty-four-year-old married woman who grew up in a large metropolitan area. She married at age seventeen and has three children or more. Her father was a high school graduate, and she has some college education or may have a B.A. degree. She is not employed in the paid labor force and is married to a small businessman or lower-level white-collar worker; her family income is $30,000 a year. She is Catholic (and may have converted), and her religion is one of the most important aspects of her life; she attends church as least once a week and occasionally more often. (1984, 197)

Perhaps more important than the demographic differences between pro-choice and pro-life activists is the fact that they view the world differently, and each group feels threatened by the other's notion of the role women should play in society. In general, pro-choice women have struggled to obtain an education and to establish a career despite the prevalence of gender discrimination in the workplace. Moreover, many have achieved career success while raising children. They want the respect that such hard work deserves and the security of knowing that they will be able to maintain their present life-style.

Pro-life activists have tended to marry at an earlier age and to forego careers outside the home; their lives revolve around their husbands and their children. They, too, feel that they have lost the respect of society because of their way of life. Each side resents—and perhaps misunderstands—the values and life-styles of the other. Each side fears significant negative consequences should the other side "win" the debate over abortion. Thus the debate concerns not only abortion but the proper role of women in society (Luker 1984).

It should be noted that to a large extent, the composition of the pro-life movement has undergone a change; increasing numbers of activists are now Protestants, Evangelicals, and Fundamentalists. The Catholic Church, although still integral to the movement, is no longer its most significant standard bearer. Furthermore, pro-life activists typically have more volunteer time to devote to their cause because they are not employed outside the home, but pro-choice activists tend to have more money to devote to their cause. It is interesting to note that despite the role of the Catholic Church in the pro-life movement, Catholic women seek abortions at higher rates than do Protestant women (Gold 1990, 19).

Most participants in the abortion debate would agree that the circumstances that lead a woman to seek an abortion are usually tragic; virtually no one is really "pro-abortion." The real issue, as defined by the courts, is: who should make the decision regarding whether the pregnancy will be continued or terminated? This was the issue emphasized by Sarah Weddington in her final arguments to the Supreme Court in *Roe v. Wade:*

We do not ask this court to rule that abortion is good, or desirable in any particular situation. We are here to advocate that the decision as to whether or not a particular woman will continue to carry or will terminate a pregnancy is a decision that should be made by that individual; that, in fact, she has a constitutional right to make that decision for herself; and that the State has shown no interest in interfering with that decision. (Craig and O'Brien 1993, 23).

The conflict between the two philosophical principles—that life begins at conception and that women have a right to control their bodies—is not resolvable. Philosophers, ethicists, theologians, policy makers, and the general public have debated this issue for decades and are no closer to reaching a common ground than they were when the debate began. Therefore, no attempt will be made to resolve it in this book. What is resolvable, however, is the question of which participants in the debate should decide who will be granted an abortion and under what circumstances.

Although the public debate on this issue has centered on the rights of fetuses and pregnant women, there are other, often overlooked, parties who may also make a claim to rights. Just as the roles of women (and especially mothers) in society have been in flux, so have the roles of men. Societal values are slowly changing; more emphasis is being placed on the role of the father in nurturing his children. This change is beginning to be reflected in public policy. For example, the Family and Medical Leave Act of 1993 provides that fathers and mothers have an equal right to parental leave to care for newborns or sick children. Twenty years ago it was almost unheard of for a father to seek child custody during a divorce. Now it is not unusual for fathers to seek and win custody, and for noncustodial mothers to pay child support. With this increasing recognition of fathers' roles in child-rearing, it is not unusual to hear assertions of their rights to have a voice in the decision concerning whether an abortion will be performed; in fact, the Supreme Court has addressed this issue. *Roe v. Wade* and a number of subsequent decisions have clearly established that until viability is established, the only party who has any legal rights in abortion decision making is the woman (with the possible exception of minors who may need to notify or even get permission from their parents).

Other family members may also feel that they have moral, if not legal, rights in this debate. Because most women seeking an abortion are young, unmarried, and have a low income, grandparents—particularly maternal grandparents—are frequently affected by the decision to forego an abortion, for it may mean that they will be called upon to help raise and support the child financially, and they may not have the financial means to contribute to such support. Some grandparents may attempt to exercise influence to prevent the abortion, regardless of who will support the child.

Health care providers would also like to claim rights in this debate. Those who participate in counseling about abortion and its procedures would like to do so without concern about being harassed at work and elsewhere by abortion opponents. Health care providers who oppose abortion would like to carry out their professional responsibilities in a work environment that is consistent with their personal values. Physicians are particularly concerned about their rights in the abortion debate. Before the *Roe* decision, statutes specified that it was a crime to perform an abortion. As Martha Field has pointed out, that decision addressed the plight of physicians, whose right to practice medicine was thus infringed on (1993, 5). Moreover, various statutes and Supreme Court decisions have required that a physician provide the woman with detailed information about informed consent, notify parents in instances where the pregnant patient is a minor, and perform viability tests if the physician believes the woman is more than twenty weeks pregnant.

Many taxpayers would like to claim rights in this debate. Those who oppose abortion object to the use of government funds to pay for abortions and abortion-related services. Many pro-choice taxpayers believe that abortions should be funded by public dollars; many taxpayers without strong feelings about abortion itself would prefer to pay for abortions rather than for childbirth, since the former are substantially less expensive and eliminate the possibility that another child will be added to the public assistance rolls. The state also has an interest in promoting the health of the pregnant woman and the potential life of the viable fetus.

This conflict of rights and interests is summarized in the joint opinion in *Planned Parenthood of Southeastern Pennsylvania v. Casey* (1992):

> Abortion is a unique act. It is an act fraught with consequences for others: for the woman who must live with the implications of her decision; for the persons who perform and assist in the procedure; for the spouse, family, and society which must confront the knowledge that these procedures exist, procedures some deem nothing short of an act of violence against innocent human life; and, depending on one's beliefs, for the life or potential life that is aborted. (at 2807)

This chapter seeks to answer the questions of who has rights and who does not, and whether such rights are positive or negative. Do certain members of society have a positive obligation to assist women in securing an abortion or is abortion a negative right in the sense that the law, although not proscribing abortion, does not actively assist women in obtaining it?

Abortion in the Nineteenth Century

In view of the intensity of the battle between pro-choice and pro-life activists, it is difficult to believe that throughout much of American histo-

ry, abortion was both legal and socially acceptable; its proscription came
about primarily as a result of reforms in the medical profession rather than
from any serious concerns about its morality (although that was a subject
of debate). From the colonial period until the early twentieth century, abortion law was governed by British common law, which did not recognize the
existence of the fetus until after quickening (the point at which a woman
feels movement of the fetus). Prior to quickening, women and their physicians could not determine whether failure to menstruate was due to pregnancy or to some type of dangerous obstruction; the techniques to remove
such obstructions were the same as those used in abortion. Rather than
have a physician perform an abortion, many women self-aborted. Information on primitive abortion techniques was available in a variety of publica-
tions, including religious magazines. James Mohr explains that juniper extract was the most common abortifacient; Laurence Tribe discusses the use
of various poisons, soap solutions, and other intrusions into the uterus
(Mohr 1978, 5-9; Tribe 1990, 29).

During the latter part of the nineteenth century, physicians launched a
successful drive to professionalize and control the practice of medicine in
the United States. They feared that they would not be able to preserve their
income level and the elite status in society that American physicians had
enjoyed throughout the seventeenth and eighteenth centuries because they
could not control common diseases (Mohr 1978, 3). Abortion procedures
were unsafe. Tribe reports that statistics on New York in the early nineteenth century indicate a mortality rate of 30 percent from infections after
abortion surgery (including operations performed in hospitals), whereas
the mortality rate from childbirth was only 3 percent (1990, 39).

Largely as a result of the inability of physicians to control disease, "irregulars" who had no medical training entered the profession between
1800 and 1840 and offered a variety of "treatments" for maladies. They
were able to succeed in this effort because most medical schools were pri-
vately run and dependent on tuition-paying students for survival; many
were degree "mills" where payment of tuition ensured receipt of a diplo-
ma (Mohr 1978, 33). Most "regular" physicians had been trained at the
better medical schools or followed the practices of those who were. The
regulars tried to organize medical societies, publish medical journals, and
encourage the maintenance of high standards in the nation's medical
schools.

The entry of irregulars into the profession, along with intense competition for patients, caused physicians' incomes to decline. The regular physicians fought back on a number of fronts, one of which was abortion. They
opposed it on several grounds. Performing or assisting in an abortion was a
violation of the Hippocratic oath. They also knew that quickening was an

arbitrarily defined point in pregnancy and had nothing to do with the physical development of the fetus. More than any other group (including ministers), they defended the principle that human life has value and should be protected. But they believed that refusing to perform or assist in abortions would prompt women to seek medical care from the irregulars, perhaps meaning a loss of patients. Moreover, women would be endangering their own lives. The best solution seemed to be to attempt to educate the public regarding the vices of abortion and to lobby state legislators to make abortion a crime (Mohr 1978).

In the mid-1840s, societal attitudes toward abortion began to change; it became an openly accepted business service, advertised in newspapers and magazines. The number of abortions performed increased dramatically; some have estimated that as many as one in every five or six pregnancies was terminated (Mohr 1978, 50; Sanderson cited in Luker 1984, 44; Petchesky 1990, 73-78). Birth rates declined from an average of 7.04 children per woman of childbearing age in 1800 to 3.56 children in 1900 (Mohr 1978, 82). It cannot be determined precisely what percentage of this decline is attributable to abortion and what percentage can be explained by increased education about contraception, however.

Prior to the 1840s, the typical abortion patient was an unmarried woman who wanted to avoid the burden and social consequences of an ''illegitimate'' pregnancy. After 1840, many middle- and upper-class married women utilized abortion as a form of birth control (Mohr 1978, 46-47). Regular physicians, among others, did not fail to notice that birth rates were higher for immigrants, particularly Catholics, than for American-born women of British and northern European ancestry. According to Tribe, regular physicians played on middle-class Protestant fears of ''race suicide'' in attempting to encourage the proscription of abortion. Regular physicians were also concerned that reproductive freedom would allow women to pursue their own interests outside the home, thus threatening traditional sex roles (Tribe 1990, 33).

Statutes enacted by state legislatures between 1821 and 1841 specified punishment for the person who performed an abortion (such as an apothecary or a physician) but not the woman seeking it. In order to prosecute, the state was required to prove that the woman was pregnant and that the intent was to perform an abortion; both were impossible to prove prior to quickening (Mohr 1978, 20). Between 1860 and 1880, at least forty anti-abortion statutes were adopted by state and territorial legislative bodies (Mohr 1978, 200). By 1900, virtually all states had passed laws prohibiting abortion. Abortion was made a crime on the part of both the provider and the woman seeking it at any time during the entire pregnancy, including the period prior to viability. Many of these statutes were still on the books and being

actively enforced nearly one hundred years later when *Roe v. Wade*
reached the Supreme Court (Mohr 1978, 226).

The Abortion Controversy Moves to the Courts: *Roe v. Wade*

In the 1960s, a decade marked by political turmoil and intensification of
the battle for equality between the sexes, abortion emerged as a pressing
issue. A number of events placed abortion at the top of the public agenda
(see Table 2-1). In 1962, the nation's attention focused on the case of
Sherri Finkbine, an Arizona mother of four young children who had taken
the tranquilizing drug Thalidomide during her pregnancy. When she became aware of news reports from Europe—where her husband had purchased the drug—indicating that it caused serious fetal deformities, she
notified her obstetrician, who recommended an abortion. He reserved the
operating room at the local public hospital but advised her to make a written request for a therapeutic abortion to the hospital's abortion committee.
Finkbine, who was then employed as the host of a local television program
for preschoolers, encouraged a friend to write a newspaper article about her
case (without identifying her), in an effort to warn others about the possible
dangers of taking Thalidomide during pregnancy (Craig and O'Brien 1993,
41; Luker 1984, 62-65).

Her anonymity was short-lived; news reporters descended on her and
her husband. The hospital denied her request and her employer fired her.
She left the United States and had an abortion in Sweden. The aborted fetus
had serious deformities and most likely would not have lived. Her well-
publicized plight was a significant agenda-setting event in the abortion debate (Craig and O'Brien 1993, 41; Tribe 1990, 37). At the same time, the
nation was hit by a Rubella epidemic that lasted until 1965 during which
time 15,000 children were born with birth defects (Tribe 1990, 37).

As public concern regarding abortion mounted, organizations began to
choose sides and new organizations were formed. In 1967, a group of clergy announced publicly that it would assist women in securing safe abortions. Several Protestant denominations, including the United Church of
Christ, the United Methodist Church, the United Presbyterian Church, and
the Episcopalian Church, endorsed the repeal of criminal abortion statutes.
Newly formed organizations, most notably NARAL, spearheaded the drive
for liberalization of abortion policy (Tribe 1990, 37-49). Groups supporting a woman's right to choose to terminate a pregnancy were organized
and sought to bring about change through state legislative action. By 1973,
Alaska, Hawaii, New York, Washington State, and the District of Columbia had legalized elective abortion. Mississippi permitted elective abortions in cases of rape, and thirteen other states allowed the performing of

Table 2-1 Agenda-setting Events in the Abortion Debate, 1962-1980

Year	Event
1962	Sherri Finkbine, a pregnant Arizona mother of four who has been taking the drug Thalidomide, seeks but is denied hospital committee approval for an abortion. She obtains an abortion in Sweden. The fetus is seriously deformed.
1962	Rubella epidemic begins, lasts until 1965; 15,000 infants are born with birth defects.
1967	Members of the clergy announce that they will assist women in securing safe abortions.
1967	The National Organization for Women adds to its Bill of Rights the right of women to control their reproductive lives.
1969	The National Association for the Repeal of Abortion Laws is founded. Name changed in 1973 to National Abortion Rights Action League. Name changed in 1994 to National Abortion and Reproductive Rights Action League.
1969	The Planned Parenthood Federation of America announces its support for the repeal of abortion statutes.
1970	Hawaii, New York, and Alaska repeal abortion statutes.
1973	The Supreme Court issues its decisions in *Roe v. Wade* and *Doe v. Bolton*.
1976	The first Hyde Amendment prohibiting the use of federal funds to pay for abortions is enacted as part of a Department of Health, Education, and Welfare appropriations bill.
1978	Pro-life groups target pro-choice senators and lobby for their electoral defeat. Senators Dick Clark (D-Iowa), Edward W. Brooke (R-Mass.), and Floyd K. Haskell (D-Colo.) are defeated. The Life Amendment Political Action Committee announces it will target other pro-choice senators for electoral defeat in 1980.
1980	Pro-choice senators John Culver (D-Iowa), Birch Bayh (D-Ind.), Frank Church (D-Idaho), Patrick Leahy (D-Vt.), George McGovern (D-S.D.), and Bob Packwood (R-Ore.) are targeted for electoral defeat by pro-life organizations. All but Leahy and Packwood are defeated.

Source: Adapted from text information in Tribe 1990, 35-51; and Craig and O'Brien 1993, 41-68.

therapeutic abortions to protect the woman's physical and mental health. Twenty-nine states allowed an abortion only to save the woman's life; Louisiana, New Hampshire, and Pennsylvania prohibited all abortions (Craig and O'Brien 1993, 75).

This was the setting in 1973, when the Supreme Court decided the landmark case of *Roe v. Wade* and its companion case, *Doe v. Bolton*. In *Roe*, the Court overturned a Texas criminal statute that prohibited abortion (except to save the life of the mother); it found that abortion fell within a woman's zone of privacy.

This right of privacy . . . is broad enough to encompass a woman's decision whether or not to terminate her pregnancy. The detriment that the State would impose upon the pregnant woman by denying this choice altogether is apparent. Specific and direct harm medically diagnosable even in early pregnancy may be involved. Maternity, or additional offspring, may force upon the woman a distressful life and future. Psychological harm may be imminent. Mental and physical health may be taxed by child care. There is also the distress, for all concerned, associated with the unwanted child, and there is the problem of bringing a child into a family already unable, psychologically and otherwise, to care for it. In other cases, as in this one, the additional difficulties and continuing stigma of unwed motherhood may be involved. All these are factors the woman and her responsible physician necessarily will consider in consultation. (*Roe v. Wade* at 153)

The Court did not, however, grant an absolute right to secure an abortion. Rather it ruled that during the first trimester, the abortion decision must be left to the medical judgment of the attending physician in consultation with the pregnant woman. During the second trimester, because the state has an interest in promoting the health of the mother, it may regulate abortion procedures in ways that are reasonably related to maternal health. In the third trimester—the stage at which the Court determined that viability existed—the state, because of its interest in preserving potential human life, may regulate and proscribe abortion except in cases where the pregnancy threatens the mother's life or health (at 114). Thus states were allowed to determine whether abortion would be legal or illegal during the last three months of pregnancy. The Court specifically declined to determine when life begins, but it did find that the word ''person'' as used in the Fourteenth Amendment did not include the unborn (at 158).

In the companion case, *Doe v. Bolton,* Mary Doe and twenty-three other individuals, including nine physicians, seven nurses, five clergymen, and two social workers, challenged a 1968 Georgia abortion statute based on the American Law Institute's Model Penal Code, which at the time of *Doe* had been enacted by approximately one-fourth of the states. The Georgia statute provided that abortions could be performed in cases where continuation of the pregnancy would endanger the pregnant woman's life or injure her health, the fetus was likely to be born with a serious defect, or the pregnancy resulted from rape. In addition, the abortion had to be performed in a hospital accredited by the Joint Commission on Accreditation of Hospitals and be approved by the hospital's abortion committee; in addition, two physicians other than the physician performing the abortion had to confirm that the abortion met the criteria specified in the statute.

Mary Doe was a 22-year-old indigent with three children. She had placed the two older children in foster care because of her inability to care for them (or even to support herself) and had given up her third child for adoption. Doe had an unstable relationship with her husband; when she did not live with him she lived with her indigent parents and their eight other children. She had also been a mental patient in a state hospital. In March 1970, she applied for an abortion at Grady Memorial Hospital in Atlanta and was denied because her situation did not meet the criteria contained in the statute.

The Supreme Court invalidated the Georgia statute, finding that the health interests of the patient did not require that an abortion at any time during the pregnancy be performed in an accredited hospital. Moreover, it found that requiring a patient to seek the approval of a hospital committee was unduly restrictive of the patient's rights and that appellants had not cited any other surgical procedures that were made subject to committee approval. On the same ground, it struck down the requirement that two other physicians confirm the need for an abortion.

The Political Response to *Roe*

The pro-life movement was quick to organize in the aftermath of the *Roe* and *Doe* decisions. It had the strong support of the Family Life Division of the National Conference of Catholic Bishops, which declared that it would not accept the two decisions and organized anti-abortion activities through its parishes (Petchesky 1990, 252). Beginning in the late 1970s, the Catholic Church received substantial support from the New Right, a sizable movement dominated by Fundamentalist religious organizations and other conservative groups that had become increasingly powerful in electoral politics through the use of political action committees and direct mail fund raising.

Although there was much common ground between the two groups, the alliance was marked by dissension. Whereas pro-life groups tended to focus on a single issue, the agenda of the conservative New Right included opposition not only to abortion but to unions, gun control, school busing, homosexuality, and women's rights. The Catholic Church, which had a long history of support for liberal causes such as civil rights, conscientious objection to the war in Vietnam, and social programs for the poor, found this agenda difficult to accept (Petchesky 1990, 254-260; Tribe 1990, 159-160).

The pro-life movement has never been monolithic in structure, but its strategies have been fairly well defined. One strategy, to seek litigation of another abortion case in the hope of reversing *Roe,* would necessitate the prior passage of state or federal legislation to be used as the legal test (Craig and O'Brien 1993, 43). If the strategy were to have any real chance of success, there would have to be a change in the makeup of the Supreme Court. A second strategy, to seek ratification of a constitutional amendment banning abortion, would necessitate massive lobbying action at both the federal and state levels, since Congress proposes amendments and the states ratify them. A third strategy was to try to persuade government officials to ignore the Court's rulings and thereby undercut *Roe* and *Doe,* and to try to prevent women from seeking abortions by making it difficult for them to enter abortion clinics (Craig and O'Brien 1993, 43). The pro-life movement pursued all of these strategies, often simultaneously.

Roe v. Wade was the catalyst for the immediate organization of such pro-life groups as the National Right to Life Committee and the American Life Lobby. They joined forces against organizations such as the Planned Parenthood Federation of America, NARAL, and the National Organization for Women (NOW), all of which were founded prior to 1973. Ordinary citizens with pro-life sentiments, but without any experience in politics, were prompted to join the political activists (Hershey and West 1983, 38). Pro-choice and pro-life groups came of age during the information revolution; thus they were able to utilize computerized direct mailing in addition to traditional tactics such as direct lobbying.

The early strategy of the pro-life movement, as designed by the Catholic Church, was to concentrate on passage of a human life amendment. In the mid-1970s, it became apparent that this strategy would fail because there were not enough pro-life votes in Congress. Therefore, its next strategy focused on getting more pro-life legislators elected; by 1978, pro-life campaign activities were in full swing. Old-fashioned electoral strategies were combined with high-tech direct mail. Candidates—especially incumbents—who were identified as pro-choice and electorally vulnerable were targeted for defeat. Iowa pro-life groups produced a leaflet designed to appeal to the emotions, depicting a fetus with a caption that read, "This little guy needs your help" (Hershey and West 1983, 45). Thousands of leaflets were distributed at churches in Iowa on the Sunday before election day in 1978. Pro-life groups also organized a voter identification program in order to establish a name bank of pro-life volunteers and to develop lists for mass mailings. The Iowa strategies were repeated by pro-life organizations in other states in the 1980 election. Right to Life organizations held electoral strategy training sessions at their national conferences and used their national newsletters to keep members informed about successful strategies. Pro-life groups were assisted in their efforts by various New Right organizations including Richard Viguerie's conservative direct mail organization (Hershey and West 1991).

Pro-life groups were euphoric in 1978 when three key senators, Dick Clarke (Iowa), Edward Brooke (Mass.), and Floyd K. Haskell (Colo.), were defeated at the polls, and in 1980, when four of six targeted incumbents met the same fate. All told, the pro-life movement gained ten Senate seats and twenty House seats in 1980, as well as a pro-life ally, newly elected President Ronald Reagan. Despite what appeared to be pro-life victories in 1978 and 1980, some political analysts have concluded that abortion was an insignificant influence on the electoral outcomes in both years. Other issues such as the economy, the government's role in the administration of social programs, the proposed equal rights amendment, defense spending, aid to minorities, tax cuts, and discrimination against women were said to be more significant than abortion in influencing voters' choices. These analysts argue that the gains made by the pro-life movement were the result of a shift to political conservatism, a shift that began to reverse in the 1982 congressional elections (Granberg and Burlison 1983; Traugott and Vinovskis 1980).

The pro-life movement's euphoria over success at the polls soon diminished when it became apparent that electoral gains would not immediately translate into substantial policy gains. The human life amendment was not proposed in Congress. The pro-life movement felt betrayed in 1981 when President Reagan (whose candidacy it had supported) appointed Sandra Day O'Connor—the first female—to the Supreme Court. Despite the movement's active lobbying against her nomination because of her voting record on abortion as an Arizona state senator, the U.S. Senate unanimously confirmed her appointment (Hershey and West 1983, 54).

Slowly, however, the fortunes of the pro-life movement began to improve. Pro-life organizations persuaded Congress and the state legislatures to chip away at the right to elective abortion by making abortion more difficult to obtain. Restrictions were added to various pieces of legislation; most notable at the federal level were the Hyde Amendments restricting the use of public funds for abortions. The movement's efforts were facilitated because President Reagan and his successor, George Bush, both announced their intentions to overturn the effect of *Roe* through federally initiated litigation and together appointed 60 percent of the federal judgeships. A 1990 study reported in the *New York Times* revealed that Reagan judicial appointees supported abortion in 77 percent of the cases before them (Lewis 1992, A13). Pro-life sympathizers could rejoice in most of the other Reagan and Bush Supreme Court appointments, particularly the elevation of Justice William Rehnquist to chief justice and the confirmations of Antonin Scalia and Clarence Thomas. A more conservative Supreme Court looked more kindly on attempts to restrict access to abortion. Although its decisions have been somewhat inconsistent (for example, sometimes upholding parental notification and sometimes overturning it), the overall impact has also been to reduce the rights enunciated in *Roe*. The Supreme Court had made it clear that it "was not the right to choose abortion that was involved, but only a right not to have abortion constitute a criminal offense. The government did not have to facilitate access to abortion" (Field 1993, 7).

Although *Roe* prohibited state bans on abortion until the third trimester of pregnancy, policy makers made it difficult for many women, particularly poor women, to obtain abortions. Before 1976, approximately 300,000 legal abortions—about 33 percent of all legal abortions—were funded annually by Medicaid (Tribe 1990, 151). This changed in 1976, with enactment of the first Hyde Amendment (named for its sponsor, Rep. Henry Hyde [R-Ill.]), prohibiting the use of Medicaid funds for abortions. Although the specific restrictions have varied from year to year, since 1976 a Hyde Amendment has been attached annually to the appropriations bill for the Department of Health, Education, and Welfare (HEW) and for that of its successor (in 1980), the Department of Health and Human Services (HHS). Most state legislatures followed the example of Congress and enacted similar restrictions on the use of state funds. As of 1994, the Hyde Amendments are still in effect and preclude the federal funding of abortion except in cases of life endangerment to the mother, rape, or incest. Similar prohibitions are in effect in two-thirds of the states.

Congress also prohibited judges and public officials from ordering recipients of federal funds to perform abortions if doing so was against the recipient's beliefs; barred lawyers participating in federally funded legal aid programs from providing legal assistance in procuring "nontherapeutic" abortions; forbade recipients of federal funds to discriminate against job applicants because of their reluctance to counsel, assist, or participate in performing abortions; prohibited the funding of organizations involved in abortions, but allowed religious organizations to receive funds to promote "self-discipline" (abstinence) as a form of birth control; and allowed employers to refuse to pay health insurance benefits for abortion except when it was necessary to save the life of the mother (Craig and O'Brien 1993, 112-113). The HHS administrative regulations issued in 1988 prohibited the use of funds allocated under Title X of the Public Health Service Act to provide abortion counseling and referral. This so-called gag rule was upheld by the Supreme Court in *Rust v. Sullivan* (1991) but was lifted by President Bill Clinton shortly after his inauguration in 1993.

State legislatures and some city councils have also sought to restrict access to abortion by enacting a variety of provisions, such as those requiring that some abortions be performed in hospitals; requiring parental notification or consent, spousal notification, and waiting periods; and denying public funding for abortions (Craig and O'Brien 1993, 79-96). The Supreme Court has upheld some restrictions but has struck down others (see Table 2-2).

The Court overturned a Missouri law requiring that abortions after the twelfth week be performed in licensed hospitals (*Planned Parenthood of Kansas City v. Ashcroft*, 1983), as well as a city ordinance that disallowed abortions in all but licensed hospitals (*City of Akron v. Akron Center for Reproductive Health*, 1983). It upheld parental notification statutes and consent statutes if they contained judicial bypass provisions (*Bellotti v. Baird*, 1976; *H. L. v. Matheson*, 1981; *Planned Parenthood of Kansas City v. Ashcroft; Hodgson v. Minnesota*, 1990; *Ohio v. Akron Center for Reproductive Health*, 1990; and *Planned Parenthood of Southeastern Pennsylvania v. Casey*, 1992), but spousal notification was found to be unconstitutional (*Planned Parenthood of Central Missouri v. Danforth*, 1976; *Planned Parenthood of Southeastern Pennsylvania v. Casey*, 1992). Requirements that abortion patients receive extensive informed consent information regarding issues such as fetal development, alternatives to abortion, and availability of child support were overturned in *City of Akron v. Akron Center for Reproductive Health* and *Thornburgh v. American College of Obstetricians and Gynecologists* (1986), but upheld in *Planned Parenthood of Southeastern Pennsylvania v. Casey* 1992) (Craig and O'Brien 1993).

Some states required waiting periods, thus typically necessitating at least two visits to the abortion clinic. The Court overturned waiting periods in *City of Akron v. Akron Center for Reproductive Health* but upheld them in *Planned Parenthood of Central Missouri v. Danforth* and *Casey v. Planned Parenthood of Southern Pennsylvania*. States and cities also restricted public funding for abortions by limiting the circumstances in which Medicaid would pay for abortions (upheld in *Maher v. Roe*, 1977, and *Beal v. Doe*, 1977), by denying poor women access to nontherapeutic abortions in public hospitals (upheld in *Poelker v. Doe*, 1977), and by prohibiting the use of public facilities for abortions that were not necessary to save the mother's life (*Webster v. Reproductive Health Services*, 1989) (Craig and O'Brien 1993). Even though the Court struck down such restrictions, the overall impact of its decisions was to make abortion more difficult and more expensive to obtain, thus creating an especially difficult dilemma for young women and low-income women, who constitute the largest categories of abortion patients.

The decisions in *Webster v. Reproductive Health Services* and *Planned Parenthood of Southeastern Pennsylvania v. Casey* merit attention because their effect has been to limit the rights originally granted in *Roe* by increasing the states' ability to regulate abortion. The two decisions should not have surprised those knowledgeable about abortion policy, however, because they reflected the significant changes in the makeup of the Supreme

Table 2-2   Significant Supreme Court Decisions Concerning Privacy and Reproductive Rights

---

Roe v. Wade, 410 U.S. 113 (1973)

A challenge to a Texas statute criminalizing the performance of abortions except those "procured or attempted by medical advice for the purpose of saving the life of the mother." Holding 7-2 that the "right of privacy . . . is broad enough to encompass a woman's decision whether or not to terminate her pregnancy," the Supreme Court severely limited a state's ability to restrict abortion. Recognition of the right to choose abortion as fundamental meant that laws interfering with reproductive decisions could only be justified by a "compelling state interest." In the abortion context, these interests—maintaining proper medical standards, protecting the life and health of the pregnant woman, and protecting potential life—become "compelling" at different points during the pregnancy. After the first trimester, a state could impose restrictions necessary to protect a woman's health; after viability, the state's interest in protecting potential life could justify banning abortion or otherwise restricting the procedure. However, even after viability, the state's interest in potential life could not be promoted at the expense of a woman's life or health. The Court explicitly refused to recognize the fetus as a "person," and rejected the argument that a state's adoption of the view that life begins at conception could justify a ban on abortion.

Doe v. Bolton, 410 U.S. 179 (1973)

A challenge to a Georgia statute banning abortions except when a pregnancy would endanger the woman's life or "seriously and permanently injure her health," the fetus would "very likely be born with grave, permanent, and irremediable mental or physical defect," or the pregnancy was the result of rape. The abortion could only be performed in a hospital after a number of other requirements had been met, including written certification of the extenuating circumstances by at least three physicians and prior approval of a hospital committee. In a 7-2 opinion issued with *Roe,* the Supreme Court found the Georgia law to be unconstitutional, but recognized that the right to choose abortion is not "absolute." Specifically, in affirming a lower court decision striking down the certification requirements, the Court held that the physician's best medical judgment concerning the necessity of an abortion includes "all factors—physical, emotional, psychological, familial, and the woman's age—relevant to the well-being of the patient."

Planned Parenthood of Central Missouri v. Danforth, 428 U.S. 52 (1976)

A challenge to a number of Missouri abortion restrictions, including a requirement that a married woman obtain her husband's written consent and an unmarried minor obtain one parent's written consent prior to an abortion; a mandate that a physician preserve the life and health of a fetus at every stage of pregnancy; and a prohibition on the use of saline amniocentesis as a method of abortion. In a 6-3 decision, the Supreme Court invalidated the spousal consent provision, holding that the state may not provide a third party with an opportunity to veto a woman's decision whether to have an abortion; the same majority struck down both the prohibition on the particular abortion method and the physician requirement concerning protection of fetal life. Finally, a 5-4 majority of the Court struck down the parental consent requirement for unmarried minor women, reasoning that it too provided an unconstitutional veto power to a third party.

Bellotti v. Baird, 428 U.S. 132 (1976)

A challenge to a Massachusetts law requiring a woman under the age of 18 to obtain the consent of both parents prior to an abortion; should one or both parents refuse to consent to the procedure, the young woman may seek the consent of a judge. A unanimous Supreme Court held that the federal district court should have abstained from ruling on the constitutional issues raised in this case. The Supreme Court held that because the statute could be read in a manner that did not conflict with *Danforth,* the lower court should have certified the case to the Massachusetts Supreme Judicial Court for an interpretation of its meaning. Specifically, the Court noted that the statute could be construed to allow either a "mature minor" or a minor whose "best interests" would be served by obtaining an abortion to seek a court order allowing the procedure without first consulting her parents.

Maher v. Roe, 432 U.S. 464 (1977)

A challenge by two Medicaid-eligible women to Connecticut's limits on state Medicaid benefits for first trimester abortions. Under the challenged regulations, a physician must certify an abortion is "medically necessary"; the procedure must be performed in an accredited hospital or clinic; the woman must submit a written request for the procedure (if she is a minor, her parent or guardian must submit the request); and the Department of Social Services must preauthorize the abortion. In their lawsuit, the women noted that similar restrictions did not apply to other medical procedures, particularly those associated with childbirth. In a 6-3 ruling, the Supreme Court found that "[t]he indigency that may make it difficult—and in some cases, perhaps, impossible—for some women to have abortions is neither created nor in any way affected by the Connecticut regulation." Further, the Court held that the stringent level of constitutional protection afforded to the right to privacy in the context of a criminal abortion statute did not extend to a state benefits scheme. The Court also stated that a state may constitutionally promote childbirth over abortion in its Medicaid program.

Beal v. Doe, 432 U.S. 438 (1977)

A challenge by several Medicaid-eligible women to Pennsylvania's limitation of coverage for abortions to those certified as "medically necessary"—defined to be situations in which "documented medical evidence" shows that a woman's health is threatened by continued pregnancy, an infant may be born with "incapacitating physical deformity or mental deficiency," or continuance of a pregnancy resulting from rape or incest threatens a woman's "mental or physical" health. In each instance, two physicians in addition to the attending doctor must certify the medical necessity in writing and the procedure must be performed in an accredited hospital. Deciding this case along with *Maher v. Roe,* the Supreme Court's 7-2 majority upheld the challenged provisions, but sent the case back to the lower courts for a review of the two physician certification requirement.

Poelker v. Doe, 432 U.S. 519 (1977)

A challenge by a low-income woman who was denied an abortion at one of St. Louis's two city-owned public hospitals, pursuant to a city policy prohibiting the performance of abortions unless continued pregnancy would result in a woman's physiological injury or death. Citing the reasoning in *Maher v. Doe,* a per curiam opinion expressing the views of six justices upheld the city policy. The Court held that, "as a policy choice,"

continued

Table 2-2   Continued

St. Louis may "provide publicly financed hospital services for childbirth without providing corresponding services for nontherapeutic abortions."

Colautti v. Franklin, 439 U.S. 379 (1979)

A challenge to a Pennsylvania statute requiring a physician performing an abortion to "preserve the life and health of the fetus [as though it were] intended to be born and not aborted" when the fetus is viable or where there was "sufficient reason to believe [it] may be viable." In a 6-3 decision, the Supreme Court found the law unconstitutionally vague because it did not distinguish between "may be viable" and the definition of viability established in *Roe.* Moreover, the Court noted that the statute did not "clearly specify . . . that the woman's life and health must always prevail over the fetus' life and health when they conflict."

Bellotti v. Baird, 443 U.S. 622 (1979)

A challenge to a Massachusetts law requiring a woman under the age of 18 to obtain the consent of both parents prior to an abortion; should one or both parents refuse to consent to the procedure, the young woman may seek the consent of a judge. (See *Bellotti I* on page 45 for earlier case history.) Eight justices voted to strike down the law, which the Massachusetts Supreme Judicial Court interpreted to (1) require consent from available parents for any nonemergency procedure, (2) require notice to an available parent of a court proceeding, or (3) allow a court to withhold consent even if "the minor is capable of making, and has made, an informed and reasonable decision." Four justices found fault with the "judicial bypass" procedure because it required parental consultation in every case and allowed the court to override the decision of a "mature minor." In contrast, the other four justices found the statute unconstitutional because it provided either a parent or a judge with an absolute veto over the decision to have an abortion.

Harris v. McRae, 448 U.S. 297 (1980)

A challenge to the Hyde Amendment, first enacted by Congress in 1976 as part of the fiscal year 1977 appropriation for the Department of Health, Education, and Welfare. As applied to the Medicaid program, the Hyde Amendment barred the use of federal funds for abortions except in extremely limited circumstances. In a 5-4 decision, the Supreme Court upheld the funding restriction, finding that "the Hyde Amendment . . . places no governmental obstacle in the path of a woman who chooses to terminate her pregnancy, but rather, by means of unequal subsidization of abortion and other medical services, encourages alternative activity deemed in the public interest." The Court further found that "[t]he financial constraints that restrict an indigent woman's ability to enjoy the full range of constitutionally protected freedoms of choice are the product not of governmental restrictions on access to abortions, but rather of her indigency." Finally, the Court found that states participating in the Medicaid program are not required by Title XIX of the Social Security Act to fund "medically necessary" abortions for which federal funds are not available.

H. L. v. Matheson, 450 U.S. 398 (1981)

A challenge to a Utah statute requiring a physician to notify the parents of a dependent, unmarried woman under the age of 18 prior to performing an abortion. In a 6-3 decision, the Supreme Court upheld the law on narrow grounds as applied to an unmarried, "immature" minor who lives with and is dependent on her parents. At the same time, the Court distinguished this measure from the ones at issue in *Bellotti* and *Danforth,* finding that parental notice is not equivalent to consent and that Utah law did not give parents or a judge veto power over a young woman's decision to obtain an abortion. The Court did not reach the issue of the constitutionality of the law as applied to mature and emancipated minors.

City of Akron v. Akron Center for Reproductive Health, 462 U.S. 416 (1983)

A challenge to an Akron city ordinance requiring that abortions performed after the first trimester be performed in a hospital; that a woman obtaining an abortion delay at least twenty-four hours after giving written consent and receiving from the attending physician specific information, including that "the unborn child is a human life from the moment of conception"; that a woman under the age of 18 notify one parent at least twenty-four hours prior to an abortion; that a woman under the age of 15 obtain the "informed" written consent of one parent twenty-four hours prior to an abortion; and that fetal remains be disposed of in a "humane and sanitary" manner. In its 6-3 opinion, the Supreme Court struck down all of the challenged provisions, finding that they unconstitutionally interfered with the right to choose abortion established in *Roe.*

Planned Parenthood Association of Kansas City v. Ashcroft, 462 U.S. 476 (1983)

A challenge to a number of Missouri provisions, including a requirement that all abortions after the twelfth week of pregnancy be performed in hospitals; a requirement that a second physician be present during any abortion performed after the point of viability to provide "immediate medical care for a child born as a result of the abortion"; and a mandate that a woman under age 18 obtain the "informed" written consent of one parent or a court prior to an abortion. Citing *Akron,* a 6-3 majority of the Supreme Court found the second trimester hospitalization requirement to be unconstitutional. However, five members of the Court upheld the second physician requirement and the parental consent provision.

Thornburgh v. American College of Obstetricians and Gynecologists, 476 U.S. 747 (1986)

A challenge to several requirements of the Pennsylvania Abortion Control Act: a woman seeking an abortion must receive specific information from her attending physician and be told of the availability of state-printed materials, including details about the fetus at various stages of pregnancy, before giving her "informed" consent to the procedure; abortion providers must file reports with the state, including the identities of the performing and referring physicians, details about the woman obtaining the abortion, and the method of payment; a physician performing a post-viability abortion must use the "degree of care" required to preserve the life and health of child intended to be born and to use the method of abortion most likely to preserve the life of the fetus, unless it would present a "significantly greater medical risk to the life or health of the pregnant woman"; and a second physician must be present during abortions where it is possible for the fetus to survive the procedure, regardless of whether an emergency exists. In a 5-4 opinion strongly reaffirming *Roe,* the Supreme Court invalidated all of these measures, finding that "our cases long have recognized that the Constitution embodies the promise that a certain private sphere of individual liberty will be kept largely beyond the

continued

Table 2-2   Continued

reach of government. . . . That promise extends to women as well as men. Few decisions are more personal and intimate, more properly private, or more basic to individual dignity and autonomy, than a woman's decision . . . whether to end her pregnancy.''

Webster v. Reproductive Health Services, 492 U.S. 490 (1989)

A challenge to a Missouri statute, which included a preamble stating that human life begins at the moment of conception and that state law must be interpreted to provide "the unborn child . . . all the rights, privileges, and immunities available to other persons, citizens, and residents" of the state. The law prohibits the use of public funding, employees, or facilities in "encouraging or counseling" a woman to have an abortion not necessary to save her life, as well as the use of public employees or facilities in performing or assisting in these procedures; it also requires a physician to determine "the gestational age, weight, and lung maturity" of any fetus suspected of being more than twenty weeks prior to performing an abortion. Claiming to be leaving *Roe* "undisturbed," the Supreme Court, in a 5-4 opinion, relied on *Poelker, Mayer,* and *McRae* to uphold the provisions relating to public employees and facilities. Five justices also found the viability testing requirement valid and stated that it was unnecessary to reach the constitutionality of the preamble because it "does not by its terms regulate abortion or any other aspect of [the plaintiffs'] medical practice." All nine justices agreed that the dispute over the restrictions on "encouraging or counseling" was moot because Missouri claimed, and plaintiffs agreed, that the measure did not affect any medical personnel's speech. This case marked the first time that only four justices—less than a majority—voted to uphold *Roe* in its entirety.

Hodgson v. Minnesota, 497 U.S. 417 (1990)

A challenge to Minnesota's two-part statute concerning parental notification prior to a young woman's abortion. The law required written notice to both of an unemancipated minor's parents at least forty-eight hours prior to the procedure, except in extremely limited circumstances; a second portion of the law provided that, should this requirement be found unconstitutional, the requirement would be enforced with the addition of a judicial bypass proceeding. In its 5-4 opinion, the Supreme Court struck down the first portion of the statute, stating that "the requirement that *both* parents be notified, whether or not both wish to be notified or have assumed responsibility for the upbringing of the child, does not reasonably further any legitimate state interest." Although unable to agree on a specific reasoning, five justices found constitutional the parental notification provision that provided for a judicial bypass.

Ohio v. Akron Center for Reproductive Health, 497 U.S. 502 (1990)

A challenge to an Ohio statute requiring a physician to notify or obtain the written consent of one parent at least twenty-four hours prior to performing an abortion on an unmarried and unemancipated minor; should the woman and an adult sibling, stepparent, or grandparent each certify that the minor fears physical, sexual, or severe emotional abuse from one of her parents, notification can be given to that adult relative. The statute also contained a bypass mechanism through which a court could either grant a minor the right to consent or provide constructive authorization through its inaction. In a 6-3 decision issued with *Hodgson v. Minnesota,* the Supreme Court found the statute constitutional.

Rust v. Sullivan, 111 S. Ct. 1759 (1991)

A challenge to federal regulations prohibiting recipients of family planning funds under Title X of the Public Health Service Act from providing counseling about or referrals for abortions, and from engaging in activities that "encourage, promote or advocate abortion as a method of family planning"; grantees that provided abortions with non-federal funds were also required to keep these activities "physically and financially separate" from their Title X project. In a 5-4 decision, the Supreme Court upheld the regulations, finding that they violated neither the Constitution's guarantees of freedom of speech and the right to privacy nor the language of the federal statute authorizing Title X.

Planned Parenthood of Southeastern Pennsylvania v. Casey, 112 S. Ct. 2791 (1992)

A challenge to requirements that all women seeking abortions delay at least twenty-four hours after receiving mandated information from a physician, including the probable gestational age of the fetus and its development, the availability of state-funded social service programs, a list of health care facilities that can help ensure healthy birth, and a statement that the putative father may be liable for child support; a married woman must notify her husband of her abortion choice except in very limited circumstances; a young woman must bring a consenting parent to the clinic or obtain judicial approval prior to an abortion; and abortion providers must file detailed reports with the state. The law's definition of "medical emergency," which allowed for the requirements to be waived, was also at issue in this case. In a fractured decision, a majority of the Supreme Court upheld all of the challenged measures, except the husband notification requirement.[a] Asserting that it was maintaining the "core" holdings of *Roe,* the Court, in a joint opinion, abandoned the trimester framework outlined in that decision, finding that a state may assert its interest in potential human life throughout pregnancy. At the same time, the Court explicitly overruled its decisions in *Akron* and *Thornburgh* and abandoned *Roe*'s "strict scrutiny" standard. In its place, the Court adopted an "undue burden" standard under which states cannot impose abortion restrictions that have "the purpose or effect of placing a substantial obstacle in the path of a woman seeking an abortion." Making clear that the Pennsylvania husband notification requirement was unconstitutional because it would be an "undue burden" on some women seeking abortions, the Court further reiterated that bans on abortion, even if they contain exceptions, also remain unconstitutional.

Bray v. Alexandria Women's Health Clinic, 113 S. Ct. 753 (1993)

A lawsuit filed by the National Organization for Women (NOW)[b] and nine women's health clinics seeking injunctive relief under federal civil rights statutes from threatened blockades of abortion providers in the Washington, D.C., area. The Supreme Court, in a 6-3 opinion, ruled that the district court had improperly used the statute, 42 U.S.C. sec. 1985(3), to enjoin abortion opponents from blocking access to the health clinics. Specifically, the majority held that plaintiffs did not meet the requirements for a claim under the law because (1) opposition to abortion does not constitute "invidiously discriminatory animus" against women as a class; and (2) based on the decision in *Geduldig v. Aiello,* 417 U.S. 484 (1974), discrimination against abortion, as with discrimination based on pregnancy, is not sex discrimination.[c] The Court also held that

continued

Table 2-2   Continued

the plaintiffs failed to demonstrate that the purpose, rather than the effect, of the blockades was to interfere with the right to interstate travel.

Source: Table supplied by Center for Reproductive Law and Policy, 1994.

[a] Justices Sandra Day O'Connor, Anthony Kennedy, and David Souter were joined by Justices Harry Blackmun and John Paul Stevens in invalidating the husband notification provision. Justices O'Connor, Kennedy, and Souter were joined by Chief Justice William Rehnquist and Justices Byron White, Antonin Scalia, and Clarence Thomas in upholding the statute's twenty-four-hour delay and mandated physician information. The same seven justices voted to uphold the parental consent provision, whereas only Justice Blackmun refused to join the ruling in favor of the reporting requirements and the definition of medical emergency. Chief Justice Rehnquist and Justices White, Scalia, and Thomas indicated that they would have overruled *Roe* completely.
[b] The National Abortion Federation was dismissed by the district court.
[c] The opinion further cited *Maher v. Roe,* 432 U.S. 464 (1977), and *Harris v. McRae,* 448 U.S. 297 (1980), in which the Court found that the federal government's decision to favor childbirth over abortion was also not discriminatory.

Court. In *Webster,* a 1986 Missouri statute was challenged by five health care professionals employed by Missouri public facilities and two nonprofit corporations that provided abortion services. The statute provided in its preamble that life begins at conception; that "unborn children" have protectable interests in the preservation of life, health, and well-being; and that other Missouri statutes are to be interpreted as granting "unborn children" the same rights as those granted other persons. The statute also prohibited the use of public employees and facilities for performing abortions (except when necessary to save the woman's life), prohibited the use of public funds to counsel women or encourage them to have abortions, and required that physicians perform viability tests on fetuses whose gestational age was believed to be twenty or more weeks.

In a plurality opinion, the Supreme Court upheld the statutory prohibition on the use of public facilities and employees for performing or assisting in abortions. The Court reasoned that because such a prohibition did not deny women the opportunity to secure abortions but only prevented them from obtaining abortions in *public* facilities, it did not constitute a violation of the due process clause of the Fourteenth Amendment.

> Nothing in the Constitution requires States to enter or remain in the business of performing abortions. Nor, as appellees suggest, do private physicians and their patients have some kind of constitutional access to public facilities for the performance of abortions. (*Webster v. Reproductive Health Services* at 510)

The Court refused to rule on the preamble because it did not actually regulate abortion, but could be read as simply expressing a value judgment favoring childbirth over abortion. The Court did, however, find the requirement of viability tests to be constitutional:

> The tests that [the statute] requires the physician to perform are designed to determine viability. The State here has chosen viability as the point at which its interest in potential human life must be safeguarded. . . . [W]e are satisfied that the requirement of these tests permissibly furthers the State's interest in protecting potential human life. . . . The Missouri testing requirement here is reasonably designed to ensure that abortions are not performed where the fetus is viable—an end which all concede is legitimate—and that is sufficient to sustain its constitutionality. (at 519-520)

The issue of counseling by publicly funded organizations was declared moot because health care professionals offering abortion services or pregnancy counseling had withdrawn their claims from their federal action (at 512-513). In a strongly worded dissent, Justice Harry Blackmun, who more than a decade earlier had written the majority opinion in *Roe v. Wade,* argued that the plurality opinion in *Webster* was an invitation for state legislatures to further restrict abortion rights. "The signs are evident and very ominous," he wrote, "and a chill wind blows" (at 560).

That chill wind was still blowing in 1992. In *Planned Parenthood of Southeastern Pennsylvania v. Casey,* a sharply divided Supreme Court further modified the basic principles established in *Roe.* The case concerned a Pennsylvania statute requiring that women seeking an abortion be advised by the physician of the gestational age of the fetus, the risks of and alternatives to abortion, and the availability of medical assistance for childbirth, child support, and state-funded programs such as adoption. After the patient received this information (the informed consent "lecture") from the physician, a twenty-four-hour waiting period was required before she could obtain an abortion. The statute also required the consent of one parent if the pregnant woman was a minor (but allowed judicial bypass), spousal notification, recordkeeping by the abortion facility, and confidential reporting of abortions to the state. The Court upheld all provisions of the statute that were contained in the appeal, with the exception of spousal notification and its related reporting provisions.

The Supreme Court did not issue a majority opinion in *Casey.* Rather, in a joint opinion, written by Justices Sandra Day O'Connor, David Souter, and Anthony M. Kennedy, and concurred with in part by Justices Harry Blackmun and John Paul Stevens, the Court affirmed that abortion would continue to be legal, but with significant restrictions. Chief Justice

William Rehnquist and Justices Antonin Scalia, Clarence Thomas, and Byron White dissented from the joint opinion and remained strong in their opposition to legalized abortion. It should be noted that although *Roe* was, in essence, upheld, the *legal principles* enunciated in the joint opinion differed greatly from those emphasized in the majority opinion in *Roe*. In *Roe,* the Court developed the trimester concept and relied on constitutional rights to privacy as the basis for the right to seek an abortion during the first two trimesters. It allowed state regulation, including the proscription of abortion—except when abortion was necessary to save the life or preserve the health of the woman—during the last trimester because at that stage, viability had been attained and therefore the state had a compelling interest in promoting potential human life. A state that sought to interfere with a woman's choice to have an abortion would have to show a ''compelling interest'' as a justification, and the Court recognized only two: the promotion of maternal health during pregnancy and the promotion of fetal life after viability (Center for Reproductive Law and Policy 1992a, 5). Moreover, even when the state could show a compelling interest, it was required to use the least restrictive alternative to achieve that interest.

In the joint opinion, the Court abandoned the trimester approach in recognition of more recent findings of medical science—specifically in the areas of prenatal and neonatal care—indicating a reduction in the gestational age at which viability occurs. Rather, it held that a woman has the right to obtain an abortion prior to viability, but not necessarily without limitation. State laws that imposed ''undue burdens'' (placed a substantial obstacle in the way of the woman seeking the abortion of a nonviable fetus) were prohibited. Other limitations were deemed constitutional. The Court found that the provisions concerning informed consent (including the required physician's presentation of information on alternatives to abortion), a twenty-four-hour waiting period, parental notification, and recordkeeping did not constitute undue burdens. Spousal notification was found to constitute an undue burden, however, and was ruled unconstitutional.

> Regulations which do no more than create a structural mechanism by which the State, or the parent or guardian of a minor, may express profound respect for the life of the unborn are permitted, if they are not a substantial obstacle to the woman's exercise of the right to choose. . . . Unless it has that effect on her right of choice, a state measure designed to persuade her to choose childbirth over abortion will be upheld if reasonably related to that goal. Regulations designed to foster the health of a woman seeking an abortion are valid if they do not constitute an undue burden. (*Planned Parenthood of Southeastern Pennsylvania v. Casey* at 2821)

Table 2-3 Americans' Attitudes toward Abortion, 1975-1992 (responses in percentages)

Year (Month)	Legal under any circumstances	Legal under certain circumstances	Illegal in all circumstances
1992 (June)	34	48	13
1992 (Jan.)	31	53	14
1991 (Sept.)	33	49	14
1991 (May)	32	50	17
1990 [a]	31	53	12
1989 (July)	29	51	17
1989 (Apr.)	27	50	18
1988	24	57	17
1983	23	58	16
1981	23	52	21
1980	25	53	18
1979	22	54	19
1977	22	55	19
1975	21	54	22

Source: Gallup Poll data reported in Nevitte, Brandon, and Davis 1993, 21.

[a] The 1990 findings are based on two askings of this question, April 5-8 and 19-22, 1990.

The Court based its position that a pregnant woman is entitled to a legal abortion prior to viability on the concept of liberty as defined in the Fourteenth Amendment.

At the heart of liberty is the right to define one's own concept of existence, of meaning, of the universe, and of the mystery of human life. Beliefs about these matters could not define the attributes of personhood were they formed under compulsion of the State. . . . Though abortion is conduct, it does not follow that the State is entitled to proscribe it in all instances. That is because the liberty of the woman is at stake in a sense unique to the human condition and so unique to the law. The mother who carries a child to full term is subject to anxieties, to physical constraints, to pain that only she must bear. That these sacrifices have from the beginning of the human race been endured by woman with a pride that ennobles her in the eyes of others and gives to the infant a bond of love cannot alone be grounds for the State to insist she make the sacrifice. Her suffering is too intimate and personal for the State to insist, without more, upon its own vision of the woman's role, however dominant that vision has been in the course of our history and our culture. The destiny of the woman must be shaped to a large

Table 2-4 State Allocation of Funds for Abortion Services, by Circumstance

State	Life endangerment only[a]	Life, rape, and incest only	Life, rape, incest, and limited health circumstances only	All or most circumstances
Alabama	x			
Alaska				x
Arizona		x		
Arkansas		x[b]		
California				x[c]
Colorado		x[b]		
Connecticut				x[c]
Delaware		x		
District of Columbia				x
Florida		x		
Georgia		x		
Hawaii				x
Idaho				x[c]
Illinois				x[b, d]
Indiana		x		
Iowa		x[e]		
Kansas	x			
Kentucky	x			
Louisiana		x[b]		
Maine		x		
Maryland				x
Massachusetts				x[c]
Michigan		x[b]		
Minnesota				x[f]
Mississippi	x			
Missouri	x			
Montana		x[b]		
Nebraska	x[b]			
Nevada		x		
New Hampshire		x		
New Jersey				x[c]
New Mexico				x
New York				x

extent on her own conception of her spiritual imperatives and her place in society. (at 2807)

While the pro-life movement was seeking to have *Roe* overturned in the courts, anti-abortion direct action organizations were seeking to prevent individual women from obtaining abortions by staging public demonstrations outside abortion clinics. Demonstrators blocked entrances to clinics and vandalized them by pouring glue or honey into their door locks, at-

State	Life endangerment only[a]	Life, rape, and incest only	Life, rape, incest, and limited health circumstances only	All or most circumstances
North Carolina				x
North Dakota	x			
Ohio		x		
Oklahoma		x		
Oregon				x[c]
Pennsylvania		x		
Rhode Island		x		
South Carolina		x		
South Dakota	x			
Tennessee		x		
Texas		x		
Utah	x			
Vermont				x[c]
Virginia			x	
Washington				x
West Virginia				x[c]
Wisconsin			x	
Wyoming		x		
Total (Number of states plus District of Columbia)	9	22	2	18

Source: National Abortion and Reproductive Rights Action League (NARAL) 1995.

[a] These states are not in compliance with a federal law prohibiting participating states from excluding abortion from the Medicaid program in cases of life endangerment, rape, and incest.

[b] A court has ruled that this state must comply with a federal law prohibiting the exclusion of abortion from Medicaid in cases of life endangerment, rape, and incest.

[c] A court has ruled that the state constitution prohibits the state from restricting funding for abortion while providing funds for costs associated with childbirth.

[d] A court has ruled that the state constitution prohibits the enforcement of a state law restricting funding to the extent it bars funding for an abortion necessary to preserve the woman's health.

[e] This statute also provides funding in some cases for fetal deformity.

[f] A trial court has ruled that the state constitution prohibits the state from restricting funding for abortion while providing funds for costs associated with childbirth. The state has appealed the ruling.

tempted to intimidate pregnant patients and health care workers, and harassed potential abortion patients at their homes. As in earlier displays of passive resistance, many demonstrations ended with mass arrests. Operation Rescue, the most widely known such anti-abortion group, was fined $500,000 in 1989 because of its activities; in that year, there were at least 200 of the group's members in jail at any one time (Rubin 1991, 248). In 1993, the Supreme Court ruled in *Bray v. Alexandria Women's Health Clinic* that Operation Rescue had not violated any civil rights law because there was no proof that the demonstrators had an "animus" against women (Center for Reproductive Law and Policy 1993b, 1). The struggle over abortion turned to violence with the fatal shooting of Dr. David Gunn outside an abortion clinic in Pensacola, Florida, in March 1993. This event, as well as other controversial anti-abortion activities, received extensive media coverage; they have also caused division within the pro-life movement. The National Right to Life Committee has disassociated itself from Operation Rescue and does not report its activities in NRLC publications; it publicly condemned the shooting of Dr. Gunn.

Abortion in the 1990s

Despite the massive efforts made by the pro-life movement to influence electoral politics and institute litigation, and its staging of direct action demonstrations, the number of abortions performed in the United States, and the attitudes of Americans as measured by public opinion polls, have not changed substantially (Gold 1990; Ladd 1989; Nevitte, Brandon, and Davis 1993). Nevitte, Brandon, and Davis noted a moderate shift in attitudes toward abortion between 1975 and 1992 (see Table 2-3 on page 53). In 1975, 75 percent of the respondents believed that abortion should be legal: 21 percent believed that abortion should be legal under any circumstances, and 54 percent believed it should be legal only under certain circumstances. In June 1992, the comparable figures were 82 percent, 34 percent, and 48 percent, respectively. These researchers also noted a reduction in Americans' approval of abortion in cases where the child is likely to be physically disabled (1993, 22). The approval rate declined from 61 percent in 1981 to 54 percent in 1990 (22). In general, however, a substantial majority of Americans consistently support legalized abortion under certain circumstances. As might be expected, the findings of public opinion polls mirror to a large extent the demographic profiles of pro-choice and pro-life activists—especially in terms of education and adherence to established religion. College graduates who rarely attend church are likely to be pro-choice, and those with a high school education or less who attend church regularly are likely to be pro-life (Ladd 1989).

Although abortion is legal until the point of viability, it is not easily obtainable for many, particularly young women and women with low incomes. In March 1994, more than thirty-six states had parental notification statutes on the books, although only twenty-four states enforced them (Andrea Miller, editor of *Reproductive Freedom News,* published by the Center for Reproductive Law and Policy; personal correspondence with the authors, February 25, 1994). The use of federal funds for abortion and abortion-related services is generally prohibited except in cases where the mother's life is at risk or in cases of rape or incest. Although all states provide funds for abortion to save the life of the mother, less than half of them provide funds in cases of rape or incest. Only eighteen states provide funds for all or most circumstances (National Abortion and Reproductive Rights Action League 1995). See Table 2-4 on page 54.

Conclusion

Abortion, perhaps more than any other issue discussed in this book, has generated an impassioned battle over rights. The debate between pro-choice and pro-life activists, with their conflicting views of pregnancy, motherhood, family, and the proper roles of women in society, has continued, with increasing intensity, for more than two decades. Other parties, such as a pregnant woman's partner and grandparents, may also claim perceived rights, but such rights have not been upheld by the courts. The decisions of the Supreme Court from *Roe* to the present reveal a pattern of negative rights. That is, a woman has the right to an elective abortion prior to viability, but the state does not have to assist her in exercising that right. In fact, the state can make it difficult for her to do so. It can stipulate that public funds not be used for abortion-related services (except in cases where the woman's life is threatened), it can mandate a waiting period, and it can require parental notification or consent.

The pattern of the Supreme Court's decisions during the past twenty years suggests that abortion will continue to be a basic right—albeit a negative one. This prediction has been given some validity by the election of President Clinton, who supports the pro-choice position, and his appointment of Ruth Bader Ginsburg, another pro-choice advocate, to the Court. Clearly, the abortion debate is far from over and the abortion issue will continue to have priority on the public agenda. Newspapers reported that in February 1994, the Catholic Church sent postcards to more than 21 million members, encouraging them to oppose the inclusion of abortion services in the Clinton health care reform package ("Abortion Fueling Health Plan Battle" 1994). At about the same time, other pro-life religious denominations were making similar plans. Thus, the conflicting groups have found a new political arena in which the battle can be fought.

C H A P T E R 3

The Right to Control Fertility: Sterilization and Contraception

Fertility control continues to be a sensitive policy issue in the United States. There are frequent complaints that safe and effective forms of fertility control are not widely available; yet many fear that these techniques are easily abused. It is likely that controversies over reproductive rights will continue, even as safe, effective, and reversible techniques for long-term fertility control become routinely available.

The debate concerning these emerging techniques began almost immediately after the Food and Drug Administration (FDA) approved the contraceptive implant Norplant in December 1990. An editorial in the *Philadelphia Inquirer* asking readers to "think about" using Norplant as a means of fighting black poverty triggered bitter criticism, prompting a retraction and an apology. A proposal was introduced in the Kansas legislature to pay welfare mothers $500 plus costs for the implantation of Norplant. The sentence imposed by a California judge on a convicted child abuser included an order that she use Norplant. More recently, the debate has widened to include the distribution, by high schools, of Norplant to sexually active students.

The debate over Norplant is the latest round of issues surrounding sterilization. Although the most contentious issues accompanying the political conflict over the right of women to reproductive privacy have been dominated by the issue of abortion; to a large extent, however, it is an outgrowth of, and parallels, earlier battles over contraception and sterilization. The issues raised in these debates are analogous to those argued in the conflict over abortion—the individual's right to have access to safe and effective fertility control, and the individual's right not to have children (that is, to have an abortion), versus the power of states to limit the individual's access and right. Considerable legislative and court action has been required to make both abortion and sterilization and contraception services available to women.

The most problematic policy issues surrounding sterilization have concerned involuntary or compulsory applications, not voluntary application as in abortion. In the early twentieth century, the conflict over sterilization centered on state policies denying certain identifiable groups, including the mentally retarded, alcoholics, prisoners, and others deemed socially "undesirable," the right to procreate. This chapter explores the issues raised by fertility control techniques, especially the reversible, long-term implants such as Norplant, which can either expand or restrict reproductive rights, depending on the motivation for their use in each case.

Fertility Control Trends in the United States

Studies of trends in fertility control practices reveal a steady increase in the use of sterilization since the 1970s. Of the 30 million American women who practiced fertility control in 1982, more than 10 million relied on sterilization—their own or that of their male partner. Almost 33 percent of the women then practicing contraception depended on sterilization (21.9 percent their own and 10.8 percent that of their partner); 28 percent depended on birth control pills (Grimes 1986, 69). The authors of a study based on 1990 data concluded that "in the United States more than two-thirds of the couples who desire no more children have been sterilized; if current trends continue, the proportion will soon approach 80 percent" (Mumford and Kessel 1992, 1203). Statistics on worldwide usage indicate that sterilization is the most prevalent fertility control strategy (see Table 3-1).

Although techniques for both males and females were introduced a century ago, voluntary surgical sterilization was used infrequently before the 1960s; not until the early 1970s did it begin to enjoy widespread use as a method of fertility control. This change can be attributed to the active mobilization of support by interest groups; liberalization of legal and policy constraints on the availability of sterilization; strong public demand for a one-time, effective means of fertility control; increased efforts to provide sterilization services; and refinements in technology, particularly that pertaining to female techniques, which made them practical for use in a wide variety of circumstances.

A growing number of Americans view sterilization as a safe and sure form of contraception. The development of oral contraceptives and intrauterine devices (IUDs) in the 1960s gave couples increased control over reproduction. Initially, both were hailed as a safe, effective means of fertility control. By 1968, however, the government was warning the public that

Table 3-1 Worldwide Prevalence of Fertility Control Methods by Percentage of Users, 1983 and 1987

Method	1983	1987
Female sterilization	26	29
Vasectomy	10	8
Intrauterine devices	19	20
Oral contraceptives	15	14
Injectable contraceptives	1	2
Condom	10	9
Withdrawal	8	8
Rhythm	7	7
Barrier	2	1
Other	2	2

Source: Diczfalusy 1993, 322.

the pill was not as safe as had been suggested and that some users were at risk for some diseases, including breast cancer. Although the percentage of favorable opinion among women is still highest for oral contraceptives (see Table 3-2), concern over health risks is likely to cause a decrease in their use. "Regardless of whether a link between OC [oral contraceptive] use and breast cancer is proved, OC use will almost certainly decline if the public perceives a link" (Trussell and Vaughan 1992, 1162).

Similarly, initial enthusiasm for the IUD in the early 1970s was soon replaced by fear when the incidence of serious (sometimes fatal) pelvic inflammatory disease was reported among some IUD users. Ironically, in some cases these infections scarred the fallopian tubes, resulting in permanent sterility. Lawsuits and legal problems primarily arising from use of the Dalkon shield resulted in the almost total end of IUD production by American companies by 1985. As of 1992, only two types of IUDs were available in the United States: the Progestasert, produced by the Alza Corporation of Palo Alto, California; and the newer copper T380A IUD, which is marketed as Paraguard, produced by GynoPharma of Somerville, New Jersey (Sivin, Stern, and Diaz 1992). The large drug companies have opted out of the market because they do not want to incur the costs of defending their products in court, even though IUDs, except for the Dalkon shield, appear to pose a minimal risk to most women. In fact, the authors of one extensive study concluded that the indictment of the Dalkon shield was a mistake and that it, too, is a safe method of fertility control (Mumford and Kessel 1992b).

In light of the controversies over the pill and IUD, developments in short-term contraceptives provide attractive options for some women. The female condom, also called a vaginal shield, is held in place by two flexible

Table 3-2 Favorable Opinions of Fertility Control Methods, 1989

Method	Percentage favoring
Pill	76
Condom	62
Vasectomy	57
Female sterilization	54
Diaphragm	30
Sponge	22
Foam	18
Vaginal suppository	18
Intrauterine device	16
Rhythm	16
Cream	14
Jelly	14
Withdrawal	10

Source: Trussel and Vaughan 1992, 1162.

plastic rings inside the shield. Because it can be inserted well in advance of anticipated intercourse and interferes less with sexual spontaneity, it might be more acceptable than the traditional male condom ("British 'Femshield' " 1988). Other short-term contraceptives include the contraceptive sponge, the postcoital pill, the nasal contraceptive, and reformulated spermicides. Although the development of these techniques allows women more of a choice in fertility control, they do not promise to be as effective or as convenient as the long-term methods.

Despite the FDA's approval of the injectable hormonal contraceptive, Depo-Provera, in October 1992, after twenty-five years of controversy over increased cancer risk, and the development of many new oral contraceptives (London 1992), the search for effective long-term methods of fertility control continues. It is estimated that contraceptive failure alone was responsible for 1.6 million to 2.0 million accidental pregnancies in the United States in 1987 and that such pregnancies account for about half of the 1.5 million abortions performed each year (Kaeser 1990, 131). Since most couples are choosing to have small families, often while they are young, they may face as many as twenty years of fertility control after completion of their family.

Rather than using a form of contraception that is, at best, inconvenient and not fully effective and is, at worst, a significant hazard to the woman's health, couples are increasingly choosing sterilization as a permanent solution to the problem of contraception. Moreover, because of the controversy over IUDs, many doctors are recommending even to healthy women who have been satisfied with the IUD and have no problems as a result of its use, that they choose another method. In the

Table 3-3   Fertility Control Methods Used by Age Group (in percentages)

		Method Used by Women at Risk			
Age group	*Women at risk* [a]	Oral contraceptives	Other reversible methods	No method	Sterilization
15-19	39.4	47.7	32.1	19.8	0.4
20-24	66.5	59.8	22.5	11.8	5.9
25-29	72.1	39.7	28.9	10.4	21.0
30-34	73.6	20.4	29.8	7.4	42.4
35-39	75.0	4.6	28.8	6.3	60.3
40-44	71.0	3.0	21.4	7.6	68.0
45-49	65.0	1.0	13.0	9.0	77.0

Source: Adapted from Trussell and Vaughan 1992, 1162. Ages 15 to 44: 1988 National Survey of Family Growth; ages 45 to 49: authors' estimate.

[a] Having sex and not pregnant, seeking pregnancy, or postpartum and not infecund.

late 1980s, approximately 2 million women fell in this category, and most of them chose sterilization (Cushner 1986, 129). As a result, what was in the late 1960s "an infrequent and commonly disapproved method [has been] transformed into the primary means of contraception in America" (Bumpass 1987, 347).

Demographic trends indicate that the demand for long-term methods of fertility control, including sterilization, is likely to increase as the population ages. Although oral contraceptives are the method of choice for most younger women, sterilization is the preferred option by age 30, and the percentage of women choosing it increases significantly after that age (see Table 3-3). As the cohorts of women over age 35 increase during the 1990s, the use of these long-term techniques will likely also increase.

One reason that sterilization has become more widely accepted by women is the higher failure rate of the other methods used. Table 3-4 shows the low failure rate of tubal ligation and vasectomy (0.40 percent and 0.15 percent, respectively). Although the IUD (6.0 percent) and the pill (6.2 percent) are far more effective than the remaining methods, their failure rates remain substantially higher than those of male or female sterilization.

Recognizing the heightened demand by couples for a safe, reliable, permanent method of contraception, a variety of organizations—in particular, the Association for Voluntary Surgical Contraception and the Planned Parenthood Federation of America—have expended considerable effort to make sterilization services available to individuals who desire them. These

Table 3-4 One-Year Contraceptive Failure Rates Per 100 Users

Method	Failure rate
Female sterilization	0.40
Vasectomy	0.15
IUD	6.00
Pill	6.20
Condom	14.20
Diaphragm	15.60
Rhythm	16.20
Spermicide	26.30
Other	22.20

Source: Ross 1989, 276.

groups have lobbied for the elimination of statutory constraints on voluntary applications. The association, through its nationwide education program, emphasizes an individual's right to know about sterilization. Planned Parenthood presents sterilization as one aspect of an overall family planning program; it has been the prime force behind the establishment of family planning clinics in the United States.

The increase in demand for and acceptability of long-term fertility control can also be traced to substantial refinements in sterilization and contraceptive techniques and procedures (Shy et al. 1992)—especially those applicable to females. Inpatient surgical procedures that formerly required general anesthesia and lengthy recovery periods are now performed on an outpatient basis with local anesthesia, thus causing minimal inconvenience for the patient. This change has also decreased the cost of sterilization relative to the long-term cost of alternative contraceptive methods. An administrative advantage of sterilization or long-term implants for family planning clinics is that they require contacting a client only once rather than on a continuing basis.

Reversible Long-Term Fertility Control Techniques

The increased incidence of divorce and remarriage of many of the individuals who chose contraceptive sterilization between the 1960s and the 1980s, along with an apparent change of priorities that led some to seek restoration of their fertility, shifted research emphasis to the development of reversible techniques. It is unlikely that a "perfect" fertility control technique will ever be found that meets all conceivable demands. This section focuses on some of the new methods that are currently available.

Contraceptive Implants for Women

Subdermal hormonal implants are a form of programmed medication. Surgically implanted rods or capsules containing the contraceptive steroid meter it into the surrounding tissue and maintain the blood level in the desired range; they are effective for approximately five years (Sivin, Stern, and Diaz 1992).

Norplant, the most extensively tested implant, was developed by the Population Council and has been manufactured by Leiras Oy in Finland since 1983. It has been used by more than 1.8 million women in fifty-one countries (McCauley and Geller 1992, 3). Six 3.4-cm silicone rubber capsules, each about the size of a match, are filled with the synthetic progestin levonorgestrel, which suppresses ovulation and causes thickening of the cervical mucus, thus inhibiting sperm penetration. After administration of a local anesthetic, the capsules are surgically implanted in a fanlike manner under the skin of the upper arm. The procedure takes approximately ten minutes and leaves no visible marks. Because the progestin is released slowly and in low doses, and because the implant contains no estrogen, the risk of overdosing and the risk of strokes and blood clots associated with some formulations of contraceptive pills are substantially reduced (McCauley and Geller 1992, 8).

Norplant has a high rate of effectiveness and high continuation rates. The pregnancy rate is 0.2 per 100 woman-years in the first and second year of use. The percentages of women who still have the implant one year after insertion range from a low of 76 percent in Scandinavian countries to 99 percent in Sri Lanka (Singh, Viegas, and Ratnam 1992; McCauley and Geller 1992, 10-13). For this reason, Norplant is welcomed by family planning clinics, which have long had to deal with the problems of education and compliance posed by techniques that require self-administered daily maintenance. Norplant and other subdermal implants are a convenient and, perhaps, safer alternative to the pill. (See Laurikka-Routte and Haukkamaa 1992 for a discussion of Progestin ST 1435.) The availability of this option may lead to a reduction in the number of tubal ligations performed in the United States.

One problem with Norplant is that the capsules are nonbiodegradable and therefore must be surgically removed upon expiration. Clinical trials of biodegradable systems that eliminate the need for removal are now under way. One biodegradable implant, Capronor, consists of a single rod containing up to 26 mg of levonorgestrel inserted under the skin of the arm or hip for eighteen months (Darney et al. 1992). Because the walls of the implant break down when exposed to tissue fluids, removal is not necessary unless the patient wishes to discontinue use before using up all of the levonorgestrel. Capronor is being developed by the Research Triangle Institute and is expected to be available on the market in the mid-1990s.

Intracervical Devices and Other Methods for Women

The intracervical contraceptive device (ICD), which is inserted in the cervical canal, has undergone successful preliminary trials in Britain (Katz, Lancet, and Shiber 1986). The main part of the mushroom-shaped device is a hollow cylinder made of inert polycarbonate plastic containing a nontoxic silicone rubber valve that prevents the ascent of sperm, while allowing exit of menstrual flux. The cap, attached to the cylinder, prevents penetration of any sperm cells that may have gained access to the area between the cervical walls and the cylinder. The device is inserted and removed with a specially designed inserter and is kept in place by two anchors of stainless steel on the outside of the cylinder.

Another form of intracervical device is now being developed in Finland. A relatively constant level of levonorgestrel is released from a Silastic reservoir that is inserted in the cervical canal and held in place by horizontal arms located in the uterine opening. Researchers are attempting to refine the design to reduce the unacceptably high rate of expulsion (Ratsula 1988).

Research is still being conducted on the Silastic vaginal ring, which the Population Council predicts will be available for worldwide distribution in the mid-1990s. One variant being tested releases a combination of levonorgestrel and estrogen that virtually stops ovulation. The ring is designed to stay in place for up to three weeks. The woman then removes it for one week and reinserts it herself. The same ring can be used for up to six months. Another variation being investigated is a low-dose vaginal ring that releases only levonorgestrel. Although it does not stop ovulation, it suppresses conception by making the cervical mucus impermeable to sperm for the two months it is in place (Liskin and Blackman 1987).

The cervical cap was approved for general use by the FDA in May 1988. This small, thimble-shaped, rubber barrier contraceptive fits tightly across the cervix, thus preventing sperm from entering the uterus (Shihata and Gollub 1992). It has been shown to be 85 percent effective in preventing pregnancy, a rate comparable to that of the diaphragm but significantly lower than that of long-term subdermal implants. The cap is inserted by the woman and remains for up to sixty hours at a time, but problems remain concerning fit and dislodgment (Klitsch 1988).

Fertility Control Methods for Men

Despite the popularity of vasectomy, the number of men electing this procedure has been steadily declining in the United States since the 1970s.

Although most research on reversible methods continues to focus on the fallopian tubes, a number of vas deferens occlusion devices have been investigated since the mid-1970s (see Martinez-Manautou et al. 1991). These techniques include reversible valves or devices that can be switched on or off to regulate passage of sperm through the vas deferens; occlusion plugs and prosthetics similar to the removable silicone plugs used by women; and a variety of clips, injectables, threads, and copper devices. Most of them never reached the stage of clinical evaluation, however, and those that did proved to be either ineffective or not sufficiently reversible.

One device that holds promise as an effective, yet reversible, sterilization technique for males has been tested in primates. The Shug consists of two elongated silicone plugs (each approximately 25 mm to 30 mm in length) that are hollow except at the tip and are connected by a 5-cm nylon thread. To implant the Shug, two holes are punctured in the exposed vas deferens. Metal styli are then inserted into each plug and the plugs are pushed through the holes into the vas deferens. The connecting thread remains partially outside the vas deferens, thus not only holding the plugs in place but allowing for removal of the Shug when reversal is desired. Removal is accomplished by exposing the vas deferens where the plugs are located and pulling the thread with a forceps. Two separate primate experiments showed that the device completely prevents sperm transport during a seven-month period. Moreover, upon its removal, all of the primates ejaculated sperm at normal concentrations and of normal motility. According to one group of researchers, these results "indicate the potential contraceptive use of the device and encourage its validation in men" (Zaneveld et al. 1988, 527).

Voluntary Sterilization: The Legal Context

The majority of sterilizations performed in the United States are voluntary. In the 1960s and 1970s, largely as a result of the development of less intrusive, safe, and effective sterilization procedures, as well as changes in the attitudes of the medical profession and the general public, a substantial effort was made to legalize voluntary sterilization. Legal action concerning voluntary sterilization for fertility control is a relatively recent development; eugenic sterilization, however, has been the subject of statutory and case law since the turn of the century (Kevles 1986).

Voluntary sterilization is now legal in all fifty states. In the first half of the twentieth century, states were hesitant to allow its use for fertility control. In a few states, it was illegal for a physician to perform sterilization for any reason other than the legally defined eugenic indication or a medical necessity. Most states had repealed their restrictions on contraceptive sterilization by 1960; Connecticut, Kansas, and Utah did not do so until the early 1970s. In those states, the restrictions resulted in inequities in access to the procedure. The age-parity formula, which stated that the woman's age times the number of her live children had to equal 100 or 120, denied the option to women who had few (or no) living children. There were also requirements that the person seeking sterilization consult at least two physicians and obtain consent of the spouse, and that the procedure be performed only in a licensed hospital.

There is considerable variation in the states' voluntary sterilization statutes; in general, however, the requirements fall in four categories:

1. Age requirements for sterilization candidates
2. A waiting period (usually thirty days between obtaining consent form and performance of sterilization)
3. Consent of spouse
4. Second-opinion consultation

In spite of these restrictions, most adults in all fifty states now have the option to undergo contraceptive sterilization.

In addition to the states' legislative actions, several court decisions have struck down some of the most constraining legal restrictions. In *Hathaway v. Worcester City Hospital* (1973), a U.S. court of appeals held that the city hospital's refusal to permit use of its facilities for sterilization operations violates the constitutional rights of a woman seeking a tubal ligation for contraceptive purposes. The court held that the Constitution protects the individual's right to both therapeutic and elective sterilizations.

In *Avila v. New York City Health and Hospitals Corporation* (1987), the Bronx County Supreme Court ruled that an institution receiving federal funds and performing sterilizations may not arbitrarily prevent a mentally competent and freely consenting individual from having the operation. Moreover, the state courts have jurisdiction to determine whether the institution's refusal to perform the requested operation is arbitrary. In *Chrisman v. Sisters of St. Joseph of Peace* (1974), a suit against a hospital operated by a religious order, however, a U.S. court of appeals held that the hospital's receipt of federal funds under the Hill-Burton Act of 1946 (which provided government grants and loans for the construction and modernization of medical facilities), tax-exempt status, and regulation by the state did not constitute sufficient public involvement to require the hospital to make sterilization available. In *Ponter v. Ponter* (1975), the New Jersey Superior Court granted Judith Ponter's right to be sterilized despite her husband's objections. In *Carey v. Population Services International* (1977), the Supreme Court invalidated New Jersey's statutory limitation on a minor's access to contraceptives; it held that this right extended to all forms of birth control, presumably including sterilization.

Although these statutes and court decisions have clarified the legal right to obtain a sterilization for fertility control in some jurisdictions, there are still some restrictions on the availability of voluntary sterilization. Publicly supported hospitals cannot refuse to perform sterilizations, but in most states they still can establish their own policies regarding waiting periods, physician consultation, and spousal consent. Furthermore, the 1973 Church Amendment (named for Sen. Frank Church) to the Hill-Burton Act gives private hospitals the right to deny sterilization on moral or religious grounds without loss of federal support for programs such as Medicare. In July 1980, the National Conference of Catholic Bishops affirmed the existence of a ban on the performance of tubal ligations, including therapeutic sterilizations, in Catholic hospitals. Such procedures can be performed only for ''grave reasons extrinsic to the case.'' The restrictions imposed by hospitals have little impact, however, because at present most sterilizations are done on an outpatient basis—often in a clinic or in the physician's office. But because physicians can also impose their own restrictions on those they consider eligible, in some localities certain categories of persons, especially minors, have difficulty obtaining voluntary sterilization. Many physicians, especially in states that have not addressed the question of minors, require that the patient be over the age of 21, be married, and have spousal or parental consent. Some states require waiting periods ranging from seventy-two hours to thirty days (the same as the waiting period for all federally funded sterilizations) to minimize the possibility that a person might change his or her mind after the procedure is completed.

Insurance policies vary in their coverage of sterilization operations. Many policies treat contraceptive sterilization as a medical procedure, whatever its motivation; others distinguish between medically indicated and elective sterilization and reimburse only the former. Some policies specifically exclude nontherapeutic sterilization. Obviously, this consideration might discourage or even prevent individuals with limited financial resources from seeking voluntary sterilization. Because Medicaid coverage for sterilization is a matter of state, not federal, jurisdiction, there is wide variation; about one-quarter of the states exclude coverage for elective sterilization.

Involuntary or Nonconsensual Sterilization: The Continuing Controversy

Early in the twentieth century, interest in sterilization was prompted by its possibilities for achieving societal control; individual choice was not a consideration. Legislators were influenced both by medical theories that mental illness was inherited and by social elitist theories stemming from social Darwinism (Kevles 1986). Since the 1930s, nonconsensual sterilization has been used as a means to achieve population control, reduce societal burdens, minimize genetic defects in the population, and as a punitive device for criminals and other undesirables; it has also been motivated by racism. Sterilization performed with the informed consent of the subject now enjoys widespread support in the United States, but sterilization performed without regard for individual choice arouses considerable controversy. Sterilization, no matter how high-minded when voluntary, is subject to abuse.

It should be noted that the term *nonconsensual* has at least two meanings. It can refer to sterilization that is not voluntary because the patient is legally incompetent to exercise informed consent. The parents of a mentally retarded woman who petition the court for permission to have her sterilized are seeking to substitute their consent for hers. This type of involuntary sterilization is always problematic because it is difficult to determine what the subject would choose if he or she were capable of informed consent. The term can also refer to sterilization that is compulsory. A person who is legally capable of informed consent is coerced to be sterilized; consent is not even requested.

Federal Government Involvement in Sterilization

The federal government funds approximately 10 percent of all sterilizations annually. It is the primary source of funding for poor women, affording them the option to exercise control over their fertility. In fiscal year 1987, the federal and state governments together spent $412 million on fertility control services for women who might not otherwise have been able to obtain them (Forrest and Singh 1990, 6). Almost all publicly funded sterilizations are paid for by Medicaid (88 percent in 1987); thus the costs are shared by the state and federal governments. Although most of these applications are voluntary and based on the informed consent of recipients, the government's involvement has aroused suspicion and been the subject of criticism. This should not be surprising, given the history of eugenic sterilization in the United States in the early twentieth century, the mistrust of many groups to state intervention (even if it is intended to be beneficial for the recipients), and instances of coerced sterilization. Welfare workers threatened recipients with a loss of benefits unless they agreed to be sterilized (Nsiah-Jefferson 1989, 30). Women were allegedly sterilized without their knowledge while they were ostensibly in the hospital for an abortion or some other operation (Mains and Poggi 1990, 284). Such reports continued to surface, even after passage of the Family Planning Services

and Population Research Act of 1970 made sterilization available in federally funded clinics. The Court alluded to them in its decision in *Relf v.
Weinberger* (1974):

> Although Congress has been insistent that all family planning pro-
> grams function on a purely voluntary basis, there is uncontroverted
> evidence in the record that minors and other incompetents have been
> sterilized with federal funds and that an indefinite number of poor
> people have been improperly coerced into accepting a sterilization
> operation under the threat that various federally supported welfare
> benefits would be withdrawn unless they submitted to irreversible
> sterilization. Patients receiving Medicaid assistance at childbirth are
> evidently the most frequent targets of this pressure. (at 1198)

Prior to 1973, the Public Health Service (which in 1953 became part of the
Department of Health, Education, and Welfare or HEW, which was re-
named the Department of Health and Human Services in 1979) funded
sterilization, along with other family planning services for the poor, under
a number of programs. The regulations imposed on state and private agencies receiving these federal grants simply required that all services, including sterilization, be ''voluntary and shall not be a prerequisite to eligibility
for or receipt of any other service or assistance from, or to participation in,
any other program of the entity or individual that provided such service or
information'' (42 U.S.C. sec. 300 a-5). After reports of abuse, HEW issued
final regulations for sterilization procedures on February 6, 1974, whose
enforcement was to be deferred at the request of the Court until March 18,
1974. These regulations permitted the sterilization of persons under the age
of 21 and persons legally incapable of giving informed consent under certain conditions that included a waiting period of at least 72 hours between
provision of written consent and performance of sterilization, and a warning about the risks and the irreversibility of sterilization. Welfare recipients
also had to be informed prior to giving consent that their benefits could not
be withdrawn should they refuse to undergo the procedure.

Almost immediately, court action was initiated to enjoin implementation of the HEW rules. On March 15, 1974, Judge Gerhard A. Gesell of the
U.S. District Court for the District of Columbia, in the combined cases of
Relf v. Weinberger and *National Welfare Rights Organization v. Weinberger,* held that they were inconsistent with the statutory requirement of voluntariness.

> No person who is mentally incompetent can meet these standards,
> nor can the consent of a representative, however sufficient under
> state law, impute voluntariness to the individual actually undergoing
> irreversible sterilization. (at 1202)

For this reason, the court permanently enjoined HEW from providing federal funds for the sterilization of individuals who were under the age of 21 or whom the courts had determined to be incompetent to give informed consent.

This injunction held until 1977, when the Court of Appeals for the District of Columbia vacated the order of the lower court in *Relf* and ruled that HEW had statutory authority to define a federal standard of voluntariness. The department subsequently published its proposed rules in the *Federal Register* and invited written comments, as well as the voicing of opinions at public hearings that were held throughout the United States. In November 1978, it issued final regulations concerning sterilization performed under programs and projects funded by its Public Health Service and Social and Rehabilitation Service.

Significantly, the regulations, which became effective on February 6, 1979, prohibit federal funding for the sterilization of persons under the age of 21, institutionalized persons, and persons legally incompetent to give informed consent. The regulations also prohibit the overt or implicit threat of loss of welfare or Medicaid benefits as a consequence of nonconsent, and prohibit the performance of hysterectomies for purposes of sterilization under federally funded programs. Sterilization on the basis of substituted consent is not permitted. Informed consent cannot be obtained while a person is in labor or under the influence of alcohol or drugs, or immediately before or after an abortion. The informed consent form must be signed by the person seeking sterilization, the person who obtains the consent, the physician performing the sterilization, and an interpreter, if one is necessary. Complete information concerning the risks, side effects, and irreversibility of sterilization, as well as alternative methods of contraception, must be given in the patient's own language, both orally and in writing. A waiting period of at least thirty days is required.

The regulations were attacked on several grounds. Liberal critics argued that they did not go far enough in preventing coerced sterilization of the poor and protecting their rights (Petchesky 1979). They also pointed out that the cutoff of federal funding of abortion and the cutback of prenatal service for poor women leaves sterilization as the only option for some of them. According to the Committee to Defend Reproductive Rights, poor women are sterilized at disproportionately higher rates than nonpoor women (1985, 1). For example, in the 1970s sterilization rates for women who were on welfare were 49 percent higher than those for women who were not. Moreover, women of color have been sterilized in higher proportions than white women: 20 percent of black women, 24 percent of Native American women, 22 percent of Chicanas, and 37 percent of Puerto Rican women were sterilized in 1979, compared with 16 percent of white women (1985, 2).

Conservatives contended that reports of abuse had been exaggerated and that the effect of the stringent regulations and arbitrary judgments by administrators was to deny sterilization to many indigents. They asserted that although the 1979 regulations' criteria of minimum age and minimum number of children were reasonable prerequisites for sterilization in order to reduce the ''regret potential'' for patients, the imposition of overly strict restrictions on women who were on public assistance prevented them from obtaining their desired form of fertility control. Most of the criticism was leveled at the thirty-day waiting period, which was viewed as paternalistic (in that it required women to delay their choice and to be guided by what authorities deemed best for them) and as reflecting a failure to acknowledge the plight of most poor women. Critics also argued that it might also subject a woman to the risk of having two surgeries, if she consented to a postpartum sterilization but delivered prematurely before expiration of the thirty-day limit, then had to return for a sterilization (Chi, Gates, and Thapa 1992).

State Legislative Action

The 1979 federal regulations have done little to reduce the frequency of nonconsensual sterilization because they apply only to operations subsidized by federal funding. Most cases of nonconsensual sterilization fall within the jurisdiction of the states, not the federal government. The states' policies regulating the sterilization of those deemed incapable of giving informed consent are inconsistent and often contradictory.

Since 1980 an increasing number of state legislatures have demonstrated renewed interest in nonconsensual sterilization statutes. Table 3-5 lists the twenty-one states that, in 1988, had statutes permitting nonconsensual sterilization; it indicates the diversity of their general provisions. Four states permit nonconsensual sterilization of institutionalized persons only; the institution's superintendent is usually the official required to initiate the request. Seventeen states permit sterilization of persons in the community as well as those in institutions. In fourteen states, parents or legal guardians can initiate sterilization proceedings; in Virginia the spouse or ''next friend'' also has that authority. Those sterilized usually include the mentally retarded or mentally ill and, in a few states, epileptics. The Delaware statute authorizes sterilization of habitual criminals.

Although all but seven states require a hearing prior to sterilization, the procedural safeguards vary considerably from state to state. Four states require only an administrative hearing, usually conducted by the director of the state department that has jurisdiction over public institutions. Nine states require a full judicial hearing prior to the performance of ster-

Table 3-5 **State Legislation for Nonconsensual Sterilization, 1988**

State	Person sterilized		Initiator		Procedural safeguards	Court order required
	Institutionalized only	Anyone	Administrator	Parent or guardian		
Arkansas		x		x	x	x
California		x		x	x	x
Colorado		x		x	x	x
Connecticut		x	x	x	x	x
Delaware		x	x		x	
Georgia		x		x	x	x
Idaho		x	x	x	x	x
Kentucky		x				
Maine		x	x		x	
Minnesota		x	x	x	x	x
Mississippi	x		x		x	
New Hampshire		x		x	x	x
North Carolina		x	x	x	x	x
North Dakota	x		x	x	x	x
Oklahoma	x		x		x	
Oregon		x	x	x	x	
South Carolina	x		x		x	
Utah		x	x		x	x
Vermont		x	x	x	x	x
Virginia		x	x	x	x	x
West Virginia		x	x	x	x	x

Source: Adapted from Association for Voluntary Surgical Contraception 1988.

ilization. They also grant to the person who is to be sterilized the right to counsel; the right to be present and to cross-examine witnesses; and the right to receive a full record of all testimony, both written and oral. Eight states permit substituted consent by the parent or guardian; several states also require such consent by the spouse of the person to be sterilized. Fourteen states require a court order before the sterilization can be performed.

These nonconsensual sterilization laws are evidence of the move away from a eugenic rationale. Only in four states does the legislation require eugenic or hereditary grounds for sterilization; the laws of three of them require other grounds as well. Increasingly, the statutory standards for sterilization include references to "the inability to care for and support children," the "best interests of the person," or the "welfare of society."

Judicial Action on Nonconsensual Sterilization

In recent years, the most conspicuous activity regarding nonconsensual sterilization has been centered in the courts and has focused on two questions: (1) Are the state statutes constitutional? and (2) In the absence of express statutory authorization, do the courts have jurisdiction to approve petitions for the sterilization of persons who are incompetent? The courts' response to the first question has generally been a qualified yes. Although the courts have not always agreed in their response to the second question, they have increasingly assumed jurisdiction by issuing orders allowing sterilization but within strict parameters.

The Constitutionality of State Statutes

The courts have tended to agree that nonconsensual sterilization statutes are constitutional, following the precedent of *Buck v. Bell* (1927), in which the Supreme Court upheld eugenic sterilization. (The majority opinion included Justice Oliver Wendell Holmes's dictum that "[t]hree generations of imbeciles are enough.") They have, however, gradually narrowed that precedent by ruling that specific statutes lack necessary due process elements such as the right to counsel, to a hearing, or to an appeal. In these cases, the courts have usually left it up to the legislatures to rewrite the laws to include both procedural and substantive protections for the targets of sterilization. In *Lulos v. State* (1990), an Indiana appellate court held that a guardian's petition for sterilization of an incompetent adult should be granted upon "clear and convincing evidence that the judicially appointed guardian brought the petition for sterilization in good faith and the sterilization is in the best interest of the incompetent adult" (at 174). The appeals court ruled that the trial court erred in using a more stringent standard of proof than the Indiana law dictated when it denied the petition for nonconsensual sterilization.

In *North Carolina Association for Retarded Children v. North Carolina* (1976), a U.S. district court left standing the right of a state legislature to enact sterilization laws, but only in certain circumstances. The court explicitly dismissed eugenic bases for mandating sterilization and rejected specific provisions of the North Carolina statute. It pointed to substantial medical opinion that sterilization might be desirable as a last resort and in relatively extreme cases. Sterilization might be warranted in cases where there were clearly identifiable genetic defects and a "significant probability'' that offspring would inherit them. Cause for sterilization might also be established if a mentally retarded person were incapable of discharging the responsibility of parenthood because of the inability to create a nondetrimental environment for his or her progeny. Other indications for sterilization, the court noted, included a person's inability to understand that the natural consequence of sexual activity is a child; a person's desire not to have children, combined with the inability to use other forms of birth control; and, in rare cases, a medical determination that sterilization would be in the best interests of either the mentally retarded person or the state, or both.

Using a somewhat different rationale, the Oregon Court of Appeals, in *Cook v. State,* 1972, upheld as constitutional an Oregon statute that authorized involuntary sterilization. The court approved the sterilization of a 17-year-old girl on the grounds that if she were to have children, they would most likely be neglected and become wards of the state because she was incapable of caring for them. The court ruled that it was therefore proper to sterilize her. In *Motes v. Hall County Department of Family and Children Services* (1983), however, the Supreme Court of Georgia declared that the state statute permitting the involuntary sterilization of mentally incompetent persons was unconstitutional because it denied those persons the right to procreate.

Equitable Jurisdiction of the Courts to Order Sterilization

Before 1980, with few exceptions, the courts generally ruled that they did not have authorization to order the permanent sterilization of incompetent persons if there had not been an express legislative grant of such power. Higher courts that assumed jurisdiction in such cases include the Supreme Court of Alaska (*In the Matter of C. D. M.,* 1981), as well as those of Colorado (*In the Matter of A. W.,* 1981), Iowa (*In the Matter of Guardianship of Matejski,* 1988), New Hampshire (*In the Matter of Penny N.,* 1980), New Jersey (*In the Matter of Grady,* 1981), Washington (*In the Matter of Guardianship of Hayes,* 1980), and Wisconsin (*In the Matter of Guardianship of Eberhardy,* 1981). Although the signals coming from the courts are not always consistent or unequivocal, there is a clear indication that courts are increasingly accepting what most of them had previously perceived as a legislative role: in the absence of authorizing statutes, they are assuming jurisdiction in matters that concern the sterilization of those incapable of giving consent. In *Conservatorship of Valerie N.* (1985), the Supreme Court of California invoked the jurisprudence of fundamental rights to invalidate a California statute that prohibited the sterilization of mentally retarded persons. In a long majority opinion, from which there was strong dissent by Chief Justice Rose E. Bird, Justice Joseph Grodin argued that the statute "impermissibly deprives developmentally disabled persons of privacy and liberty interests protected by the Fourteenth Amendment . . . and . . . the California Constitution" (at 771-772). By denying the option of sterilization to an incompetent woman, the statute deprived her of her only realistic opportunity for contraception, and consequently restricted her chances for self-fulfillment. "Since the right to elect sterilization as a method of contraception is generally available to adult women in this state, the restriction [of that right] must be justified by a compelling state interest" (at 774).

Despite the increased acceptance by the courts of their jurisdiction to approve petitions for nonconsensual sterilization in the absence of authorizing statutes, there is a hesitancy to order irreversible sterilization, except under extreme circumstances. For instance, although the appellate court in *Wentzel v. Montgomery General Hospital, Inc.* (1982) concluded that "circuit courts, acting in pursuance of their inherent *parens patriae* authority, have subject matter jurisdiction to consider a petition for an order authorizing a guardian to consent to sterilization of an incompetent minor" (at 1253), it rejected the petition for the hysterectomy of a 13-year-old girl on the grounds that the evidence did not support such drastic action.

The Irreversibility Assumption

The availability of safe and effective sterilization techniques that offer a high rate of reversibility, along with long-term subdermal implants, will create a climate of increased social pressure for nonconsensual sterilization. Sterilization no longer represents the permanent destruction of a person's reproductive capacity caused by conventional surgical sterilization, but rather a less intrusive and presumably temporary cessation of fertility. From a purely technical standpoint, nonconsensual sterilization is more easily justified under such circumstances. These same innovations that promise to make sterilization less invasive technically, however, also threaten to increase the frequency of its use for eugenic or social control purposes by eliminating the most objectionable aspect of invasion—irreversibility.

Just as advancements in sterilization techniques in the 1890s helped rationalize compulsory sterilization, so current innovations with regard to reversible procedures will make them a less objectionable means of solving social problems. Courts that have refused to order sterilizations or have vacated lower court orders for sterilization have consistently emphasized the irreversible nature of the procedure. In a 1974 case, *In the Interest of M. K. R.*, the Supreme Court of Missouri disallowed the sterilization of a woman with an IQ of 50. Judge Fred Henley explained that this "routine operation would *irreversibly* deny to a human being a fundamental right, the right to bear or beget a child'' (at 470; emphasis added). He argued that the jurisdiction to exercise the power to deprive a person *permanently* of this right may be conferred only by a special statute.

Similarly, in *Relf v. Weinberger* (1974), Judge Gesell of the U.S. district court flatly stated: ''Sterilization of females or males is irreversible'' (at 1199). The court rejected the federal government's attempts to sanction

one of the most drastic methods of population control—the involuntary irreversible sterilization of men and women—without any legislative guidance. . . . We should not drift into a policy which has unfathomed implications and which permanently deprives . . . citizens of their ability to procreate without adequate legal safeguards. (at 1204)

This argument echoes Justice William O. Douglas's opinion in *Skinner v. Oklahoma* (1942):

The power to sterilize, if exercised, may have subtle, far-reaching and devastating effects. . . . There is no redemption for the individual whom the law touches. Any experiment which the State conducts is to his irreparable injury. He is *forever* deprived of a basic liberty. (at 541; emphasis added)

Similar conclusions were reached by a U.S. district court in *North Carolina Association for Retarded Children v. North Carolina* (1976), when it voided parts of the North Carolina sterilization statute: ''Sterilization is a drastic procedure, almost impossible to reverse in females and difficult and uncertain to reverse in males, that is intended to be permanent'' (at 454). Such a drastic measure, said the court, requires that a heavy burden of proof be placed on those who institute proceedings for sterilization: ''The burden of proof put upon the petitioner [by the North Carolina Supreme Court] that the evidence must be clear, strong, and convincing strongly protects against predictive error'' (at 458). In *Wyatt v. Aderholt* (1974), a federal district court defined sterilization as ''any medical or surgical operation or procedure which results in a patient's permanent inability to reproduce'' (at 1384).

Rosalind Petchesky has taken a strong stand against the practice of involuntary sterilization in the United States, basing her argument on the assumption of irreversibility. Sterilization is a procedure that

renders a person permanently unable to bear children. . . . While the ethics of a biomedical procedure are never determined by technology alone, the virtually irreversible nature of surgical sterilization makes the choice a more drastic one than it might be otherwise. (1979, 29)

As she cogently explains in her defense of thirty-day waiting periods, although they are frequently a source of inconvenience, women need to understand fully the ramifications of having their "bodies and reproductive capacities . . . irrevocably altered" (36).

Although Petchesky's assumption of irreversibility was generally accurate in 1979, the question here is the extent to which her argument is undermined by the availability and use of technically reversible procedures, particularly subdermal implants. She argues that the ethics of a biomedical procedure are not determined by technology alone, but technology plays a major role in defining the context of decision making and the range of choices available. Petchesky notes that the permanency of sterilization makes the choice a more drastic one than it might otherwise be. This implies that when reversible techniques become available, the choice will become less drastic. The question is, how much less so?

With the emergence of reversible procedures, will the courts be prompted to reconsider their opinions and allow reversible techniques to be used, or will they attempt to devise a basis other than irreversibility to reject these new procedures? At the least, the emphasis will have to be shifted to practical irreversibility in the cases they are examining.

Such methods as Norplant may be technically reversible, but once they are applied involuntarily to a mentally retarded person, or a mother on welfare, it is unlikely that they will be reversed, no matter how effective the reversal procedure. Control over fertility is taken out of the hands of the method's user and placed in the hands of specialists in the health care profession. Only a health care professional (most likely, a physician) has the ability to remove the implant or reverse the procedure. In contrast, control over use of the pill, condom, diaphragm, and, to a lesser extent, the IUD, is retained by the user. Whatever strategy the critics adopt to challenge technological advances in reversible means of fertility control, their task in demonstrating the dangers of nonconsensual compulsory sterilization will be made more difficult by the abolition of the assumption of permanency.

Reducing the Economic Burden: Sterilizing Welfare Recipients

The economic motivation for nonconsensual sterilization is not a new one. In *Buck v. Bell* (1927), the superintendent of the State Colony for Epileptics and Feeble Minded for the State of Virginia testified that there would be a great savings to the state if girls like Carrie Buck could be sterilized and released rather than institutionalized during their childbearing years. Much of the controversy over federal funding of sterilizations and the resulting HEW regulations of 1979 was provoked by assertions of widespread coerced sterilization of women on welfare (Docksai 1981, 10).

Pressure to reduce rising welfare costs, combined with moral indignation over some well-publicized welfare abuse cases, led to the introduction in some state legislatures of measures authorizing the sterilization of women on welfare after they had had a specified number of illegitimate children. Although none of these measures has yet been passed, they continue to have the support of many state policy makers.

Opponents of the sterilization of mothers on welfare charge that it is the fundamental right of every woman to bear children and that sterilization often precludes that choice. They agree that the exercise of this right by these women might impose a financial burden on society but argue that the state exists primarily to protect the interests and rights of all socioeconomic groups. The court in *Relf v. Weinberger* concluded that maintenance of the state's fiscal integrity is not a compelling interest when a fundamental right like procreation is held in the balance. The opponents argue that any intervention that limits the procreative choice of women on public assistance is not only a wholesale violation of the woman's rights but an obvious attempt to eliminate whole groups of people by terminating their fertility.

The argument of many who advocate limiting the procreative choice of women on public assistance plays into the hands of the critics. Dwight Ingle (1973), for instance, argues that the quality of the gene pool is deteriorating because the birth rates of the educated middle class are increasing more slowly than those of the uneducated poor, and that the survival of society therefore demands intervention in the area of reproduction.

Although coerced, irreversible sterilization is antithetical to the principles of a free society, encouragement of the use of reversible methods has some merits, which must be balanced against the costs. Many children born to women on welfare are unplanned and unwanted, as evidence by the figures on abortion among these women—approximately 300,000 per year before the Hyde Amendment ended federal funding of abortions in 1978. If the premise is correct that these women wish to control fertility but have an understandable aversion to permanent sterilization, then providing access to reversible techniques that allow the woman to have ultimate control for reversal might be an appropriate solution.

The availability of reversible fertility control techniques makes it easier for many persons to rationalize their use by women on welfare, and ironically increases their potential for abuse because they are perceived as a less extreme intrusion. Reversibility might facilitate the passage of statutes similar to the measures introduced in many state legislatures, but defeated because of the irreversibility of conventional techniques.

Reversibility has raised some yet-unanswered questions. Who ultimately has the power to reverse sterilization? Although the removal of subdermal implants is likely to be a relatively simple and inexpensive medical procedure, it must be performed by a trained health care professional and thus will entail an expense. Should the government provide welfare recipients who have undergone sterilization the opportunity, and the funding, for its reversal? Under what conditions is reversal warranted? Is there a real likelihood of reversal for most women whose sterilization was funded by governmental programs as long as they remain on welfare, or must they get off welfare before reversal can be considered? These questions must be resolved if policy makers are to view reversible sterilization as a possible way of reducing the expenditure of scarce public resources in response to the taxpayers' demands to cut government spending.

Reducing the Teenage Pregnancy Rate

More than 1 million women aged 15 to 19 become pregnant every year (Smith 1994, 85). Of these pregnancies, 13 percent end in miscarriage, 40 percent are electively aborted, and 46 percent produce a live birth (Morris, Warren, and Aral 1993, 31). Despite the fact that 93 percent of all U.S. teenagers receive sex education in high school, abortion and birth rates in the United States remain high compared with those of other developed countries and have increased by at least 8 percent annually since 1988 (Sulak and Haney 1993, 2043). Moreover, of the 517,989 births to teenage women in 1989, more than 30,000 were to girls 14 years of age or younger (Henshaw and Van Vort 1989, 85). Studies have found that up to 95 percent of teenage pregnancies are not deliberate (Smith 1994, 84).

Using data from twelve separate studies, Martha Burt (1986) estimates that the cost to the public of teenage childbearing in 1985 was $16.65 billion. These funds were allocated under three governmental programs (Aid to Families with Dependent Children, Food Stamps, and Medicaid) to women who had first given birth as teenagers. Over a twenty-year period beginning in 1985, the government will pay an average of $13,902 to each family begun by a first birth to a teenager; the total cost will be $5.16 billion (Burt 1986, 221). Babies born to teenagers tend to be premature and subject to developmental deprivation. Despite remarkable advances in the capacity of medical professionals to treat these low-birthweight babies, their survival rates are, on average, low (Shankaran et al. 1988).

Pregnant teenagers are at higher risk than older women, whether they have an abortion or carry the pregnancy to term, because of their physical underdevelopment, poor nutrition, lack of prenatal care, and, frequently, smoking and drug use. Moreover, it is difficult for many teenage mothers to care for and raise their children properly. Many of these women never escape the burdens of poverty and lack of education, and their effects tend to be passed on to the women's children. Although public attention has recently been focused on teenage pregnancy, the proposed solutions—counseling, education in birth control methods, provision of free birth control services, and subsidized abortions for teenagers—have as yet done little to reduce the frequency of teenage pregnancy. The difficult question is whether stricter control of the teenagers' procreative prerogatives is the necessary (or feasible) solution.

Ironically, it has been the AIDS epidemic, to a greater extent than teenage pregnancy, that has increased public support for sex education programs in the schools. Recent surveys indicate the existence of widespread public approval for such programs, despite the opposition expressed by influential groups in many school districts. In a Gallup Poll conducted in April 1992, 63 percent of the respondents approved of making condoms available to high school students; 35 percent were opposed. An even larger majority—87 percent—approved of teaching students about AIDS and other sexually transmitted diseases in the early grades; 12 percent were opposed.* The questions of whether such public approval can be translated into education and prevention programs (which continue to be a highly charged issue) and whether such efforts will ultimately be effective in reducing teenage pregnancy remain unanswered, however (DiClimente 1993).

The widespread application of a reversible fertility control procedure such as Norplant might be effective in reducing teenage pregnancy. A woman who had reached puberty or had aborted her first pregnancy would have a subdermal implant until she was deemed physically and emotionally mature enough to provide a proper fetal environment and to raise a child. The implant would then be removed and the woman would be "allowed" to procreate.

The policy strategy to be implemented for the use of subdermal implants could range from the minimally intrusive approach of increasing the options offered by family planning services to include subdermal implants for the sexually active teenager, to the most extreme approach of requiring the placement of subdermal implants in all women at puberty (Figure 3-1). More moderate approaches include establishment of an education program to encourage the use of subdermal implants by young women, provision of free implants to teenagers who desire them, and subtle forms of coercion such as equating the use of implants with the status of womanhood. The city of Baltimore has already established a program that offers free Norplant insertions to teenage students (Hanson 1992).

A coercive approach not only raises serious moral and constitutional questions but challenges strongly held democratic principles. Who is to judge whether a young woman is sufficiently mature and responsible to bear a child? Should the decision be made by the parents, a birth control

---

* Survey no. GO 222034, conducted April 5, 1992.

Figure 3-1   Continuum of Subdermal Implant Strategies

Education	Offered by family planning service	Offered free, on demand	Subtle coercion	Required at first abortion or pregnancy	Required of all women at puberty

counselor, a physician, or a representative of the public health service? Why target only young women for forced life-style changes when
older pregnant women are at risk as well? Why should intrusive methods be directed only at the woman? Since even the safest and most effective reversible method poses risks to the subject, including some chance
of irreversibility, should any one person have the power to subject another person to that risk? Moreover, even if it seems advantageous to
institute a program for the implantation of long-term fertility control
devices in sexually active teenagers, how would such a program be administered? Whereas some young women might welcome the opportunity to
use this type of fertility control, others might view it as a restriction of
their procreative freedom. Constitutional issues will also be raised if
teenage women who desire implants are denied them, whether because of
parental opposition, lack of access, or the enforcement of strict informed
consent provisions.

Despite these questions, it is likely that the availability of long-term
contraceptive options will increase the pressure for their use in helping
reduce teenage pregnancy. If proven safe and effective, they will probably
be perceived as an attractive option by many advocates of teenage fertility
control.

The impact of any fertility control program established for teenage
women emphasizing subdermal implants will be greater on black teenagers, especially those who depend on public assistance, because the pregnancy rate among black teenagers aged 15 to 19 is double that of white
teenagers of the same ages. Furthermore, "the race contrast [is] especially
great for girls under 15: [in 1985,] the abortion rate among nonwhites was
5.4 times that among whites, and the birthrate was 6.5 times as high"
(Henshaw and Van Vort 1989, 86). Mary G. Edwards, however, argues
that early childbearing should be viewed as being economically advantageous for poor women. Therefore, "current public policies, which emphasize the prevention of early childbearing, discriminate against poor women
by attempting to interfere in this process" (1990, 12). But if the impact of
teenage pregnancy—not only on the teenager but on the family and society—is as great as the data seem to indicate, policy makers will actually do
a disservice to these young persons by not providing them access to, and
perhaps encouraging the use of, innovations in long-term fertility control

once they have been proven safe, effective, and reversible, in order to reduce the rates of teenage abortion and unwanted births.

Conclusion

Fertility control, like abortion, continues to create policy dilemmas that require concerted action. The courts, state legislatures, and, to a lesser extent, the federal government have established a largely workable policy framework for dealing with the issues of fertility control (which they have not succeeded in doing with regard to abortion) in a way that protects individual rights even though there are still some policy inconsistencies, particularly regarding the nonconsensual application of sterilization.

New technological developments, especially long-term subdermal implants, however, require a reevaluation of existing policy and a clarification of the reproductive rights of the most vulnerable segments of society, including poor and mentally retarded women. Most women now have the right to decide not to bear children as a result of their access to a variety of relatively safe and effective methods of fertility control. But because of the potential for abuse, such as coerced applications that limit the reproductive capacity and autonomy of certain societal groups, there will be a need for continued vigilance on the part of policy makers and the public.

C H A P T E R 4

Assisted Reproduction: Expanding the Right to Have Children

In 1989, the Yorks, a married couple who had moved from Virginia to California, requested that the Jones Institute in Norfolk, Va., transport a single frozen embryo left over from three failed attempts at in vitro fertilization. The Norfolk institute refused to release the frozen embryo, however, claiming that the Yorks agreed to have it thawed for placement only in that clinic. The Yorks sued in the federal district court to gain custody of their embryo and for damages resulting from unlawful retention, breach of contract, and violation of civil rights (Walther 1992). In *York v. Jones* (1989), the court ruled in favor of the Yorks, holding that neither the state's human subject research statute nor the terms of the original agreement between the parties undercut their property interest in the frozen embryo. The court also held that the most reasonable reading of the consent form was that the Yorks retained dispositional custody, including the right to remove the embryo from the Jones Institute (at 426). Had the consent form explicitly prohibited transfer, the institute could have retained custody, according to the ruling, which centered on contractual, not ethical, issues. Shortly after the court's decision, the couple had the embryo transported to California for implantation.

This case illustrates some of the novel legal issues created by the new technological capabilities in human reproduction. Both *York* and *Davis v. Davis* (1992), in which a divorced couple fought over the disposition of seven frozen embryos, have stimulated considerable public debate about the status of an embryo and have raised policy questions about the rights and responsibilities of the many parties to the "new" reproduction.

Chapters 2 and 3 focused on the right not to have children and the related issues of abortion and fertility control; this chapter's subject is the (possibly more problematic) right to have children. A review of current and developing reproductive technologies designed to enhance fertility or to compensate for infertility is followed by an examination of some of the policy issues raised by technology-assisted reproduction. Although these procedures vary in terms of both technical capabilities and the motivation for their use in specific cases, they raise similar issues: the role of the third parties they introduce in the reproductive process, the treatment of children and women as commodities, and the commercialization of procreation. The introduction of third parties complicates the rights of the participants and creates new areas of potential conflict (for example, determining access to these often expensive interventions). The procedures also focus attention on the positive rights aspect of reproduction and the proper role of government and society in providing the resources necessary to exercise the right to reproduce.

Reproduction-Assisting Technologies

The first stage of the revolution in human reproduction began in the 1960s, with the introduction of the pill and other contraceptive innovations that made possible the separation of reproduction from sexual intercourse. It continued with the development of long-term subdermal contraceptive implants such as Norplant and abortifacients such as the drug RU-486. The revolution's second stage promises to be accompanied by changes in social attitudes and behavior that are more extensive than those that took place during the first. Precipitating the second phase is an array of techniques that effectively make sexual intercourse unnecessary as a prerequisite for reproduction.

Infertility is a problem for an increasing number of American men and women. In 1992, an estimated one couple in six was infertile. Infertility for a couple can be caused by problems in the man, the woman, or in combination. The total number of women with impaired fertility was 5.3 million, or 9.1 percent of all women aged 15 to 44, but only 43 percent of them had ever obtained any infertility service (Wilcox and Mosher 1993, 122). The rate of infertility appears to have remained constant since the early 1980s; in previous years it had consistently shown a substantial increase, however, and the causes of infertility continue to be widespread in the United States (Ingram 1993, 103).

The causes of infertility are complex and still not fully understood, but they include environmental, heritable, pathological, and sociobehavioral factors (Office of Technology Assessment 1988b, 61-76). The highly sensitive oviducts are easily scarred by pelvic inflammatory disease or gynecological infections; the resulting blockage of the oviducts presents passage of the ovum through the fallopian tubes to unite with the sperm. Certain social patterns have been linked with increased infertility in women, such as the decision of many to postpone childbearing until they are in their thirties or forties, and increased sexual contact with a variety of partners. The virtual epidemic of gonorrhea and, more recently, of herpes type 2 and chlamydia among young women will probably intensify this problem (Sellors et al. 1988, 451). Drug therapy and microsurgical intervention have been effective in treating infertility in some instances, but couples are increasingly turning to a range of reproduction-assisting technologies.

Artificial Insemination

The oldest, simplest, and most widely used type of reproduction-assisting technology is artificial insemination. Although this is a relatively simple procedure, its success depends on a number of technical factors such as timing and the quality of the semen specimen. Semen obtained by masturbation is deposited by means of a syringe in or near the cervix. Because the exact timing of ovulation is uncertain, the procedure is often conducted on several consecutive days. The usual success rate is 80 percent pregnancy within several months of the start of treatment (Office of Technology Assessment 1988a, 4).

The two basic types of artificial insemination have identical procedures but differ in that the sperm used is either the husband's (AIH) or that of a donor (AID, more commonly known as donor insemination or DI). Whether the semen is provided by the husband or by a donor is biologically irrelevant, but donor insemination raises ethical, psychological, and social questions. It has been estimated that more than 500,000 children in the United States have been conceived by means of artificial insemination, most with donor sperm. Approximately 172,000 women underwent artificial insemination in 1986-1987, resulting in 75,000 births; 30,000 of these procedures utilized donor sperm (Office of Technology Assessment 1988a, 3). Artificial insemination brings into the reproductive process third parties, such as physicians and the donors of sperm. In that sense it is a form of collaborative conception.

The first reported birth to have been made possible by the use of donor insemination took place in the nineteenth century, but use of the procedure has increased in the last few decades, largely as a result of the introduction of cryopreservation, in which the sperm is frozen and can be preserved indefinitely by immersion in liquid nitrogen. In 1988, the American Fertility Society (1988a, 211) amended its therapeutic donor insemination guidelines, advising that "the use of fresh semen is no longer warranted" in response to reports of transmission of the AIDS virus through donated semen. Although there is a slightly decreased pregnancy rate using frozen as compared to fresh sperm, most professional fertility services use frozen semen (Subak, Adamson, and Boltz 1992, 1597).

In Vitro Fertilization

In vitro fertilization (IVF) is the procedure by which eggs are removed from a woman's ovaries and fertilized outside her body. The resulting embryos are kept in a culture medium for approximately two days until they reach the four- to eight-cell stage, at which point they are transferred by means of a catheter into the woman's uterus. If the procedure is successful, the embryos will implant in six to nine days, resulting in a pregnancy. Usually, the retrieval of the mature eggs by surgery using a laparascope that permits visualization of the ovaries is preceded by the induction of ovulation (or "superovulation")—the woman takes a combination of hormones that stimulate her ovaries to produce an abnormal number of eggs for retrieval and fertilization, thus increasing the chances of conception and, ultimately, pregnancy. This procedure is indicated when the oviducts are blocked, thus preventing passage of the egg through the fallopian tubes to be fertilized.

One variation of IVF is gamete intrafallopian transfer (GIFT), in which sperm and eggs are transferred separately to the fallopian tubes. Because fertilization takes place in the fallopian tubes rather than in a petri dish, GIFT is more acceptable than IVF to some religions, such as Roman Catholicism. Another variation is zygote intrafallopian transfer (ZIFT), in which the embryo is placed via catheter in the fallopian tube about eighteen hours after fertilization. Both variations can use donor ova and sperm when appropriate and are increasingly making use of cryopreserved embryos. The outcomes of in vitro fertilization and its variations, as reported by the Society for Assisted Reproductive Technology in 1993, are compared in Table 4-1. Table 4-2 shows the clinical pregnancy rates reported by users of IVF and GIFT from 1985 to 1991 and the increased use of these procedures. In 1991, approximately 4,000 clinical pregnancies were reported by the approximately 200 clinic members of the Society for Assisted Reproductive Technology who had used IVF (Society for Assisted Reproductive Technology 1992); the pregnancy rate was about 19 percent per retrieval. The corresponding figures for GIFT were approximately 1,500 clinical pregnancies and 34 percent.

In addition to its clinical application to circumvent infertility caused by blocked fallopian tubes, IVF increases the possible combinations of germinal material and thus further complicates the concept of parenthood (see Figure 4-1). Controversy has been raised over the use of IVF to enable post-menopausal women to become pregnant using donor eggs. Women as old as sixty years of age have given birth, raising questions as to whether

Table 4-1 Reported Outcomes of ART Procedures

	IVF	GIFT	ZIFT	Donor[a]	Cryopreserved ETs[b]
Cycles/procedures[c]	24,671	5,452	2,104	1,107	4,225
Cancellation	(15.2)	(19.2)	(16.0)	(5.6)	NA
Retrievals	21,083	4,474	1,808	1,045	NA
Transfers per retrieval	(87.1)	(97.7)	(83.5)	(94.1)	NA
Pregnancies	4,017	1,515	442	328	559
Pregnancy loss	(19.9)	(21.6)	(19.2)	(18.3)	(22.9)
Deliveries	3,215	1,188	357	268	431
Deliveries per retrieval	(15.2)	(26.6)	(19.7)	(25.6)	(10.2)
Singletons	(70.0)	(66.0)	(67.0)	(67.0)	(79.0)
Ectopic pregnancies	223	44	20	7	20
Ectopic pregnancies per transfer	(1.2)	(1.0)	(1.3)	(0.7)	NA
Birth defects per neonate delivered	(1.5)	(1.1)	(0.8)	(2.1)	(0.8)

Source: Society for Assisted Reproductive Technology 1993, 957.
Note: Figures in parentheses are percentages. NA means not available.
[a] Donor includes known or anonymous source but not a surrogate.
[b] Cryopreserved embryo transfer cycles not done in combination with fresh ETs and not done with donor embryos.
[c] Includes all cycles, regardless of age or diagnosis; 3 of 215 programs did not report cycles initiated.

any age limits should be set for access to IVF. There is no biological reason why the fertilized egg cannot be transferred to a woman other than the one who supplied the egg. In vitro fertilization has made possible the use of surrogate mothers who carry another genetic mother's baby to term. There is increasing evidence that an embryo produced by means of IVF might be transferred to the abdominal cavity of a male, possibly resulting in male pregnancy (Hepburn 1992, 48). The reported successful delivery by a New Zealand woman who had no uterus, and successful male procreation in other species, contribute to this expectation.

The subjection of the process of conception to the microscope of the laboratory has made possible a wide range of embryo research possibilities, as well as genetic screening, and selection and modification of embryos (Figure 4-1). Preimplantation diagnosis techniques (discussed in Chapter 6) allow for the physical division of embryos into two or more twins or clones. Cryopreservation of eggs and embryos, as well as of sperm, permits the combination of germ cell materials from persons of different generations. Embryo freezing, perhaps used in conjunction with twinning, may allow identical twins to be born years or even generations apart.

Table 4-2   Clinical Pregnancy Rates of Women Using IVF and GIFT, 1985-1991

	IVF			GIFT		
Year	Retrievals	Clinical pregnancies	Rate	Retrievals	Clinical pregnancies	Rate
1985	2,892	337	11.7	56	3	5.4
1986	3,366	485	14.4	466	108	23.2
1987	8,725	1,367	15.7	1,968	492	25.0
1988	13,647	2,243	16.4	3,080	846	27.5
1989	15,392	2,811	18.3	3,652	1,112	30.5
1990	16,405	3,057	18.7	3,692	1,093	29.6
1991	21,083	4,017	19.0	4,474	1,515	33.8
Total	65,105	11,260	17.3	13,696	4,076	29.8

Sources: For 1985-1989, Hartz, Porter, and DeCherney 1992, 257; for 1990, Society for Assisted Reproductive Technology 1992, 17; for 1991, Society for Assisted Reproductive Technology 1993, 957.

In July 1978, Louise Brown, the first baby conceived by means of IVF, was born in England. In January 1980, after considerable political debate, Norfolk General Hospital in Virginia obtained state governmental approval to make the technique available in the United States. On December 28, 1981, Elizabeth Carr was born—the first baby in the United States to have been conceived using IVF. By 1990, more than 200 clinics in the United States were offering the procedure. The United States In Vitro Fertilization Registry has documented, since 1985, 70,000 stimulation cycles, resulting in approximately 8,200 deliveries and 10,600 babies ("MRI, SART, and AFT" 1990). The number of clinical pregnancies resulting from the use of GIFT increased from 3 to 1,515 between 1985 and 1991; success rates now average about 30 percent for each attempt (Table 4-2).

Most clinics in the United States continue to have waiting lists of women who are willing to pay $4,000 to $6,000 for a chance to become pregnant. The total expenses they incur in a series of attempts at pregnancy, including travel, lodging, and loss of employment for the duration of the treatment, may well be as high as $50,000 (Ingram 1993, 104). Despite this investment, approximately 90 percent of the women who undergo IVF do not give birth to a child (Neumann et al. 1994, 239). In addition to significantly different success rates among IVF programs there is substantial variation between patients with specific indications. Success rates are particularly reduced for couples in which the male is infertile (5.9 percent), for women who have only one ovary (8.0 percent), and for women who are over 40 years of age (4.0 percent) (Haan et al. 1991, 587). There is also some evidence to suggest that success rates are exaggerated because of spontaneous pregnancies occurring during treatment. Studies of women

Figure 4-1   Applications and Extensions of IVF

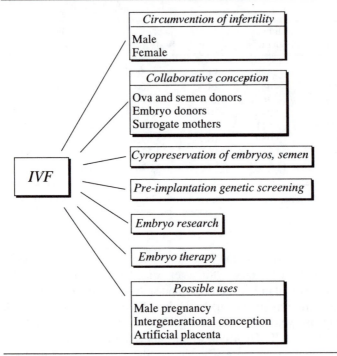

accepted for IVF programs show that 7 to 28 percent conceive naturally either before receiving treatment or within two years after discontinuation (Wagner and St. Clair 1989, 1028). These data on women who became pregnant independent of IVF treatment suggest that success rates are masking at least some proportion of births that cannot be attributed to IVF. Nevertheless, as more technologies become available and are viewed effective, their more widespread use is assured (especially if their costs are reimbursed by third-party payers), because the pool of candidates for assisted procreation is a growing one.

Because the IVF procedure is designed to circumvent the natural reproductive mechanisms, questions have been raised about its safety. The rate of congenital abnormalities of babies conceived by means of IVF does not seem to be significantly higher than that of babies conceived naturally, however, although there is some evidence that the former have a higher incidence of low birth weight (Bonnicksen 1989, 85). The damage might be traced to the development of the ovum (especially if superovulation is induced), the selection of sperm (the female reproductive tract selects against some types of abnormal sperm), the fertilization itself,

Table 4-3 Rates of Conception and Multiple Gestation
Relative to Number of Oocytes Transferred

Oocytes transferred	Number of procedures	Pregnancy rate	Multiple gestation rate
1	14	7.1	0
2	40	10.0	0
3	82	32.9	14.8
4	272	33.6	25.3
5	136	41.6	24.6

Source: Nelson et al. 1993, 119.

and the use of freezing techniques to preserve gametes or embryos. Risks to the woman who undergoes IVF include ovarian hyperstimulation syndrome (which in rare cases has been fatal) and heightened incidence of breast, genital, and hormone-dependent cancer linked to superovulation (Schenker and Ezra 1994, 412). Furthermore, the procedures for retrieval of the woman's eggs may cause bleeding, infection, or injury to blood vessels (Wagner and St. Clair 1989, 1028). Ironically, considerable research is needed to test for safety of the embryo, but ethical concerns about such research have in the past precluded adequate testing in humans (see Chapter 8).

One problem associated with IVF and GIFT is the increase in multiple pregnancies that can lead to a wide array of medical and psychological complications (Nijs et al. 1993, 1245). The practice of transferring multiple embryos is used in order to maximize pregnancy success rates; the more embryos transferred, the higher the probability of multiple gestation (see Table 4-3). Although there are other factors such as maternal age that contribute to this problem, the vast majority of multiple pregnancies (63 to 80 percent) are a direct result of reproduction-assisting technologies (Callahan et al. 1994, 244). While assisted births represent only 2 percent of singleton pregnancies, they represent 35 percent of twin and 77 percent of triplet pregnancies (Collins and Bleyl 1990, 1384).

This problem is of particular concern because multiple pregnancies are associated with complications for both pregnant women and the fetus/newborn. The incidence of infant mortality for triplets and quadruplets is almost ten times that of singletons (Seoud et al. 1992, 825). Children who are part of multiple pregnancies are also likely to be premature, thus increasing their chances of problems linked to low birth weight and increasing the need for neonatal care (Luke 1994, 105). Moreover, particularly for older women undergoing IVF, multiple pregnancies might produce an unbearable overload for the cardiovascular and renal functions, among other body systems (Schenkler and Ezra 1994, 418).

One response to the increased rates of multiple pregnancies produced by IVF is the highly controversial procedure of selective reduction or termination of pregnancies. Usually this entails an injection of potassium chloride into the heart of the fetus (or fetuses) to be aborted. In some cases, selective termination has been carried out in multiple pregnancies where one of the fetuses has been diagnosed through ultrasound as abnormal (Zaner and Fox 1993, 120). More frequently it is used in the first trimester to reduce the number of fetuses a woman is carrying in order to reduce the risk of pre-term delivery. In one study,

> at the time of the procedure 88 women had triplets, 89 had quadru-
> plets, 16 had quintuplets, and 7 had from 6 to 9 fetuses. These preg-
> nancies were reduced to 189 sets of twins, 5 sets of triplets, and 6
> singletons. . . . The incidence of intrauterine growth retardation was
> not increased over that anticipated in a population of twins
> (Berkowitz et al. 1993, 17).

Selective termination has been shown to be effective in reducing both maternal risk and risk to the surviving infants; however, because it does so by selectively aborting healthy fetuses, it has been attacked by opponents of abortion. It has been suggested that the number of embryos transferred be limited to a maximum of two (Nijs et al. 1993, 1249).

Extensions of Reproduction-Assisting Technologies

A variety of new techniques for assisting reproduction are currently being developed. Micromanipulation allows the insertion of one selected spermatozoan into the egg's outer membrane (Boldt 1988). In April 1989, the first baby conceived by the use of micro-manipulation sperm transfer was born in Singapore. An extension of this technique is the microsurgical removal of extra male pronuclei (a condition that is a potential complication of IVF with a reported incidence of 4 percent to 5 percent depending on the superovulation process initiated) (Rawlins et al. 1988).

Some reproduction-assisting technologies overlap with screening and selection technologies. Use of sperm separation techniques in conjunction with DI and IVF can maximize conception of a child of the desired sex. The ability to carry out fertilization under the microscope in the laboratory increases the likelihood that increasingly precise genetic diagnostic and therapeutic techniques can be used to study and treat the embryo before it is transferred for implantation (see Chapter 6). The fusion of the nuclei of two eggs could eliminate the need for the male contribution to procreation; two women could each contribute an egg, thus producing a daughter with two mothers and no father.

The Commercialization of Assisted Reproduction

The rapid increase in demand for reproduction-assisting innovations has drawn the attention of investors, many of whom are involved in the development of some of the techniques. In an economy in which the marketplace is relied upon as a broker of demands and of the supply of goods and services, this demand would soon be met, but the commercialization of these technologies may have adverse consequences. They include the viewing of children as products of increasingly sophisticated intervention methods; the intrusion of the profit motive into a process as unique and human as procreation; and the exploitation of vulnerable and often desperate consumers. Barbara Rothman (1986) sees developments in the area of reproductive technology as reflecting a general trend—the treatment of people and parts of people as commodities:

> The new technology of reproduction is building on this commodification. Rather than buying whole bodies, we can now buy the parts. Sperm is relatively cheap. . . . Egg donations are being done only on an experimental basis now: will they eventually become purchasable too? And what of embryo transplants. . . . How long will it be before human embryos, like some animal embryos, are up for sale? (2)

Donor insemination and the marketing of embryos are useful examples of technologies adversely affected by this trend toward commercialization.

Donor Insemination, Ovum Donation, and Cryobanks

Donor insemination in the United States has always had a financial element. Virtually all the practitioners of DI responding to the Curie-Cohen (1979) survey paid for semen samples: 90 percent paid between $20 and $35 per ejaculate, and 7 percent paid as much as $100. As a result of its 1987 survey, the Office of Technology Assessment estimated the average to be $70 to $80 (1986b, 48). George Annas prefers the term sperm "vendor" rather than "donor"; he argues that the consent form that is signed is, in actuality, a contract in which the sperm vendor agrees to deliver a product in return for payment of a specified sum. The term "consignor" refers to men who "transfer their semen to another's charge or custody" (1980, 6). This transfer normally involves a fee, though it may not. Also, the semen might be held in a cryobank for later transfer to one or more recipient women. The consignor would likely be paid for such a transfer, but if it were a transfer to the few sperm banks that exist primarily for eugenic purposes, the motivation might be something other than money.

The commercialization of DI increased significantly with the introduction of techniques of cryopreservation. The concept of human semen banking was introduced in 1866; the first successful technique for preserving human semen was developed in 1953. Since the mid-1960s, the introduction of more advanced cryopreservation methods has led to the establishment of cryobanks. (They were initially intended for sperm; only later did they accept embryos and ova.) There are approximately 400 hospital-based cryobanks in the United States. In addition there are a growing number of commercial cryobanks that sell sperm to DI practitioners (Kaplan and Tong 1994, 227). Commercial interest was at first based on the (largely unrealized) expectation that millions of men planning to undergo vasectomy would elect to store their semen as a form of "fertility insurance." Cryobanks have diversified and now offer many services, including timed multiple inseminations with a donor's sperm and a wide selection of germ cell material for purchase. A few cryobanks have made a name for themselves because of their special goals or clientele. The Sperm Bank of Northern California is a feminist-run facility that provides DI to single or lesbian women. The Repository for Germinal Choice has an eugenic mission of providing sperm of men of prominence to specially selected couples in order to produce "superior" children (Kaplan and Tong 1994, 228).

Despite initial concern about the possibility of long-term genetic damage to sperm during freezing and a decrease in the fertilization capacity of frozen sperm, its use in DI is widespread. In 1988, the total number of births made possible by the use of frozen sperm was estimated to be more than 30,000. Most practitioners of DI (74 percent) who use frozen sperm obtain it from commercial sperm banks (Office of Technology Assessment 1988a, 43). The need for more inseminations with frozen sperm to achieve pregnancy is outweighed by the convenience of frozen sperm because the donor need not be physically present to provide the sample. Also, the freezing of sperm tends to depersonalize the process of DI, thus making it more acceptable to some individuals. In addition, the use of frozen sperm allows more thorough screening of donors and of the sperm sample directly—considerations that are particularly important in an era of AIDS.

It has been estimated that there is a potential clientele of more than 100,000 women who, for a variety of medical reasons, might benefit from ovum donation (Braverman 1993, 1216). Since the practice was introduced in 1983, its use has increased dramatically; more than fifty such programs are currently in operation. Women who donate eggs must endure uncomfortable procedures and they earn an average of $2,000 per donation; (Goodwin 1992, 276). Ovum donation raises questions about the psychological impact on both the offspring and the families as well as questions of consent and parentage.

The Marketing of Human Embryos

The most publicized method of assisted reproduction is in vitro fertilization. Donor insemination continues to have a considerably wider application, but IVF has sparked more debate (Bonnicksen 1989). Books and articles about IVF written for mass consumption are now commonplace. Although it is no longer front page news, the production of test-tube babies continues to be of interest to the American public. As recently as 1978, however, the most common references to IVF were not in the press but in science fiction. The birth of Louise Brown in July 1978 stimulated public interest in reproduction technology and triggered a spate of research activity. The rapid proliferation of assisted reproduction services and techniques can be traced to that single success, which had been preceded by seven years of failed attempts.

Chris Raymond points to the increasing commercialization of IVF: "Buffeted by the pressures of commercial interests and near-desperate patients searching for a technological miracle, the technique has become a major player in an increasingly lucrative fertility market" (1988, 464). There is no doubt that reproductive technology has tremendous profit-making potential. The estimated potential clientele is 1 million persons with an estimated income (in 1990) of $2 billion (Bonnicksen 1989, 25).

In 1987, $70 million was spent in attempts to use IVF, which translates into 7,000 couples paying an average of $10,000 each for the technique. About one-fourth of the more than 200 IVF centers in the United States are currently private, for-profit clinics (Raymond 1988, 464). Increasingly, these private centers are using aggressive marketing techniques and some have been accused of inflating their success rates. At least two chains of private IVF centers have been established; such clinics "recruit patients by mass mailings to gynecologists, advertisements in professional journals, and packaged brochures" (Bonnicksen 1989, 26).

This already substantial demand for IVF services is certain to intensify if IVF pregnancy success rates increase and the technique becomes more widely available. The mounting pressure on insurance companies to cover all or part of the costs of IVF and other fertility services has resulted in the passage of state laws mandating such insurance (Ingram 1993). Although these statutes exempt payment by Medicaid for individuals without insurance, claims for such coverage are inevitable. Moreover, as the costs are increasingly reimbursed all or in part by third-party payers, the demand for such services will intensify.

This trend toward the commercialization of assisted reproduction raises serious questions as to the future of American society. On a practical level, as infertile couples, and indeed all parents, come to be viewed as potential consumers of a growing array of reproductive technologies and services, society will have to consider the possibility of regulations designed to protect their interests. As noted earlier, this need is compelling because many of these persons are desperate and willing to try anything that promises results.

To defer fully to the marketplace on matters of reproductive technology is to evade social responsibility. The transformation of procreation from a matter of intimacy between two persons to yet another market enterprise makes it imperative that there be a careful analysis of how this revolution in thinking, as well as in technique, will affect human relationships. How will this trend alter societal views of parental responsibility? Of children? And of women?

Regulating Reproduction-Assisting Technologies

The proliferation of reproduction-assisting services, the trend toward commercialization of these services, and the potential conflicts among the many parties involved in the new reproduction methods raise concerns about regulation. In practice the issues surrounding these innovations have been resolved on a case-by-case approach only when legal conflicts have arisen, primarily with regard to custody. Although Congress has held many hearings on reproduction-assisting technologies, they have not resulted in the establishment of a national policy. In 1987 and 1988, four separate House subcommittees held preliminary hearings relating to the implications of these technologies for families and children (U.S. Congress, House, 1987c), access to reproductive technologies (U.S. Congress, House, 1987b), and consumer protection issues (U.S. Congress, House, 1988). The House Subcommittee on Regulation and Business Opportunities surveyed all IVF centers in the United States in 1989 and published comparative data in a booklet that is available to the public. Two major reports on fertility services issued by the Office of Technology Assessment (1988a, 1988b) helped spark awareness among members of Congress.

Despite the appearance of reproduction-assisting technologies on the national agenda in the late 1980s, the regulation of infertility services has largely rested with the states through their authority to protect the public health and their power to control familial relations, medical practice, the licensing of health personnel and facilities, and contracts. As a result, attempts to regulate assisted reproduction services are inconsistent and at

Table 4-4   Selected Provisions of State Donor Insemination Statutes

State	Physician must inseminate	Refers only to married women	Mentions husband consent	Legitimizes offspring	Requires record-keeping
Alabama	x	x	x	x	x
Alaska		x	x	x	
Arkansas	x	x	x	x	
California	x		x	x	x
Colorado	x			x	
Connecticut	x		x	x	x
Florida			x	x	
Georgia	x			x	
Idaho	x		x	x	x
Illinois	x		x	x	
Kansas			x	x	x
Louisiana				x	
Maryland		x	x	x	
Michigan		x	x	x	
Minnesota	x			x	
Montana	x	x	x	x	x
Nevada	x	x	x	x	x
New Jersey	x			x	
New Mexico	x		x	x	x
New York	x	x	x	x	
North Carolina			x	x	
Ohio	x		x	x	x
Oklahoma	x		x	x	x
Oregon	x		x	x	x
Tennessee		x	x	x	
Texas		x	x	x	
Virginia	x	x	x	x	
Washington	x		x	x	x
Wisconsin	x		x	x	x
Wyoming			x	x	x

Source: Adapted from Office of Technology Assessment 1988b, 243

times contradictory from one state to the next. Table 4-4 indicates the range of provisions of state statutes regulating donor insemination. Although these statutes have helped clarify the legal context of DI, many state legislatures have yet to address even the basic issues concerning screening requirements, the legal status of the various parties, and access both to the services and to information.

There has been little statutory regulation of DI, which has been practiced for a century, and even less of more recent and provocative innovations such as IVF and GIFT,. Most of the current laws affect IVF only indirectly. Several statutes (such as those of Pennsylvania) have recordkeeping and reporting provisions but largely defer to the professional guidelines of the American Fertility Society and the American College of Obstetricians and Gynecologists.

Public policy makers have frequently deferred to professional organizations to develop and apply guidelines for assisted reproduction services. The two organizations that have been most active in promulgating relevant standards of practice are the American Fertility Society and the American Association of Tissue Banks. Since 1986 the society has prepared ethical guidelines concerning these technologies, issued position papers on insurance coverage for fertility services, and published revised procedures for performing DI, IVF, GIFT, and other relevant services (American Fertility Society 1988a, 1988b). Most recently it has published guidelines for therapeutic DI (1993a), guidelines for oocyte donation (1993b), and guidelines for minimal genetic screening for gamete donors (1993c). In 1992, the American Fertility Society and the American College of Obstetricians and Gynecologists founded the National Advisory Board on Ethics in Reproduction to "fill the vacuum created by the lack of systematic reflection on the ethical questions raised by reproductive research and medicine."

Although the standards promulgated by professional organizations are valuable because they provide some control over the use of these technologies, the problem with guidelines (as opposed to regulations) is that they do not have the force of law and there is no legal authority to ensure compliance with them. Organizations thus must rely on accreditation privileges and ethical sanctions. There is little to stop the establishment of non-sanctioned cryobanks, fertility clinics, or DI/IVF/GIFT clinics. Even though lack of compliance to voluntary guidelines by nonmember businesses carries some risk, in the emerging highly lucrative and competitive fertility industry, such guidelines alone are not sufficient to protect all parties. One strategy is for the states to restrict the performance of these services to those facilities that comply with the American Fertility Society guidelines. (Louisiana passed such a statute in 1986.) Another strategy would be to use these guidelines as a framework for establishing a national policy.

Assisted Reproduction and Reproductive Rights

As discussed earlier, assisted reproduction shifts emphasis from the right not to have children to the questions of whether there is a complementary right to have children and, if so, whether qualifications can be imposed as to the number or "quality" of those progeny. Do prospective parents who carry genetic disease have a duty to refrain from contributing from their own eggs or sperm and instead to utilize collaborative conception technologies such as DI or embryo transfer? If there is a right to have children, to what extent does it include a claim of access to reproduction-assisting technologies? These technologies have the potential to expand the right to have children significantly, but only if those persons who need it have access to it.

Reproduction-assisting technologies give rise to the logical extension of reproductive autonomy as a positive right—a claim on society to guarantee, through whatever means possible, the capacity to reproduce. If the right to procreate is interpreted as a positive one, then an infertile couple might have a constitutional claim for access to these technologies. Under such circumstances, individuals who are unable to afford the treatments necessary to achieve reproductive capacity could expect society to guarantee access to them. A woman with blocked fallopian tubes would have a claim to corrective surgery or IVF. An infertile man could claim access to DI or corrective surgery, if possible.

Once procreative rights are stated as positive, however, drawing reasonable boundaries becomes difficult. Does a woman who is unable to carry a fetus to term because of the absence of a uterus or the existence of a high-risk condition have a legitimate claim to have a surrogate mother do so? No matter where the lines are drawn, some individuals are likely to have a limited opportunity to have children. The adoption of a positive rights perspective will intensify the already growing demand for these technologies, encourage entrepreneurs to provide a wide variety of reproduction-assisting services, and, perhaps most important, put increasing pressure on the government to fund these services.

Technology-assisted reproduction thus raises questions concerning the exercise and scope of reproductive rights. Although these technologies give hope to many infertile persons and provide the means to exert more control over the characteristics of their progeny, they may also give rise to conflicts among the rights of the many parties involved in their application. Each technology has a variety of possible clinical, social, and eugenic applications, depending on the prime motivation for its use. And, depending on the specific application, the technologies can either extend or constrain the reproductive rights of the users.

One problem arising from these technologies is that by creating new categories of mother and father they have produced the likelihood of conflict among such categories. At least five parents are now possible. The most significant and novel distinction is that between the genetic mother, who contributes the ova, and the gestational or biological mother, who carries the child to term. In addition, the process may include a separate nurturing mother who cares for the baby once it is born. Moreover, the woman who carries the baby to term might do so in order to give the baby to another woman to raise, in which case the gestational mother becomes a "surrogate" mother (see Chapter 7). Similarly, DI creates a distinction between genetic fatherhood and legal fatherhood, thus raising critical legal questions about paternity. Technologies such as egg fusion and twinning promise to add to these categories of parents and to challenge traditional notions of maternal and paternal rights.

In vitro fertilization has produced another category of potential rights holder. Before it became possible to fertilize, freeze, and store human embryos, there were no questions concerning either the rights of the "owner" of the embryo or the possible "rights" of the embryo because it was, in effect, part of the woman throughout the gestation period. With this new technology, however, have come new dilemmas about the legal and moral status of the embryo and a growing number of court cases concerning them (see Goodwin, 1992). In *Davis v. Davis* (1992), the genetic father fought with the genetic mother after their divorce about the disposition of seven frozen embryos that remained after their earlier attempt to use IVF. Reversing the lower court decision, which held that the embryos should not be destroyed, the Tennessee Supreme Court ruled that the father's right not to be a parent superseded the mother's right to have the embryos transferred to her uterus and to carry any resulting fetus(es) to term.

Other legal claims have concerned the rights of "orphaned" embryos (Rios case, Australia); the rights of a couple to custody of "their" embryos being held by a fertility clinic (*York v. Jones*, 1989); the rights of a widow to be inseminated by the frozen semen of her deceased husband; and the right of death row prisoners to have children by means of artificial insemination so they could pass on their genes. These cases constitute what is likely to be a torrent of challenging and unfamiliar legal questions.

In sum, the definition of legal parentage and parental rights is becoming increasingly difficult. In addition to giving rise to conflicts over rights of access to particular applications of assisted reproduction, cumulatively these new capabilities raise more general concerns about the rights of certain categories of people. The impact of reproductive technologies on children and women, and the related issue of access, are analyzed in the next two sections.

The Children of Technology-Assisted Reproduction

Conspicuously absent from much of the debate about reproductive technologies is any discussion of the impact of these innovations on children: individual children who are products of specific applications and society's perception of children. The child is the person most affected by the decision to utilize a specific assisted reproduction technique, even though the child is not a party to the decision. A case can be made that the child would favor the decision of the parent(s) to use that technique, because otherwise he or she would not exist. The desired outcome of assisted reproduction is the deliberate creation of a child, often with specific genetic characteristics. Therefore, "in making decisions and undertaking procedures to fulfill the wishes of the would-be parents, it would be improper to forget that some child must live with the consequences of those decisions and procedures" (Snowden, Mitchell, and Snowden 1983, 25).

The first issue regarding children of assisted reproduction is whether they should have access to information as to who their genetic parents are. Ethicist Leon Kass points out that "clarity about who your parents are, clarity in the lines of generation, clarity about who is whose are indispensable foundations of a sound family life, itself the sound foundation of civilized community" (Grobstein 1981, 65). Although some applications of assisted reproduction reinforce the genetic link by enabling infertile persons to have a child of their own, other practices such as DI, egg donation, and embryo transfer "challenge the notion that genetic parenthood guarantees familial relationship" (Stanworth 1987, 21). The increased use of these practices raises the question of whether children have a right to know the identity of their genetic parents. Reports frequently appear in the media of children born by means of DI now searching for their genetic fathers, the semen donors who were guaranteed anonymity. One donor, who was opposed to these searches, said, "I did not do it to get fifty cards on Father's Day; I did it for the money." As the children produced by means of egg donation or marketed embryos in the 1980s and 1990s reach maturity, it is likely that some of them will also claim a right to know their genetic heritage. If such a right is recognized, there may be an end to much of the secrecy currently surrounding assisted reproduction with donor semen, ova, and embryos.

The second issue regarding the impact on children born as a result of assisted reproduction is the extent to which these innovations change the value society places on the child. Prospective parents have always wanted children for a variety of personal reasons, but before the development of procreative technologies, by and large they took responsibility for the children they bore. When fate dealt them a child with imperfections, they accepted it and coped as well as they could. As a result of the expanding selection of intervention possibilities available today, many parents are no longer satisfied with a child whom they view as less than the best or even average. To some observers, it seems that "the search for a perfect baby is leading us further and further back into pregnancy" (Klass 1989, 45).

This emphasis on technological "perfection" raises questions concerning the purpose of children. It is not surprising that terms such as "quality control" and children as "products" of particular techniques are commonplace in current debates about the reproductive process. This possible treatment of children as commodities must be contrasted with the reproductive rights of the potential parents who will use these techniques.

Reproduction-Assisting Technologies and Women's Rights

Assisted reproduction has affected the reproductive rights of women, both as consumers of these services and in the aggregate.

> The new reproductive technology has a paradoxical effect on reproductive freedom, particularly the reproductive freedom of women: on the one hand, it appears to enhance our capacity to make choices, but on the other hand, a closer examination suggests that there are many ways in which reproductive technology may serve to reduce the choices we can make. (Overall 1987, 198)

In part this paradox might follow from the varied motivations and uses of these techniques, which could include a coercive dimension, and in part it is a predictable result of all applications of such revolutionary interventions.

Although individual women might benefit from reproductive technologies, the cumulative effect might be to jeopardize women's freedom. When "choices" become available to women, they tend to become compulsions to "choose" the alternative endorsed by society (Hubbard 1982, 210).

> The "right to choose" means very little when women are powerless. . . . Women make their own reproductive choices, but they do not make them just as they please; they do not make them under conditions which they themselves create but under social conditions and constraints which they, as mere individuals, are powerless to change. (Petchesky 1980, 685)

Furthermore, because it requires third-party involvement and encourages dependence on medical technique, assisted reproduction may force a woman to surrender control over procreation.

The division of motherhood such that one woman donates the egg, a second woman carries the fetus to term, and a third raises the child weakens a woman's claim to maternity and destroys the integrity of motherhood. "In this dismemberment of maternity, women may lose one of our few (potential) sources of power" (Arditti 1985, 582). Reproductive technologies have been vehemently indicted as inherently sexist:

> Sexist biases permeate the new reproductive technologies and genetic engineering at all levels. In general, they imply that motherhood,

the capacity of women to bring forth children, is changed from a creative process, in which woman cooperated with her body as an active human being, to an industrial production process. In this process, not only is the symbiosis of mother and child disrupted, but the whole process is rationalized, objectified, planned and controlled by medical experts. More than ever before the woman is objectified and made passive. (Mies 1987, 332)

Moreover, because the woman is no longer considered an entity but is rather treated as a comprising object that can be isolated, examined, recombined, sold, hired, or simply thrown away, her integrity as a human being is destroyed (Mies 1987, 332). Thus the commercialization of assisted reproduction might lead not only to the treatment of children as commodities but to the creation of a value context where gametes, embryos, and women are viewed as commodities to be "banked, bought, sold, and rented as a means to procreation" (Office of Technology Assessment 1988b, 327).

One example of the medicalization of reproduction is donor insemination where the woman is cast in the role of a patient to whom treatment is given even though she has no medical condition that requires treatment. If anything, her spouse, who is not involved in the procedure other than to give his consent, is the patient in absentia. At best, the medical setting legitimizes the use of DI for the woman and for society. Ironically, research into male infertility might have a higher priority if DI were not so easy and, as some feminists claim, done to the woman (Corea 1985b). In a growing number of cases, DI is carried out because the husband had earlier undergone sterilization voluntarily, only to change his mind as circumstances changed.

Moreover, IVF is increasingly being used on healthy, fertile women to enable them to have children by their infertile male partners. Because IVF requires a smaller proportion of viable sperm than required in natural fertilization, men with very low sperm counts (that is, men who are functionally infertile for uterine fertilization) might father a child if their spouse undergoes IVF. This particular application of IVF is yet another indication that the "choices" opened up to women by reproductive technology are frequently illusory.

To some extent, the fact that women bear the risks of reproductive technology is explained by their biologically central role in pregnancy. Nevertheless it has been argued that women are a deliberate target of new reproductive technologies that can be "powerful socio-economic and political instruments of control" (Klein 1987, 65). Many feminists assert that the problem is exacerbated because the majority of researchers and clinicians are male (Stanworth 1988, 3). Although women are most affected by these technologies, they are virtually absent from the legal, scientific, and governmental bodies that are involved in the research, development, and delivery of the technologies.

Access to Assisted Reproduction

The increase in assisted reproduction services throughout the United States has raised critical questions of access, especially in the market-oriented health care system. Answers to these questions turn on the prevailing conception of reproductive rights. If there is a positive right to have children, to what extent is a woman or a couple entitled to expect the medical community or the government to provide the resources necessary to exercise that right? The high costs of many of these techniques, especially IVF, have created economic barriers that, at least initially, meant that only those persons with adequate financial resources were able to undergo treatment. However, the heightened concern about access has resulted in the establishment of what is, in effect, an economic screening mechanism that determines which infertile couples will have the opportunity to have children.

Insurance Coverage

There are currently no comprehensive data available that would enable a comparison of the proportion of assisted reproduction costs paid out of pocket with the proportion reimbursed by private insurers. An increasing number of carriers are providing routine coverage for IVF and other reproduction-assisting treatment if it is medically indicated (Neumann and Johannesson 1994). For instance, employees covered by BlueCross Blue-Shield in Delaware have an option to purchase IVF coverage (no minimum waiting period, $25,000 lifetime maximum). The Prudential medical insurance programs nationwide recognize infertility as an illness and routinely cover virtually all related services, including performance of AIH and IVF, as long as the services conform to the standards of the American College of Obstetricians and Gynecologists and are determined to be medically necessary (Office of Technology Assessment 1988, 151). Many group insurance plans do not cover IVF, however, usually on grounds that it is experimental. This inconsistency in coverage for IVF has led to lobbying efforts by groups such as RESOLVE for enactment of state legislation requiring third-party coverage.

The courts have given mixed signals regarding insurance coverage. In *Witcraft v. Sundstrand Health and Disability Group Benefit Plan* (1988), the Iowa Supreme Court held that the dysfunctioning of the insured's reproductive organs was an illness. Since the plan covered ''expenses relating to'' illness, the court ruled that the claim for IVF expenses was valid. In *Egert v. Connecticut General Life Insurance Company* (1990), the United States Court of Appeals for the Seventh Circuit held that the claim was invalid. In *Kinzie v. Physician's Liability Insurance Company* (1987), however, an Oklahoma appellate court denied recovery on the grounds that IVF is elective and was not required to cure or preserve the insured's health. Moreover, the court did not deem it medically necessary to a woman's health that she give birth to a child (Ingram 1993, 104).

At least six states (Arkansas, Connecticut, Hawaii, Maryland, Massachusetts, and Texas) have adopted legislation requiring insurance carriers operating in their states either to routinely provide coverage for IVF and related services or to offer an optional package that includes such coverage. Massachusetts enacted legislation (1987 Mass. Acts. H. 3721) requiring all insurance plans that provide pregnancy-related benefits to cover medically indicated expenses of diagnosis and treatment of infertility to the same extent that they cover other pregnancy-related procedures. The regulations promulgated under this act require insurers to provide benefits for all nonexperimental infertility procedures (211 C.M.R. Sections 37.01 to 37.11). These include, but are not limited to, AI, IVF, and other procedures recognized as nonexperimental by the American Fertility Society, or by other infertility experts recognized by the state commissioner of insurance. Surrogacy, reversal of voluntary sterilization, and procurement of donor eggs and sperm are specifically excluded. The insurers may establish reasonable eligibility requirements, information about which is to be made available to the insured.

Despite this legislative activity, most states have no policy concerning third-party coverage for assisted-reproduction services. In the absence of state regulations, the majority of health insurance plans and health maintenance organizations (HMOs) specifically exclude coverage for IVF. Its potentially high cost and its low success rate, combined with the common perception of it as a procedure of uncertain benefit to the few at the expense of the many, deter many insurers from entering this market. It is not surprising, therefore, that groups demanding such coverage have gone to the state legislatures.

Expansion of insurance coverage for fertility treatment will expand accessibility, but there is little evidence that Medicaid recipients or the millions of women without health insurance will have access to assisted reproduction even though, on average, infertility is more prevalent among poor women than middle-class women. There has been little effort by the states or by Congress to fund assisted reproduction, and they are unlikely to do so in a time of continued budget scarcity (Clayton 1991, 92). For those women who are unable to obtain assisted reproduction because of insufficient financial resources, reproduction as a positive right remains unfulfilled.

Exclusionary Policies

Even the negative right to have children is problematic for women who are denied access to assisted reproduction services because they are not married, especially if they are lesbians. Although these women might have the financial resources, they are effectively barred from using services that are available only to married couples or heterosexual couples in "long-term stable relationships." Some observers (Kern and Ridolfi 1982) argue that this practice is a violation of these women's fundamental right to procreate and bear a child under the Fourteenth Amendment. But as mentioned earlier, the right to have children has not been firmly established and remains controversial, even among feminists. As a result, it is doubtful that the courts will act to guarantee access to commercial fertility services.

Exclusionary practices based on marital status or sexual orientation have forced some women to conclude third-party arrangements with known or anonymous donors (Achilles 1992, 10). It has been reported that at least 1,500 unmarried women a year in the United States are having children by means of DI despite the difficulty of gaining access to mainstream DI services (*Harvard Law Review* 1985, 671). Unfortunately, women denied the anonymity and screening capabilities provided by professional services are more at risk for legal problems and possibly for health problems. In *Jhordan C. v. Mary K.* (1986), the appellate court upheld a semen donor's request for visitation rights with a child born to a lesbian mother. The court stated that the woman could have avoided this situation if a physician had obtained the semen as provided by statute, but it did not query whether she would have had access to such professional services.

The debate over making assisted reproduction services available to nontraditional families often includes arguments concerning a child's right to have both a mother and a father. In *C. M. v. C. C.* (1979) a semen donor was awarded parental rights and responsibilities because the court declared that it was in the best interest of the child to have two parents. Some observers have asserted that if a stable marriage is no longer considered a precondition for DI, then the social and psychological implications for babies born in households where no males are present must be seriously considered. They explain that this is "not to say that lesbian couples or cohabiting women should be denied the right to have a baby by AID, but to point out the need for rules within which the service is to be provided if the practice is not to change the basis of social organization—the family" (Snowden, Mitchell, and Snowden 1983, 13).

A case brought in California is indicative of the confusion over parental roles that can follow use of reproductive technologies. Two lesbians who wanted to have a baby obtained sperm, which one of them inserted into the uterus of the other, using a poultry baster. In a custody battle that followed the breakup of the couple several years later, one woman argued that she was in fact the ''father'' since she physically inseminated the ''mother.'' Moreover, she argued, it was their mutual intention to share the parental roles. This case was dismissed, but in a similar case credence was given to the argument of the plaintiff and joint custody was awarded.

Reproductive technologies promise to revolutionize the family structure even more if the demands of some transsexual groups (genetic males who have undergone hormonal and surgical treatment to become females) are ultimately met. Some of these individuals are demanding more government funding of research into male procreation to facilitate more rapid development of applications so that they can experience ''womanhood to its fullest.'' If transsexual women have access, it seems unlikely that any man who desires to experience ''motherhood'' can be denied it.

Ultimately, the resolution of issues regarding access to assisted reproduction technologies depends on how broadly the right to have children is defined if, indeed, there is agreement that such a right exists. Because of the need for access to professional services, and in some cases (such as IVF) teams of medical specialists, procreation is no longer a private matter, nor is it inexpensive. This raises important questions concerning the allocation of medical resources. What priority should these costly treatments have, in comparison with preventive measures and research to discover the underlying causes of infertility? Although society has put a high priority on reproductive rights, debate continues about the exercise of these rights when it requires significant public resources.

Conclusion

The technological context of human reproduction is rapidly changing. Assisted reproduction offers many persons some hope of overcoming fertility problems and having the children they so desperately desire. The new capabilities also create important policy problems and have the potential to engender conflict among the many parties and interests involved. Some of the issues related to reproductive technology have reached the public policy agenda, but by and large policy makers have been hesitant to become embroiled in an area that has traditionally been viewed as a private matter between a man and a woman.

The professional guidelines established by the American Fertility Society and other organizations appear to be generally appropriate and may in fact be the most reasonable and workable means of regulating reproductive services; however, many questions are still unresolved because of the absence of a national policy. Is reproduction a positive right, and if so, how far should the national government go in guaranteeing access to reproduc-

tion-assisting technologies? Given the potential threats to children, wom-
en, and families in this changing reproductive environment, what, if any,
national policies should be instituted to maximize the beneficial uses while
maintaining the control necessary to minimize the negative consequences?
Although case law and a few states have addressed these issues, there is a
need for for an informed national debate about the implications of this
second stage of the reproductive revolution.

C H A P T E R 5

Surrogate Motherhood: Redefining the Family

In October 1991, Arlette Schweitzer gave birth to twin grandchildren. Present at the delivery were her husband and her daughter, Christa Uchytil, for whom Schweitzer had served as a gestational surrogate. The delivery room in 1991 was far different from the family home, built by Schweitzer's grandfather, where Arlette had been born forty-two years earlier, unattended by a physician. The Schweitzer-Uchytil partnership and other instances of surrogate motherhood raise a number of ethical and legal questions. Are the twins Schweitzer's children, since she gave birth to them? Or are they her grandchildren, since they are the product of her daughter's ova fertilized in vitro by her son-in-law's sperm? Is Christa Uchytil a sibling of the twins or is she their mother?

Biological surrogacy typically consists of artificial insemination of a surrogate with the sperm of a man whose wife is infertile, or for other reasons, cannot or will not bear a child. This form of surrogacy does not require sophisticated medical technology; it is a social and legal arrangement whereby the surrogate agrees to provide one-half of the genetic material, carry the fetus to term, deliver the baby, and surrender it to the father and his wife. But the term ''surrogate'' in this scenario is a misnomer because the ''surrogate'' is providing one-half of the genetic material and therefore is, in reality, the mother. To avoid confusion, in this chapter surrogates who provide the ova and gestate the fetus are referred to as ''biological surrogates.''

Recent developments in technology have made possible other forms of surrogacy. In *gestational surrogacy,* the surrogate agrees to carry a fetus to which she typically has no biological relationship. For example, if the wife produces ova but cannot become pregnant, her ova can be removed surgically, fertilized in vitro with her husband's sperm, and implanted in a gestational surrogate. Or if the wife is capable of becoming pregnant, but is unable to carry the fetus to term, the embryo can be surgically removed from the biological mother and implanted in the gestational surrogate.

In gestational surrogacy, it is possible for the child to have three mothers: the woman who provides the genetic material, the woman who gestates the fetus, and a "social" mother if the child is raised by someone other than the biological or gestating mother. The birth of James Alan Mack, Jr., in January 1993, was made possible by the contributions of several family members. Linda Mack was unable to have children because of a hysterectomy necessitated by endometriosis. Family members offered to assist her and her husband after a planned adoption arrangement had proved unsuccessful. Linda's sister, Anne, provided ova that were fertilized in vitro with James Mack's sperm, and his sister Kathy served as the gestational surrogate. The three families lived in different states but met at a fertility center in California to perform the insemination. James, Jr. was delivered by cesarean section; Linda and her husband, along with Kathy's husband, were present (Linda Mack, telephone interview with author, February 17, 1994). It is also possible for a child to have three fathers: the man who provided the sperm, the husband of the surrogate, and a social father.

Although surrogacy arrangements have received much publicity—particularly if they have been the subject of dispute—surrogacy is not widespread in the United States. The first reported birth of a child as the result of a surrogacy arrangement was in 1976; by 1988 the number of such births was estimated to be between 750 and 1,000 (New York State Task Force on Life and the Law 1988, 25). The Center for Surrogate Parenting reported in 1993 that there had been approximately 4,000 surrogate births since the late 1970s and that only 11 of them had given rise to custody litigation (1993, 1). These statistics would seem to indicate that the overwhelming majority of these cases came to a conclusion without dispute: the pregnancy went well, the surrogate relinquished her parental rights, the baby went home with the father and his wife, and the surrogate received her fee.

On the surface, surrogacy arrangements seem to be an ideal solution for an infertile couple who would like a child genetically related to at least one of them. There are significant social, ethical, and legal questions surrounding that "solution," however. In the area of assisted reproduction, and particularly in matters related to commercial surrogacy, public policy is sorely lacking in that the rights of the various actors are poorly defined. Specifically, do the intending couples have positive rights once surrogacy agreements have been signed? Does the surrogate have a legal duty to the couple as a result of the contract? Should the state enforce such contracts, thus enforcing the rights of the couple and the duties of the surrogate? What role should third parties play in this legally and ethically complex effort to create a family? In this chapter we analyze the characteristics of various actors in surrogacy and the potential conflicting rights among those actors, look at the impact of surrogacy on the nuclear family, discuss the exploitation of women, and conclude with an analysis of statute law and litigation.

Surrogates and Couples: Who and Why?

Some couples faced with infertility choose to pursue adoption, but it is a well-known fact that there are more couples seeking to adopt than there are children to be adopted—especially healthy Caucasian infants. Moreover, since infertility is often the result of waiting until mid-life to attempt creation of a family, many couples are excluded by adoption agencies that prefer younger parents.

Some couples may seek surrogacy arrangements at one of the approximately fifteen surrogacy centers in the United States. These centers are typically staffed by lawyers and administrators and may also employ physicians and psychologists. The Center for Surrogate Parenting in Beverly Hills, California, was founded in 1980 by attorney William Handel as a matching service for couples seeking surrogates and women wishing to serve as surrogates. The center provides comprehensive case management. Couples and surrogates are screened and psychological counseling is required. Surrogates must also attend monthly group counseling sessions from the time they enter the program until after delivery. Credit and criminal record checks are conducted on potential surrogates, although not on potential fathers or their wives. As of June 1993, the center had been involved in the births of nearly 200 infants through its biological surrogacy program and more than 50 infants through its gestational surrogacy program. As of late 1994, all infants had been willingly surrendered to the intended parents, and no litigation resulted.

One of the largest services in the United States is managed by attorney and surrogacy entrepreneur Noel Keane, who has offices in New York, Indiana, and California. As of July 1993, his centers had been involved in nearly 500 pregnancies (Keane 1993). He does not screen clients and accepts all intended parents who can pay his fees (Keane telephone interview with author, June 7, 1989). His centers conduct medical and psychological screening of potential surrogates, and voluntary counseling is available.

Keane's New York office served as the broker for William Stern and surrogate Mary Beth Whitehead, whose dispute over custody of Baby M made headlines internationally in 1987. The facts of this case have been related countless times, in newspapers, popular magazines, on television talk shows, and in a made-for-television movie. William Stern had contracted with Mary Beth Whitehead to bear his child. But shortly after Whitehead gave birth she refused to surrender the child and fled to Florida. A bitter legal battle ensued, and ultimately custody was awarded to Stern and his wife, with visitation rights awarded to Whitehead.

A surrogacy center usually attracts clients and surrogates by advertising, and then acts as a broker between them. It provides the client with names of potential surrogates and also with the contract. The contract between Whitehead and Stern stated that Whitehead would be inseminated with Stern's sperm. Other provisions stipulated that during the pregnancy, she would not smoke, drink alcoholic beverages, use illegal drugs, or take medication without written consent from her physician. She would submit to prenatal testing, and if it was determined that the fetus had defects, she would have an abortion if Stern so demanded. She would not abort under other circumstances unless the inseminating physician determined that such an abortion was necessary for her physical health. She would also assume all risks, including the risks of death and post-partum complications.

The Whiteheads would not form any parent-child bonds and would agree to termination of their parental rights, thus allowing Stern's wife to adopt the child. They would surrender the child to Stern immediately after delivery, and if Stern died prior to delivery, custody would be surrendered to his wife. Stern would assume legal responsibility for the child even if there were handicaps or defects. The contract did not say, however, that he would accept physical custody.

Mary Beth Whitehead would be paid a $10,000 fee for her "services." But if she miscarried prior to the fifth month, there would be no compensation, and if she miscarried after that month or if the child was stillborn, she would be paid $1,000. Stern agreed to pay any medical expenses not covered by her health insurance. In a separate contract, he agreed to pay the Infertility Center of New York (ICNY) a nonrefundable $7,500 fee for assisting him in the selection of a surrogate (*In re Baby M* 1988, 1265-1273; Merrick 1990).

The fees paid for surrogacy arrangements differ now depending on the broker used. Contracts provided by the Center for Surrogate Parenting have a significantly different payment structure from that included in the Stern-Whitehead agreement. In the former, the surrogate receives the same fee whether the child is stillborn or live-born. She also receives the fee if she refuses to surrender the child, although if a custody battle ensued and the contract was held to be unenforceable, it is unlikely that the father would be required by the court to pay the fee and most likely he would not do so voluntarily.

Moreover, the total costs of surrogacy arrangements are now substantially higher than the costs incurred by William Stern. For example, in

1991 actress Deirdre Hall and her husband incurred expenses in excess of $35,000 in contracting with a surrogate through the Center for Surrogate Parenting. This expense is typical at the Beverly Hills center, where $16,000 is paid for case management, and $10,000 to $12,000 is paid to the surrogate; she is also reimbursed for "business" expenses, such as medical costs not covered by her insurance and travel and daycare expenses related to the pregnancy. These figures are consistent with estimates of $30,000 to $50,000, with about one-fourth of the money going to the surrogate (Office of Technology Assessment 1988, 276). Keane's centers currently charge an agency fee of $16,000 and a surrogate's fee of $13,000 or more; total costs range from $40,000 to $45,000 (Keane 1993).

A number of studies have been conducted to develop typical profiles of couples and surrogates, and their findings are similar. A 1987 study conducted by the Office of Technology Assessment revealed that the typical couples are white, married, and in their late thirties or early forties. Sixty-four percent reported household incomes of more than $50,000 per year, and more than half had attended graduate school. The study also showed considerable differences in the backgrounds of couples and surrogates. The average surrogate was younger (between 26 and 28 years of age), most (60 percent) were married, less than 35 percent had attended college, and most (66 percent) reported family incomes of less than $30,000 per year (Office of Technology Assessment 1988, 274).*

Philip Parker's 1983 study of 125 women who had applied to be surrogates at Keane's Michigan infertility center in the early 1980s indicated that 40 percent were unemployed or receiving some form of financial aid. A large proportion (35 percent) had had an abortion prior to becoming a surrogate, and 9 percent had previously relinquished a child for adoption. Most significantly, 89 percent would not have agreed to act as surrogates had they not been promised a substantial fee, although the fee alone was not a totally sufficient reason for becoming a surrogate. On the basis of his study, Parker concluded that surrogates' decisions were based on (1) the perceived desire and need for money, (2) the perceived degree of enjoyment and the desire to be pregnant, and (3) the perception that the advantages of relinquishment outweighed the disadvantages.

This last factor consisted of two motivational components. First, the women often expressed a strong wish to give the gift of a baby to a parent who needed a child. Second, the women felt (often uncon-

---

* It is important to note that the largest surrogacy center in the United States, which is run by Keane and accounts for about one-third of all surrogacy births, did not respond to the survey (Noel Keane, founder of Infertility Centers of New York and Michigan, telephone interview with author, June 7, 1989a). Therefore the data may be skewed.

sciously) that surrogate motherhood would help them master unresolved [depressive] feelings they had regarding a voluntary loss of
fetus or baby through abortion or relinquishment (Parker 1983, 118).

In her study of surrogates and couples at a Los Angeles surrogate motherhood program, Hilary Hanafin found that the women had a variety of
motives for serving as surrogates. The vast majority (72 percent) enjoyed
being pregnant and also wanted to help a childless couple (68 percent).
More than half (54 percent) stated that they were also motivated by the
monetary payment, and for some (12 percent), unresolved feelings about a
prior loss played a role. Thirty-seven percent of the surrogates had had
abortions (Hanafin 1987).

Conflicting Rights

Surrogacy raises a number of complex social and ethical questions. For
the most part, they concern the potentially conflicting rights of the child, of
the surrogate and her family, and of the biological father and his wife.

Rights of the Child

Clearly, the children in these arrangements are the most vulnerable because they cannot speak for themselves and are not parties to the contract.
Were it not for the surrogacy arrangement, they would not have been born,
so surrogacy has given them life, which in and of itself has value.

Perhaps the most difficult question regarding the welfare of the child is
whether surrogacy involves the sale of a child. The National Organ Transplant Act, passed in 1984, prohibits the sale of human organs. Parents cannot buy or sell custody rights during a divorce. All states prohibit baby
selling, and thirty-six states prohibit the charging of fees in adoption over
and above expenses.

So how can it be legal to exchange a baby for a fee in a surrogacy agreement? One argument is that the arrangements are made before conception
and delivery and thus do not constitute baby selling because there is no
coercion on a vulnerable pregnant woman to surrender her child. At the
time that surrogacy agreements are made, the child has yet to be conceived.
This argument is complicated, however, by the fact that all states prohibit
pre-birth adoption agreements, and adoption by the father's wife is generally necessary in cases of biological surrogacy in order for her to become
the legal mother.

Some have argued that surrogacy arrangements are business contracts—
for example, a rental contract between the father and the surrogate. But this

argument collapses under careful scrutiny. In biological surrogacy, the surrogate, who is in reality the biological mother, provides half of the genetic material. Her role in the pregnancy and delivery goes far beyond womb rental, however. Most reasonable people would not argue that in marriage a husband rents his wife's womb, even though he may pay all of her expenses and provide her with spending money. Yet in reality, a pregnant wife and a pregnant biological surrogate play synonymous roles in a pregnancy. In gestational surrogacy, the "renting the womb" argument is also flawed. The gestational surrogate provides the nutrition for the fetus; her life-style has a decisive effect on its health and welfare; and the fetus knows no other home (and no other mother) than the woman within whose body it resides for nine months.

Another argument is that the father has a contract for the surrogate's services—that is, he is paying for her time and effort. Most surrogacy contracts have structured pay scales, however. A lower fee is paid when the child is stillborn than when it is live-born, as was stipulated in the Stern-Whitehead contract. Yet the surrogate's "service" is the same regardless of the outcome at delivery. Moreover, no fees are paid until the child is surrendered to the father and the surrogate's parental rights are terminated. But the service is the same whether she surrenders the child or not. In a successful pregnancy, a baby is produced regardless of where gestation occurred. Thus, arguments based on the existence of a contractual relationship between the father and the surrogate break down when one examines the role played by the surrogate in the pregnancy and the contribution she makes to the development and health of the child.

Regardless of how we characterize the surrogacy transaction, it involves the exchange of money. Therefore, some questions to be asked are: Does this exchange commercialize and commodify pregnancy and childbearing, and make commercial objects of the children themselves? Does the exchange of money devalue the children born of surrogacy arrangements, and in fact devalue the worth of all children in society?

Eventually the children of biological surrogates will have to be informed of their beginnings and will have to deal with the fact that their *mothers*—the women in whose bodies they were created—conceived them without ever intending to raise or possibly even to know them, gave them to a couple they most likely knew very little about, and agreed from the very outset to do this for financial gain. Generations of adopted children have had to face the realization that their parents gave them up, as, predictably, will the children of surrogacy. One wonders if these arrangements will damage the children's self-esteem, and if these children will worry that in the future their parents might give them up again.

These issues are not as prominent in cases of gestational surrogacy because the ethics are much less controversial. Children of gestational surrogacy who are raised by their biological parents do not have to deal with the question of why their biological mothers surrendered them because in fact they did not. But more complex issues of parenthood may arise. In the case of *Anna J.* (discussed in more detail later in this chapter), the gestational surrogate, who had no genetic relationship to the child, fought for custody in the California courts. Both the surrogate and the biological mother met the statutory definition of motherhood, but ultimately the California Supreme Court enforced the surrogacy contract and disallowed parental rights for the surrogate.

In another complex case, triplets born after conclusion of a gestational surrogacy agreement became the subject of a 1994 custody battle between the biological parents, Ronald and Pamela Soos, when they decided to divorce. The gestational surrogate, who had no genetic relationship to the children, voluntarily surrendered them to Ronald Soos, and subsequently Pamela Soos, the genetic mother, filed for custody. At the time of this writing, the Arizona courts have not yet ruled on custody ("Judge to decide" 1994).

In analyzing the rights of the child, questions of parental commitment to the child should be examined. Is the commitment of the parents—both biological and gestational—reduced as a result of the surrogacy arrangement? Clearly the answer with regard to the biological surrogate is yes, for she enters into the agreement with the understanding that, after giving birth, her parental rights will be terminated and she will probably never see the child again. The same is true of the gestational surrogate, although typically there is no question about her willingness to surrender the child because she is not the biological mother.

But the biological father and his wife have probably made a sizable financial commitment to obtain this child. We can assume they likely have also made a considerable personal commitment. They are typically older, well educated, and financially stable. But the circumstances surrogacy imposes might work to counteract their commitment. When one considers that the father in a surrogacy situation is extremely detached from the pregnancy and from the birth experience, it is clear that a lack of commitment is a real possibility. He does not love the surrogate mother and probably does not see her on a daily basis. She may live in another state (or even in another country), and he may never have met her. He does not participate in childbirth classes and usually is not present during delivery.

An interesting situation occurred in Ionia, Michigan. Patty Nowakowski agreed to serve as a biological surrogate and became pregnant with twins. Shortly before the birth, the father-to-be stated that he only wanted a girl and would refuse to accept a male child. If both twins were male, he would refuse them both. Initially, the twin girl went home with the father, and her brother was placed in foster care. Shortly thereafter, the Nowakowskis took him into their home and named him Aaron Nowakowski, Jr., after Patty's husband. Eventually, the couple gained custody of the female twin as well (Andrews 1989, 250).

There can be additional problems when children are born with defects. Surrogacy contracts generally have a clause requiring prenatal testing, as well as abortion upon demand by the father in the event birth defects are detected. Although this clause is legally unenforceable as a result of *Roe v. Wade,* it points to the fact that the biological father expects a child free of mental and physical disabilities. Both biological and gestational surrogacy arrangements can give rise to sharp accusations when children are born with disabilities. What if the child has a genetic defect transmitted from the biological surrogate? What if a defect is due to smoking, alcohol consumption, or substance abuse on the part of the biological or gestational surrogate? Will the father and his wife want to raise a child with defects they perceive as being caused by the surrogate's actions?

These concerns were raised in 1983, when Judith Stiver entered into a surrogacy agreement with Alexander Malahoff and the child was born with both microcephaly (abnormally small head, an indicator of mental retardation) and a life-threatening strep infection. Neither Malahoff or Stiver wanted him. It was reported that Malahoff had refused to give permission to treat the infection, and the hospital had then obtained a court order. Malahoff denied paternity and therefore responsibility for the child; the Stivers disputed his claims and also denied responsibility for the child (Capron 1987, 691; Corea 1985, 219). Ultimately a paternity test—the results of which were announced on the Phil Donahue television talk show—showed that the child was not Malahoff's but was probably the son of Stiver's husband. Nevertheless, at birth neither Malahoff nor Stiver knew that, and neither wanted the child at that time.

Another case—involving an AIDS baby—was reported in the *New England Journal of Medicine.* In 1986, a couple contracted with the wife's sister to be their surrogate, unaware that she had a history of substance abuse. After she was successfully inseminated she tested positive for the HIV antibody, and at birth, the child tested seropositive for the HIV antibody. Both the father and the surrogate refused to accept custody (Frederick 1987, 1352).

The home environment of the intended parents obviously has a bearing on the child's welfare. Most surrogacy brokers do little screening of the intended parents. No one screens the home environment when a couple has children without assisted reproduction, but when a child is to be raised outside its biological family—as in adoption or foster care—or when divorcing parents cannot agree on custody, home studies are the norm in the United States. At present, only New Hampshire and Virginia have statutes requiring evaluation of the home environments of the intended couples. Amy Overvold's research on surrogacy centers provides some insight here. She points out that there is

a lack of hard, clinical data defining the components of proper screening. And in the absence of such data [surrogacy centers] vociferously defend their individual screening processes, no matter how cursory the process appears to be. Some, especially those with training in psychology or social work, said they base a lot of their decisions on "intuition" and "trust" (Overvold 1988, 168).

Thus the rights of the child are not clearly defined and are potentially in conflict with the rights of other parties in these surrogacy arrangements. The child most likely will never know its biological mother, if born as a result of biological surrogacy, or the woman who carried him prenatally, if the arrangement was gestational surrogacy. The child is exchanged for a fee and may be more vulnerable to parental rejection, particularly if born with defects or a serious illness.

Rights of the Surrogate and Her Family

Surrogacy arrangements also raise questions concerning the needs and rights of the surrogate and her family. If commercial surrogacy transforms children into commodities, does it similarly transform surrogate mothers? A biological surrogate who was a respondent in Parker's 1983 study indicated that she was "only an incubator"—a material object (Parker 1983, 118). In September 1988 the following advertisement appeared in *USA Today*, next to the automobile advertisements: "Surrogate Mother Needed to legally carry loving infertile couple's child. $10,000 plus expenses paid. Confidential. Blue or green eyes. 5'2" to 5'8" preferred. Call collect" ("Surrogate Mother Needed" 1988).

Briefs filed in a Michigan surrogacy case indicated that fees varied depending on the "quality" of the surrogate. The problem was how to determine the assignment of "a Saks Fifth Avenue price tag for one woman as opposed to a K-Mart price tag for another" (Brief for the Attorney General in *Doe v. Kelley,* 106 Mich. App. 169, 307 N.W. 2d 438 (1981) cited in Field 1987, 489). The notion that a woman's body can be "rented" and that the price depends on her physical and intellectual characteristics is degrading and does a disservice to women who are struggling to achieve equality in a society long dominated by men. Women—like men—should be valued for their intrinsic worth and their achievements, not for their reproductive capabilities.

A couple profiled by Overvold (1988) wants nothing to do with their biological surrogate. Neither partner wants to meet her. They are angered when the broker tells them of her physical discomfort and the difficulty she is having in explaining the situation to her young daughter. They want her out of the picture as soon as possible and are upset that the surrogacy center will allow her to visit, in the hospital, the child to whom she has just given birth. The "humanness" of the biological surrogate (who is, in reality, the biological mother) appears to be ignored by the couple; she is merely a device to obtain the baby they so desperately want.

A surrogate may also suffer psychological damage. It has been pointed out that many women

> regret the decision they made to relinquish the child to the sperm donor. These mothers tell of being coerced, manipulated, exploited, betrayed and lied to by the baby broker and the sperm donor. They share feelings of sorrow and anguish caused by severe strain on their nuclear family. . . . These women's lives and the lives of their families have been shattered and forever altered by the greed and indifference of an industry which seeks only to satisfy its own desires (National Coalition Against Surrogacy).

Elizabeth Kane (a pseudonym) has told of her own experiences as one of the first commercial surrogates in the United States. Initially, she viewed surrogacy as a wonderful gift to an infertile couple, but this "gift" turned into a disaster for her and her family. She felt that she had been exploited, lied to, and manipulated by the Kentucky brokers who handled the arrangements. Her marriage suffered under the strain of community criticism, and her children developed emotional problems; she had nightmares and suffered from depression and other psychological disorders. She continued to show compassion for infertile couples, but took a strong stand in opposition to surrogacy:

> I now believe that surrogate motherhood is nothing more than the transference of pain from one woman to another. One woman is in anguish because she cannot become a mother, and another woman may suffer for the rest of her life because she cannot know the child she bore for someone else (Kane 1988, 275).

But there are legitimate arguments on the other side of this issue as well. Lori Andrews argues that women have the right to make reproductive choices that include contraception, abortion, and pregnancy. Should not surrogacy be one of those choices as well? Women are rational and need not be protected from making their own decisions. Because surrogates may later regret surrendering their children is not a sufficient ground for banning the practice (Andrews 1988).

Andrews' point is well taken. People make many decisions that they later regret—such as marriage, divorce, and relinquishing children for adoption—but society does not ban these practices. In *Johnson v. Calvert* (1993), the California Supreme Court upheld a contract for gestational surrogacy, noting that the surrogate was educated, experienced, intelligent, and capable of making an informed decision whether to enter into a surrogacy agreement. Andrews also raises the question of the rights of the "other woman" in biological surrogacy—the father's wife. Should society also be concerned with her emotional welfare? Surrogacy arrangements are voluntary; the surrogate chooses to enter the agreement and the father and his wife choose to pay the expenses and fees (Andrews 1988).

Surrogacy arrangements also affect other members of the surrogate's family. The surrogate's husband watches his wife grow large carrying another man's child. He may participate in childbirth classes and be present for the delivery. His responsibilities for family chores and care of the other children in the family may increase. Moreover, he may eventually raise the other man's child (or children) as his own, as did Aaron Nowakowski.

The surrogate's other children may suffer embarrassment when their peers learn of their mother's arrangement and be confused when their brother or sister is given away to someone they do not even know (Kane 1988; Overvold 1988). They may fear that they, too, might be given away if they are bad or if Mommy needs the money.

Rights of the Biological Father and His Wife

The father and his wife in a surrogacy arrangement also have rights and needs. They may have experienced years of frustration and despair as a result of infertility and be disappointed with adoption agencies. But a surrogacy arrangement may present problems as well. Both husband and wife may worry that the surrogate will not relinquish her parental rights, or that they will be criticized by family and friends.

Overvold's research shows that an infertile wife may feel very vulnerable as a result of the surrogacy arrangement. She may experience feelings of guilt because of the expense and the emotional strain of knowing that another woman is carrying her husband's baby because she cannot or does not want to do so. But adding this child to her family will not eliminate the feelings of inadequacy she may have as a result of being infertile. Biological surrogacy means that the wife has no genetic connection to the child—yet after delivery she will most likely be the parent who is primarily responsible for its care. She may be in a state of emotional and social limbo.

It is difficult for these women to find a place for themselves in a process in which someone else has assumed their natural role (Overvold 1988, 88). Moreover, surrogacy may have negative consequences for the family unit that is created; when a child is genetically linked to only one parent, an asymmetry exists in the family that may weaken the bond between the unrelated parent and child (New York State Task Force on Life and the Law 1988, 81). But despite the potential problems for the intended couple, surrogacy may be the only way for them to have children, and most likely the fears and emotional and financial difficulties will be outweighed by the joy of receiving the child.

In addition to the conflicting rights of the actors, the impact on society at large is also a consideration. We turn now to a discussion of the potential effects of surrogacy on the nuclear family and on the socioeconomic exploitation of women.

Social Impact of Surrogacy

Impact on the Nuclear Family

In assessing the effect of surrogacy on the various parties involved, we should consider how it impacts the nuclear family, whose unity has already been jeopardized by high rates of divorce, out-of-wedlock births, and couples living together without the legal sanction of marriage. Children born of biological surrogacy arrangements are permanently separated from one of their genetic parents. Divorce and giving a child up for adoption are usually sad events, but they are not intentional efforts to raise children apart from their biological parents. Surrogacy has that intent at its heart; Sidney Callahan argues that this will create deeper problems in American society:

> Already epidemics of divorce, illegitimate conceptions, and parental irresponsibility and failures are straining the family bonds necessary for successful childrearing. If we legitimate the isolation of genetic, gestational, and social parentage and govern reproduction by contract and purchase, our culture will become even more fragmented, rootless and alienated (New York State Task Force on Life and the Law 1988, 81).

Children born of biological surrogacy arrangements are usually raised by their biological fathers and their wives, who in reality are stepmothers. They are part of a nuclear family in the same way that adopted children and children in stepfamilies are part of nuclear families. But the biological father and the surrogate mother will always be tied to each other in some sense through their child, and the child will eventually have to resolve this. As Barbara Heyl points out with regard to Baby M, "the flaw in this plan is that the lives of these biological parents are in fact bound together through the baby, who is alive and well and who will, as she grows up, make her own judgments of all this cutting apart of what is connected'' (1988, 11).

Socioeconomic Exploitation of Women

Socioeconomic class differences are typical of surrogacy arrangements. As previously noted, most surrogates have less education and a lower income than the contracting fathers. The surrogate's fee is usually about $10,000—which, according to an *amicus* brief filed by the Rutgers University Women's Rights Litigation Clinic in the Baby M case, amounts to $1.57 per hour (Isaacs and Holt 1987, 30). Most of the surrogates studied by the Office of Technology Assessment in 1987 had moderate family incomes. This study contradicts the popular perception that surrogates are destitute and need the fee to pay for the necessities of life although the 1983 Parker study, primarily of surrogates referred to Parker by Keane, showed 40 percent of them to be unemployed or receiving financial aid, or both (Office of Technology Assessment 1988; Parker 1983).

William Stern had a Ph.D., and his wife had both Ph.D. and M.D. degrees. They reported an annual family income in excess of $90,000. Mary Beth Whitehead was a high school dropout who was married to a sanitation worker. They reported a joint annual income of $28,000 and were undergoing foreclosure proceedings on their house during the custody battle. As mentioned earlier, the typical contracting father incurs expenses ranging from $30,000 to $50,000, of which the surrogate receives about one-fourth. It is clear that a couple must have substantial income or assets to be able to afford such an arrangement; the option is seemingly reserved for the financially secure.

The 1987 case of Alejandra Muñoz is a classic example of socioeconomic exploitation. A Mexican citizen, she was reportedly brought to San Diego illegally to participate in an embryo transfer for her infertile cousin, Natie Haro, and Natie's husband, Mario. She has claimed that after she was inseminated, she was told the embryo transfer could not be completed and that she would have to bear the child. She signed a handwritten agreement stating that she would be paid approximately $1,500, well below the typical surrogacy fee. Muñoz has claimed that someone added the statement, ''I will give up my rights to the baby,'' after she signed the agreement. Several months after the birth, she contacted the Haros, demanding a higher fee; a custody battle ensued (Steven Cummings, attorney for Haros, telephone interview with author, June 12, 1989). Muñoz does not speak English, has a second-grade education, and is not able to read handwriting. The child now lives with the biological father, and Muñoz has visitation rights (Arditti 1987, 44-45; U.S. Congress, House 1987, 37-43).

Surrogacy and the Law

Legal Issues

The legal status of commercial surrogacy is as problematic as the social and ethical questions it raises. The Baby M case was a triggering mechanism in the states' agenda-setting process. In 1987, in its aftermath, seventy-two bills pertaining to surrogacy were introduced in twenty-six state legislatures and the District of Columbia. Bills were also introduced in 1988 and 1989. The arena of conflict regarding commercial surrogacy has included both the courts and state legislatures. The provisions of state statutes vary widely and have created a confusing patchwork of public policy. This is not unusual because of the federalism inherent in the American political system and, in the case of surrogacy, because of the national government's reluctance to enter the field of family law.

As of December 1993, less than half the states had statutes or state supreme court decisions dealing with surrogate motherhood (National Conference of State Legislatures 1993; see also Robinson 1993 for a thorough analysis of the state statutes). Thirteen states (Arizona, Florida, Indiana, Kentucky, Louisiana, Michigan, Nebraska, New Hampshire, New York, North Dakota, Utah, Virginia, and Washington) prohibit commercial surrogacy or make commercial surrogacy contracts unenforceable. In some of these states, violation of the prohibition is a misdemeanor; in others, it is a felony.

Arizona, North Dakota, and Utah, in addition to prohibiting surrogacy contracts, provide that the surrogate is the legal mother, and her husband is presumed to be the father. Florida, New Hampshire, and Virginia prohibit commercial surrogacy but specifically allow surrogacy without compensation (Robinson 1993, 209). Surrogacy contracts have been ruled unenforceable by the New Jersey Supreme Court, but were ruled enforceable by the California State Supreme Court. Arkansas and Nevada have statutes that allow for surrogacy, although the baby-selling statutes in Nevada probably preclude payment to the surrogate in that state (National Conference of State Legislatures 1993).

Some states distinguish between biological surrogates and gestational surrogates. In North Dakota, the genetic mother is not considered to be the legal mother. The New Hampshire statute provides that in noncommercial surrogacy, the "intended mother" is the legal mother whether she is genetically related to the child or not, unless the surrogate changes her mind within seventy-two hours of the birth, in which case the birth mother is the legal mother. The Virginia statute allows the surrogate to change her mind and terminate the contract during pregnancy or up to 180 days after the last assisted reproduction (Robinson 1993, 210). (See Table 5-1 for a summary of state policies.)

Since most states lack any statutory provision for surrogacy, some scholars have argued that part of the problem is a lack of available law. Harvard law professor Martha Field takes the contrary position, arguing that problems arise because there is an *excess* of available law, which includes contract law, baby-selling law, adoption law, laws governing the rights of biological fathers not married to the biological mothers of their children, and laws concerning the rights and obligations of sperm donors (Field 1988, 7-8). Thus, according to Field, the judge must determine which area of law is most appropriate.

Litigation in the area of commercial surrogacy is complex. Thus far, three such cases have been decided by state supreme courts; none has reached the United States Supreme Court. In 1986, the Kentucky Supreme Court found that commercial surrogacy did not violate the state's baby-selling laws if agreements were made prior to conception, and if the mother was allowed to change her mind before relinquishing her parental rights (*Surrogate Parenting v. Commonwealth ex rel. Armstrong*). The Kentucky legislature subsequently prohibited surrogacy agreements.

Most public attention has focused on the legal struggles in *Baby M* (1988) and *Anna J.* (1993). The facts of the Baby M case were discussed earlier in this chapter. William Stern and his wife, Elizabeth Stern, contracted with the Infertility Center of New York to retain a surrogate. Mrs. Stern believed that she had a mild form of multiple sclerosis (although she had not been clinically diagnosed) and that pregnancy would worsen her condition. Mr. Stern had a strong preference for a biological child, since both his parents were dead and other family members had been killed in the Holocaust.

Mary Beth Whitehead presented a starkly contrasting image. She was a young mother who had dropped out of high school as a teenager, married, and shortly thereafter had two children. The family moved often and at times had lived with relatives. Her husband, Richard, had admitted having alcohol problems and had an unstable employment record. At the time of Baby M's birth, on March 27, 1986, Richard was a sanitation worker earning $28,000 per year (Merrick 1990).

William Stern and the Whiteheads signed a contract on February 6, 1985, and Mary Beth Whitehead was successfully impregnated with Stern's sperm through artificial insemination. For the most part, relations between the Sterns and the Whiteheads were cordial during the pregnancy, but they deteriorated shortly after the child's birth. William Stern named the child Melissa, but Mary Beth Whitehead named her Sara; thus began a legal battle.

Table 5-1 State Statutes Concerning Surrogate Motherhood

State	Noncommercial surrogate motherhood legitimated	Commercial surrogate motherhood legitimated	Contract declared void and unenforceable	Definition of mother	Custody disputes decided by court
Arizona	no	no		gestational	
Arkansas	yes	unclear	unclear	social [a]	
Florida	yes	no	commercial only		x
Indiana	no	no	yes		
Kentucky	no	no	yes		
Louisiana	no	no	yes		
Michigan	no	no	yes		x
Nebraska	no	no	yes		
New Hampshire	yes	no	commercial only	gestational	
New York	no	no	yes	gestational	x
North Dakota	no	no	yes	gestational	
Utah	no	no	yes	gestational	x
Virginia	yes	no	compensation only	social/genetic [a]	
Washington	no	no	yes	gestational	x

Source: Robinson 1993, 224.

[a] The social mother is the mother of the child in court-approved surrogacy arrangements. The genetic mother is the mother of the child in surrogacy arrangements that did not have court approval.

A few days after the birth, Mary Beth Whitehead appeared at the Sterns' home in a state of hysteria, pleading for permission to take the child home with her for a week, to which the Sterns agreed. Whitehead subsequently notified them that she would not surrender the child. The Sterns obtained a court order, but when they appeared at the Whitehead home with the police, the baby was handed out a back window. Shortly thereafter, the Whiteheads fled to Florida, leaving their older children in the care of relatives. They moved from place to place for nearly three months before they were located by authorities. During this time on the run, Mary Beth Whitehead telephoned William Stern and threatened to kill both herself and the child if Stern pursued his plans to obtain custody. The child was finally found in Florida and was returned to New Jersey, where both the Sterns and the Whiteheads had resided. The Sterns filed for custody.

The trial court issued its decision on March 31, 1987. It upheld the surrogacy contract as enforceable and found that because Mary Beth Whitehead had been pregnant before, she knew the risks involved. Moreover, the court pointed out that she had entered the agreement willingly, had had the benefit of some legal advice prior to signing the contract, and had then changed her mind and broken the contract. Citing Whitehead's instability, the court ruled that it was in the best interest of the child to live with the Sterns. Mary Beth Whitehead's parental rights were terminated, and Elizabeth Stern was allowed to adopt the child (*In re Baby M* 1987, 1175).

On appeal, the New Jersey Supreme Court ruled unanimously, on February 3, 1988, that the contract between Stern and the Whiteheads was unenforceable because it violated New Jersey laws prohibiting baby-selling, monetary inducement for adoption, and pre-birth adoption agreements.* The New Jersey court focused extensively on the financial remuneration aspects of the contract, finding that "Mr. Stern knew he was paying for the adoption of the child; Mrs. Whitehead knew she was accepting money so that a child might be adopted; the Infertility Center knew that it was being paid for assisting in the adoption of a child" (at 1241). This is clearly baby selling, and it is illegal, and perhaps criminal, said the court. It is "the sale of a child, or, at the very least, the sale of a mother's right to her child, the only mitigating factor being that one of the purchasers is the

---

* All states prohibit baby selling, monetary inducement for adoption, and pre-birth adoption agreements. Thirty-four states allow the birth mother a grace period after delivery to revoke her decision in private placement adoptions. This grace period conflicts with the intent of the biological surrogacy contract, which is to prevent the biological mother from changing her mind and keeping the child. In numerous decisions, the U.S. Supreme Court has recognized the right of natural parents to the care and custody of their children (see New York State Task Force on Life and the Law 1988, 63).

father. Almost every evil that prompted the prohibition on the payment of money in connection with adoptions exists here'' (at 1248).

The court ruled that Mary Beth Whitehead was the legal mother because she had done nothing to justify having her parental rights terminated. Interpreting family law to determine custody, it found that it was in Baby M's best interest to live with the Sterns because their life-style was stable, and they had provided a loving home for the child during the custody dispute. The court noted that Mary Beth Whitehead's life-style was more erratic, that she had not been consistently truthful during the custody dispute, and that she appeared to be unaccepting of the need for psychiatric help, which the court said was needed. Moreover, the court considered the fact that during the custody dispute, Mary Beth Whitehead became pregnant by another man, divorced her husband, and soon remarried. Although Whitehead was denied custody, she was granted visitation rights.

The issues in *Anna J.* were significantly different from those in *Baby M,* and the findings of the California Supreme Court in the former were significantly different from those of the New Jersey Supreme Court in the latter. Mark and Crispina Calvert, he a Caucasian and she of Filipino ancestry, sought a surrogacy agreement because Crispina had undergone a partial hysterectomy, for removal of her uterus but not her ovaries. Anna Johnson, a 29-year old African-American single mother who worked as a licensed practical nurse at the hospital where Crispina worked as a registered nurse, agreed to serve as their gestational surrogate.

On January 15, 1990, the Calverts and Johnson signed an agreement that provided that Johnson would be implanted with zygotes created in vitro from Mark's sperm and Crispina's ova. The Calverts agreed to a schedule of payments to be made to Anna during the pregnancy, with final payments to be made after delivery. They also agreed to purchase a $200,000 life insurance policy on Anna's life. Anna agreed to relinquish the baby upon delivery so that it would be raised by the Calverts. Later that month, three zygotes were implanted in Johnson, resulting in a single pregnancy.

But difficulties arose between the Calverts and Johnson. The couple discovered that Johnson had not disclosed a medical history of miscarriages and stillbirths. Johnson claimed that the Calverts were late with their payments and had not assisted her in getting to the hospital when false labor began. She also claimed they had not purchased the life insurance policy as promised.

On September 19, 1990, Johnson delivered a healthy baby boy. The Calverts named him Michael Ryan, Johnson named him Matthew; as in the Baby M case, it was the beginning of a legal battle. The Calverts filed suit in the Superior Court of Orange Country, California, asking to be named the legal parents. Johnson also filed suit, asking to be named the legal mother. The parties agreed to abide by a court order that gave temporary custody of the infant to the Calverts and stipulated that the child was genetically related to the Calverts and genetically unrelated to Johnson.

In a six-day hearing in October 1990, the Superior Court granted legal parenthood to the Calverts, recognizing them as the "genetic, biological, and natural" parents. It denied Johnson's claim to parenthood and terminated her visitation rights. The surrogacy contract was found to be enforceable and payment of the fee was found to be legal. Johnson appealed to the California Court of Appeals for the Fourth District, which affirmed the trial court decision (*Anna J. v. Mark C.* 1991).

On appeal, the California Supreme Court focused on identification of the legal mother. Both women had presented acceptable proof of maternity. Crispina Calvert provided the genetic material and Anna Johnson underwent gestation, labor, and delivery. Therefore, both women passed the test of "statutory motherhood." Interpreting contract law to decide the question of intent, the court said that the surrogacy agreement, as well as the parties' actions, clearly indicated that their intents had been for Crispina to serve as the child's mother and raise him in her home. There was no intent on the Calverts' part to "donate" a zygote to Johnson so that she could raise the child. The Court found that

> although [statutory law] recognizes both genetic consanguinity and giving birth as means of establishing a mother and child relationship, when the two means do not coincide in one woman, she who intended to procreate the child—that is, she who intended to bring about the birth of a child that she intended to raise as her own—is the natural mother under California law (*Johnson v. Calvert* 1993, at 782).

The Court also ruled that statutory prohibitions on payment for consent to adoption were not violated because gestational surrogacy differs in important respects from adoption, and because the surrogacy payments were not intended as payments in exchange for surrendering parental rights but rather as compensation for Johnson's services in gestating the fetus and undergoing labor. Johnson's arguments regarding involuntary servitude were dismissed, as were arguments regarding the general exploitation of women and the treatment of children as commodities. Crispina Calvert was declared to be the legal mother and Johnson's claims to motherhood were dismissed. The Court did not comment on whether its findings would have differed had Johnson been the biological mother.

A number of other issues, not directly addressed in either *Baby M* or *Anna J.*, merit discussion. Although the life-style clauses of surrogacy contracts have not yet been litigated, it is questionable whether the substantial restrictions placed on surrogates are enforceable. Although the typical clause stipulates that the intending couple can demand that the surrogate undergo abortion if a prenatal diagnosis indicates fetal defects, *Roe v.*

Wade has given all decision-making power regarding termination of pregnancy to the pregnant woman.

But can the contract legally bind the surrogate to refrain from drinking, smoking, and other activities that can potentially harm the child? Must the surrogate submit to amniocentesis? Bodily integrity is well grounded in both ethics and the law in the United States. Invasion of a patient's body without consent constitutes battery by the physician. If the surrogate refuses medical procedures requested by the couple, can she be ordered by the court to submit? If not, can she be sued for breach of contract, particularly if her choice results in miscarriage or injury to the fetus?

> Assume the contract required a specific dietary regime or series of medical examinations during pregnancy, which the surrogate failed to perform, leading to provable damage to the child. This action might void the contract for nonperformance or lead to an assessment of damage to compensate the couple for their added expense in caring for the child (Capron 1987, 696).

Can the surrogate be sued if she becomes pregnant with her husband's sperm instead of the intended father's sperm? In the Stiver-Malahoff case, discussed earlier, Malahoff filed suit against the Stivers claiming that since Judith had become pregnant not with his sperm but with that of her husband, Malahoff had been ''denied the love, services, affection, and happiness'' of the child that Judy had promised to bear for him (Andrews 1989, 45).

There are a number of constitutional issues to be considered here. Does the Constitution guarantee couples a positive right to be parents? The right to privacy and the right to procreate were clearly established by the Supreme Court in *Skinner v. Oklahoma* (1942), *Griswold v. Connecticut* (1965), and *Eisenstadt v. Baird* (1972). But do these rights protect a surrogacy contract? There are at least two mitigating circumstances that counter this notion. First, the surrogacy arrangement includes a fee; second, the right to procreate is not the same as the right to care for and have custody of a child. In biological surrogacy, the question is not whether a woman can be artificially inseminated. Rather, it is whether she can legally be paid a fee to terminate her parental rights, and whether an agreement stipulating that she revoke her right to the care and custody of her child before that child is conceived is legally enforceable.

Another constitutional issue centers on the equal protection clause of the Fourteenth Amendment. Is equal protection violated if women cannot sell their procreative abilities through surrogacy, yet men can sell their procreative ability through sperm banks? The trial court judge in the Baby M case adopted this argument in upholding the Stern-Whitehead contract, as did the Kentucky Supreme Court. However, the analogy seems inappropriate because there are substantial differences between selling sperm, and carrying a fetus and delivering a child. Donating sperm is a risk-free procedure that takes a few minutes of a man's time. If the donation is made to a sperm bank, the donor typically never knows whether the sperm is used or, if it was, whether the birth of a child resulted. The risks in pregnancy can be serious and extensive, the gestation period is nine months plus recuperation, and delivery is usually painful. The correct analogy to sperm donation is the donation of an unfertilized ovum (Capron 1987).

Another argument based on the equal protection clause suggests that prohibiting surrogacy contracts discriminates against infertile couples because "the state may not draw arbitrary distinctions between persons who are similarly situated, and [it] requires substantial reasons for any such distinction that interferes with persons' fundamental rights" (Field 1987, 497). Field argues that it is difficult to support this argument in favor of surrogacy, however, because it is not state action that has made the couple infertile. In essence, then, Field is arguing that infertile couples have a negative right; they have the right to have children, but not the right to have the government assist them: "In one sense, the state has one rule for all: that all can have children naturally but not for hire, and that rule is probably not vulnerable as a matter of equal protection" (1987, 497).

If the contracts are found to be illegal or unenforceable, in most cases custody will be determined by the "best interests of the child" principle, as was true in *Baby M*. Determining the child's interests is particularly difficult in a surrogacy situation because it involves a newborn who has never lived with either parent. Despite the existence of male domination in society, family law places fathers at a severe disadvantage in custody disputes, particularly those involving newborns. The New Jersey Supreme Court awarded custody to William Stern and his wife, but it noted:

> When a father and mother are separated and disagree, at birth, on custody, only in an extreme, truly rare, case should the child be taken from its mother . . . before the dispute is finally determined by the court on its merits. The probable bond between mother and child, and the child's need, not just the mother's, to strengthen that bond, along with the likelihood, in most cases, of a significantly lesser, if any, bond with the father—all counsel against temporary custody in the father. A substantial showing that the mother's continued custody would threaten the child's health or welfare would seem to be required (*In re Baby M* at 1261).

As family law attorneys will attest, temporary custody usually develops into permanent custody—as it did in the Baby M case—since judges are reluctant to disrupt children's lives by shifting them between contesting parents.

The position of the father in a surrogacy situation may be stronger than that of a divorcing or an unwed father seeking custody. The contract—should it be upheld—favors his interests, and most likely he has the resources necessary to hire attorneys, psychologists, and expert witnesses. Because of his higher level of education, he may be more knowledgeable about the legal system. He can provide a higher standard of living and more material goods for the child than can the surrogate. The stable life-style that the Sterns could offer was a major factor considered by both the trial court and the New Jersey Supreme Court in awarding them custody.

When custody battles arise, they typically involve child support and visitation issues. If the father wins custody, it is unlikely that the surrogate will be required to pay child support because of the disparity in incomes. Should the surrogate win, however, support from the father is likely to be required, and a contract probably will not relieve him of this obligation since the support is owed to the child and not to the mother (Carbone 1988, 156). In at least two surrogacy custody disputes, fathers have been obligated to provide child support. In 1988, Barry Huber was ordered to pay support to surrogate mother Laurie Yates while she had custody of twins born as a result of their surrogacy agreement. Ultimately, however, Huber won custody. Mario Haro also made small support payments to Alejandra Muñoz for a time as a result of their custody dispute. Eventually he also received custody.

Conclusion

As in other areas of reproductive rights, public policy is nonexistent concerning the practice of surrogacy. Surrogacy is clearly an issue in American society, but it lacks clearly defined ethical or legal frameworks within which to resolve disputes between parties whose claimed rights conflict. For the most part, the desires of these parties are well intentioned. The couple wants a child genetically related to one or both of them and, usually for medical reasons, has not been able to attain this goal. It is natural and reasonable to want to create a family that includes children who are biologically related to at least one of the parents.

Surrogates also have needs and rights, although their motivations for participating in surrogacy arrangements are not always clear. Although research indicates that a desire to help an infertile couple sometimes plays a role, it is reasonable to assume that most commercial surrogates would not participate unless a substantial fee were provided. The impacts on the other parties, including the surrogate's husband and children, must also be considered. The situation is complicated by the intervention of surrogacy brokers, third party players in this game who are in it for financial gain. As discussed in Chapter 1, reproductive issues are complicated by the interaction of public and private actors who have different, but sometimes overlapping, agendas.

Surrogacy, like other forms of assisted reproduction, has redefined the traditional notion of family and increased the number of players, who have different backgrounds and different motivations with regard to the surrogacy agreement. Thus the potential for conflict is great. For better or for worse, the nuclear family as depicted in Norman Rockwell's paintings is rapidly being superseded by a new generation of nonnuclear families.

C H A P T E R   6

Prenatal Intervention: Choosing the Characteristics of Unborn Children

Earlier chapters have focused on the right to have children and the conflicts that arise in assisted reproduction and surrogacy. This chapter is concerned with the question of whether there is also a right to attempt to maximize the "quality" of unborn children—to design them by choosing their sex and other characteristics. A growing array of prenatal technologies permit diagnosis of the health of the fetus and thus allow for increasing parental control over the quality of their progeny. With the development of more sophisticated forms of genetic intervention, the prenatal period will increasingly become a critical time for reproductive choices to be made.

These new capabilities in human genetic and prenatal intervention raise many questions. Do parents have a responsibility to utilize technologies that might enhance the health of their potential children or lead to selective abortion of affected fetuses? If a child has the right to be born with a "sound mind and body," what does this require of the pregnant woman? What impact will such emphasis on technologies designed to maximize production of healthy children have on society's perceptions of children who do not fulfill the heightened expectations? Finally, how might these technologies affect how society views persons with disabilities who are already alive?

Prenatal intervention has not attained a place on the formal governmental agenda. As with disputes over assisted reproduction, many of the disputes over the use of these technologies have been resolved by the courts. The federal government has been more active in funding research on prenatal techniques (largely through the National Institutes of Health) than in financing development of the reproductive technologies discussed in Chapter 4. Public funding, especially for the Human Genome

Initiative (discussed later in this chapter) and related research, has been substantial.

"Abortion politics, filtered through such activities as grant-making and basic research, [has] influenced the development of these technologies" (Brigham, Rifkin, and Solt 1993, 31). It is no coincidence that genetic screening and prenatal diagnosis became widespread only after *Roe v. Wade* in 1973. Such techniques continue to arouse controversy. Moreover, because of the large number of interest groups with strong positions on these issues (including religious, health, and advocacy groups representing a variety of genetic diseases and conditions), there have been vocal demands for government action ranging from mandate to prohibition.

Prenatal Diagnosis

Prenatal diagnosis has become an important component of clinical prenatal care and is now a medical standard for certain women at risk for producing abnormal offspring. Of the more than 3.5 million infants delivered in the United States annually, about 0.50 percent suffer from a chromosomal abnormality, 1 percent have a dominant or X-chromosome-linked disease, 0.25 percent have a recessive-gene disease, and about 9 percent have an irregularly inherited disorder (Scriver 1985, 96). Although many genetic diseases are very rare, collectively they are a significant cause of infant mortality. In addition, between 30 percent and 50 percent of the hospitalized children have diseases of intrinsic origin—birth defects and single-gene or gene-influenced diseases. "The cost of rehabilitation programs for the severely handicapped [is high]. The family tragedy is immeasurable" (D'Alton and DeCherney 1993, 114).

Many prenatal diagnostic technologies are currently being used in the United States to reduce the incidence of birth defects. An increasingly routine technique for the detection of genetic disorders in utero is *amniocentesis*. Although one study indicates that amniocentesis at the twelfth week of pregnancy is a viable option for potential parents desiring early prenatal genetic diagnostic information (Hanson et al. 1992, 1707), amniocentesis is usually performed between sixteen and eighteen weeks after the beginning of the last menstrual period. The procedure involves inserting a long needle attached to a syringe through the lower wall of the woman's abdomen and withdrawing approximately 20 cc of the amniotic fluid that surrounds the fetus and that contains some live body cells shed by the fetus. These cells are placed in the proper laboratory medium and cultured for approximately three weeks. Karyotypes of the chromosomes are then made in order to identify any abnormalities in the chromosomal complement as well as the sex of the fetus. If necessary, specific biochemical assays can be

Table 6-1   Proportion of Patients with Indications for Amniocentesis

Indication	Percent of patients
Maternal age	91.7
Family history or prior child with chromosomal abnormality	4.1
Maternal anxiety	2.7
Family history or prior child with neural tube defect	0.6
Prior child with multiple congenital abnormalities	0.2
Fetal abnormality on ultrasonography	0.2
Other	0.2

Source: Hanson et al. 1992, 1708.

conducted to identify up to 120 separate metabolic disorders and approximately 90 percent of neural tube defects. More than 90 percent of the women who undergo amniocentesis are informed that the fetus is normal. In the event a fetus is diagnosed having a severe chromosomal or metabolic disorder, the woman may opt for a therapeutic abortion.

Nearly all amniocenteses are done on the approximately 5 percent of all pregnant women who are over 35 years of age (Table 6-1). This reflects the current standard of care—to offer amniocentesis to women over the age of 35 because the rate of chromosomal abnormalities increases with increases in maternal age (Table 6-2). At variance with this pattern, approximately 80 percent of all children with Down syndrome (where an extra chromosome 21 is present) are born to women under the age of 35 (Platt and Carlson 1992, 637). For this reason, some observers argue that prenatal diagnosis should be offered to all pregnant patients, thus giving all women a choice as to whether to have such information. The projected cost of $1 billion annually would be offset by the savings that would result from the termination of pregnancies in which an anomoly was detected (Druzin et al. 1993, 617).

Chorionic villus sampling is a procedure in which a biopsy is taken from the placenta, whose deoxyribonucleic acid (DNA) is identical to that of the fetus. There are two kinds of sampling: *transabdominal,* in which a needle is inserted through the pregnant woman's abdomen to extract a small amount of placental tissue (Jackson et al. 1992); and *transcervical,* in which a pump-type sampler is used to aspirate a specimen of placental tissue under direct view of a laparoscope. The advantage of chorionic villus sampling over amniocentesis is that it can be conducted as early as the

Table 6-2   Maternal Age and Estimated Rate of Chromosomal Abnormalities

Age	Down syndrome	Other chromosomal abnormalities
20	1/1667	1/526
25	1/1250	1/476
30	1/952	1/385
35	1/385	1/202
37	1/227	1/129
40	1/106	1/65
45	1/30	1/20
49	1/11	1/7

Source: D'Alton and DeCherney 1993, 115.

ninth week of pregnancy, thus enabling a first-trimester diagnosis (Kickler et al. 1992, 1407). Early studies of the use of such sampling found elevated miscarriage rates, but improvements in its technique have resulted in more optimistic findings, suggesting that it is just as safe as amniocentesis for both mother and fetus (Williams et al. 1992, 1023). From 1985 to 1990, there was a shift from use of amniocentesis to use of chorionic villus sampling, a trend that is likely to continue as more women choose it (Brandenburg et al. 1992, 239). The advantage for the pregnant woman is to give her the same information at a time when a safer abortion is possible; with amniocentesis, abortions are generally performed at midterm.

A technology that is more widely used than either amniocentesis or chorionic villus sampling and has become indispensable in prenatal diagnosis is *ultrasound,* or ultrasonography. High-frequency, nonionizing, nonelectromagnetic sound waves are directed into the abdomen of the pregnant woman to obtain an echo-visual image of the fetus, uterus, placenta, and other inner structures (Smith and Bottoms 1993, 490). It is a noninvasive procedure that is painless for the woman and reduces the need for X-ray scanning procedures. Extensive studies have found no harmful long- or short-term hazards to the fetus from use of diagnostic sonography. Its routine use, however, should be weighed against the possibility of a false positive or negative diagnosis and the considerable monetary investment required to screen large numbers of low-risk pregnancies (Berkowitz 1993, 875). For instance, in 1990-91, a study of more than 15,000 low-risk pregnant women found that routine ultrasound screening did not improve the perinatal outcome in comparison with its selective use on the basis of clinical judgment (Ewigman, Crane, and Frigoletto 1993, 821).

In addition to its use in conjunction with amniocentesis to determine fetal position, fetal age, and amniotic fluid volume, ultrasound can be used to observe fetal development and movement as well as to detect spina bifida (Platt et al. 1992, 1328) and some musculoskeletal malformations and major organ disorders (Bronshtein et al. 1993, 225). More sophisticated devices can show images of fetal organs, such as the ventricles and intestines, and in some cases identify fetuses with Down syndrome (Lockwood, Lynch, and Berkowitz 1991, 349). Ultrasound is essential in fetoscopy, placental aspiration, and fetal surgery. Finally, ultrasound used in combination with magnetic resonance imaging has the potential to facilitate detailed diagnosis of nervous system abnormalities (Williamson et al. 1989, 952).

A wide variety of hereditary disorders, including hemophilia and possibly Duchenne's muscular dystrophy, that cannot be detected using amniotic samples might be identifiable by means of *fetoscopy*. Fetoscopy is an application of fiber optics technology that allows direct visualization of the fetus in utero. The fetoscope is inserted in an incision through the woman's abdomen, usually guided by ultrasound. Although only a small area of fetal surface can be examined because of current limitations in instrumentation, the fetoscope can be maneuvered around in the uterus to examine the fetus section by section. Fetoscopy is also used to sample fetal blood from a fetal blood vessel on the surface of the placenta (Shulman and Elias, 1990). This is accomplished by inserting a small tube into the uterus and aspirating a minute quantity of blood for diagnostic testing. Fetoscopy also has direct therapeutic use in the intrauterine transfusion of fetuses and considerable potential for the introduction of medicines, cell transplants, or genetic materials into fetal tissues in order to treat genetic diseases.

Although substantial advances have been made in fetoscopy and fetoscopic aspiration since the mid-1980s, they are still classified as applied research because of the hazards they pose for the fetus (D'Alton and De Cherney 1992, 117). Escalated rates of prematurity and a miscarriage rate of between 3 percent and 5 percent are associated with these procedures and must be reduced considerably before fetoscopy can be considered a routine medical practice. Also, because of major advances in ultrasonography, some procedures (such as fetal blood sampling) that were initially performed by fetoscopy are now accomplished using ultrasound (Ghidini et al. 1993, 1339). Nevertheless, fetoscopy is a vanguard technology for future attempts to treat genetic disease in utero and for fetal surgery.

Another prenatal diagnostic technique, *maternal serum alpha-fetoprotein testing*, has been used to detect neural tube defects and, more recently, Down syndrome (Haddow, Palomaki, and Knight 1992, 588). The level of alpha-fetoprotein is determined either from amniotic fluid or from maternal serum, usually collected between the twelfth and twentieth week of pregnancy. Although the FDA has approved the sale of diagnostic kits, controversy has arisen because of the high rate of false positives, the crude nature of a particular test, and the possibility that women might be encouraged to abort fetuses solely on the basis of this preliminary screening device. Furthermore, because higher levels of maternal serum alpha-fetoprotein have been found in pregnant black women who are not carrying a fetus affected by open spina bifida than in pregnant white women, an adjustment must be made in the procedure when used on black women (Johnson, Palomaki, and Haddow 1990). In 1986, California's legislature enacted a bill requiring physicians to inform pregnant patients of the availability of alpha-fetoprotein tests (Steinbrook 1986, 5).

A method that is on the cutting edge of diagnostic techniques is *preimplantation embryo testing,* in which a biopsy is performed on one or more cells removed from a four-to-eight cell embryo produced by IVF before it is transferred to the uterus (Simpson and Carson 1992, 951; Handyside et al. 1992, 905). There are several techniques for performing the biopsy; usually it entails stabilizing the embryo with a holding pipette, making an opening in the wall with a micro-needle, and aspirating the cell into a catheter (Tarin and Handyside 1993, 943). The DNA of the cell is then enlarged to enable analysis of sufficient material on the basis of a genetic probe for the particular disorder in question. If the biopsied cell is free of the disorder, the embryo is transferred to the woman. If the cell has the flawed gene, the embryo is either destroyed or frozen for later study (Bonnicksen 1992, 55).

To couples at risk for genetic disease, preimplantation embryo testing offers distinct advantages over conventional techniques. Ethical objections have been raised, however, concerning the moral status of the embryo and the manipulations required (it may be possible in the near future to diagnose some inherited diseases in human embryos by means of noninvasive methods) and the procedure's eugenic implications and potential for the positive engineering of offspring traits (Robertson 1992, 3). Despite these concerns, and largely because of the potential benefits, there has been significant government support for the Human Genome Initiative discussed later in this chapter.

Preselection of Sex

Interest in sex selection is certainly not new. Infanticide has long been practiced in many cultures to enable choice of gender. There is evidence that, because American couples are in general having fewer children, they are increasingly considering the use of technologies that offer them control over the characteristics of their progeny. Although a preference for a particular gender is less clear in the United States than in some other cultures, survey data from the United States indicate a preference for a son as the first child born and a daughter as the second (Veit and Jewelawicz 1988, 939).

Estimates vary as to when sex preselection techniques will become widely available to couples, but sex selection kits have been marketed in the United States since 1986 by Pro-Care Industries under the name Gender Choice. These "child-selection kits," which are available in pink and blue and have sold for $49.95, contain directions, thermometers, and the paraphernalia necessary to monitor vaginal mucus. The kits were withdrawn in 1987, when the FDA declared that some of the implied claims stated on the packages and in advertisements had not been substantiated.

Each sperm cell carries either an X chromosome or a Y chromosome; the sex of progeny is determined by which type of sperm fertilizes the egg. The goal of sex preselection is therefore to control which type of sperm fertilizes a particular egg. Some recently discovered characteristics of these two types of sperm are useful in this regard. In any male ejaculation, there are more Y-bearing sperm than X-bearing sperm. In addition to being more numerous, the Y-bearing sperm are smaller, less dense, and move faster than their X-bearing counterparts. But the Y-bearing sperm die sooner and are more readily slowed down by the normal acidic secretions of the vagina. They are less inhibited by the alkaline environment of the uterus, once they have passed the vagina, however.

Most sex preselection research is aimed at developing accurate and reliable sperm separation techniques. Techniques currently being used include various sedimentation processes, centrifugation, and electrophoresis. Once the desired sperm concentrations are isolated, they are inserted into the recipient woman's uterus by means of artificial insemination. Gametrics sold franchises for an albumin density gradient method (the patent for which is held by Ronald Ericsson), based on the principle that Y-bearing sperm swim faster than X-bearing sperm. Gametrics reports that centers using this technique have a success rate of 86 percent for male selection and 74 percent for female selection, although Sandra Ann Carson (1988, 17) disputes these figures.

At least seventy clinics in the United States are currently using variations of the sperm separation procedure to select sex chromosome-specific sperm. Although most fertility clinics are more experienced in choosing Y-bearing (male-producing) sperm, several are working with both sex chromosomes. A 1988 survey found that 14 percent of DI practitioners regularly offer the sperm separation procedure for preconception sex selection (Office of Technology Assessment 1988a, 41). The procedure allows a couple not only the possibility of overcoming infertility problems but an opportunity to select the sex of their hoped-for progeny with a high degree of accuracy.

Although the ultimate scope of sex preselection applications in the United States is unclear at present, and no simple, reliable method enjoys wide acceptance by the research community, the demand for such procedures is accelerating as reports of their success are given more coverage by the mass media. The potential market for a reliable and less intrusive method is not limited to a small proportion of the public, as it is for IVF and other techniques. Unfortunately, this also seems to be an area where the latent desires of many persons to control the gender of their offspring can be exploited by an industry that markets sex selection products and services.

Policy Issues Raised by Prenatal Diagnosis

Since the mid-1970s, there has been an increase in the number and type of prenatal diagnostic techniques available to women to identify fetal anomalies. Amniocentesis, chorionic villus sampling, and ultrasound have become standard clinical procedures—in some cases before their safety and efficacy have been fully evaluated (Oakley 1988, 41). These technologies can enhance a woman's reproductive freedom by providing information that helps her decide how to manage the pregnancy, but as with all reproductive technologies, anything that can be done voluntarily can also be coerced.

Moreover, coercion can take many forms, from subtle "pressures" to conform to accepted medical practice and to follow the technological imperative, to legally defined duties. Even though a 1984 joint report by the National Institutes of Health (NIH) and the Food and Drug Administration (FDA) (Office of Medical Applications of Research 1984, 669) found no clear benefit to be gained from routine use of ultrasound, at least one-third of all pregnant women in the United States undergo that procedure annually, and there is some evidence that the proportion is substantially higher (Petchesky 1988, 66). The new images of the fetus made possible by prenatal technologies are making the public aware of the "unborn" as people, "but they do so at the cost of making transparent the mother." Furthermore, a "diagnostic technology that pronounces judgments halfway through the pregnancy makes extraordinary demands on women to separate themselves from the fetus within" (Rothman 1986, 114). Even in the absence of legal coercion, then, the culturally imposed sanctions favoring medical intervention in pregnancies exert a strong influence.

One issue surrounding these techniques as currently used is that although they increase the ability to reduce the incidence of genetic disease, they do so primarily by eliminating the affected fetus through selective abortion, not by treatment of the disease. Future developments in gene therapy might shift the emphasis toward treatment, but for the most part prenatal diagnosis can be expected to expand maternal choice only to the extent that it allows the pregnant woman to terminate the pregnancy of an affected fetus. Thus, it will continue to be a policy issue congruous with abortion.

The issue becomes more immediate, however, if gene therapy is available in conjunction with the diagnosis, as in the case of Rh incompatibility. In *Grodin v. Grodin* (1980), a Michigan appellate court recognized the right of a child to sue his or her mother for having failed to obtain a pregnancy test. The logic of this ruling implies that a child would also have the right to sue his or her mother for failing to monitor the pregnancy and to identify and correct threats to the child's health during gestation. "The issue in such a case would be whether the mother's failure to seek a test was negligent in light of the risks that the test posed to her and the fetus and the probability that the test would uncover a correctable defect" (Robertson 1983b, 448). Technically, prenatal diagnosis could be specifically mandated by state statute with criminal sanctions for women who failed to comply with the law.

Fetal rights advocates have argued that state authorities could justify such a statute on public health grounds (Robertson 1983b, 449), but this seems most unlikely, given the absence of any national health insurance that would guarantee access of all pregnant women to such technologies. It would be illogical and most unfair to hold a pregnant woman liable for failing to utilize a medical procedure that she was unable to afford. Other observers argue that the state should never intervene to override the decision of the pregnant woman (see Johnsen 1986, McNulty 1988). Attempting to control a woman to protect the fetus is "unwise and unconstitutionally burdens the woman's right to reproduce" (Field 1989, 124). Moreover, fetal rights advocates ignore the fact that women have fundamental rights that preclude the kind and degree of government intervention they propose (Gallagher 1987, 12).

Fetal Surgery

Until the late 1970s a woman given a prenatal diagnosis of a fetal disorder usually had only two options: carry the affected fetus to term, or abort it. In some cases, blood transfusions were performed to treat Rh incompatibility. (They have been used successfully for this purpose since the early 1960s.) Now, however, there are three basic approaches to the treatment of an endangered fetus. The first is to administer medication (biotin, digitalis, cortisone, or related hormone drugs) or other substances indirectly to the fetus through the mother's bloodstream. The second is to induce timely delivery so that the infant's problem can be treated immediately outside the womb. The third, and newest, approach is to perform surgery on the fetus in the womb. Fetal surgery has been made possible by new developments in ultrasound, amniocentesis, and fetoscopy and also by the development of sophisticated surgical instrumentation designed specifically for performing these intricate procedures on fetuses.

The first reported fetal surgery was performed in April 1981, on a 31-week-old fetus twin suffering from a severe urinary tract obstruction (Golbus et al. 1982, 383). In a similar case, surgeons operating with the assistance of ultrasound treated a urinary tract obstruction in a 22-week-old fetus by draining with a needle an accumulation of fluid from a large cyst that threatened the life of the fetus (Harrison et al. 1982, 591). Also using ultrasound, doctors in several parts of the United States have implanted miniature shunting devices in the brains of fetuses that had been diagnosed as having hydrocephalus, a dangerous buildup of fluid in the brain. These shunts allow the fluid to be drained from the upper ventricles of the brain into the amniotic sac. In one case, surgeons inserted a four-inch-long shunt to permit continued drainage during the last three months of pregnancy. Other applications of fetal surgical methods have enabled drainage of a collapsed lung that had become filled with fluid and drainage of excess fluid from a fetus's chest and abdomen. In utero surgery has been termed practical in two respects:

> First, *in utero* surgery takes place in a surgical field (the amniotic fluid) that is sterile at the onset. Second, the fetus responds in a fundamentally different way to injury than an adult. Fetal wounds heal without scarring, inflammation, fibrosis, or contraction that affect adult wound healing. (Pergament 1993, 141)

Ex utero surgery was conducted on a 24-week-old fetus to repair a diaphragmatic hernia (Harrison et al. 1990, 1582). The mother's abdomen was opened surgically and the left side of the fetus was brought outside the uterus. After a fifty-four minute surgery, the uterus was closed in three layers, a fibrin glue having been applied between them, and the amniotic fluid was replenished. At thirty-two weeks of gestation, seven weeks after surgery, a healthy baby boy was delivered by cesarean section.

It should be stressed that notwithstanding these successes, fetal surgery is still a high-risk procedure whose use is limited to fetuses otherwise in danger of dying either before or soon after delivery. It is improbable that effective treatment for many disorders will be developed in the foreseeable future. Furthermore, the danger of precipitating preterm delivery or abortion is a serious constraint on all but the most routine in utero interventions, despite the strides that have been made in prevention of some disorders. And though fetal surgery may "save" a fetus who otherwise would die, a seriously disabled newborn may survive (Pergament 1993, 144).

Conflicting Interests

One of the most difficult legal problems to be faced in the near future is how to balance the rights of the mother and the medical needs of the fetus when they are contradictory. The basic question is whether the fetus is a patient separate from its mother in cases where the fetus can be treated either medically or surgically. Prior to these recent developments in fetal surgery, the fetus was considered, at most, a medical patient and certain problems were treated by administering medication to the mother or directly into the amniotic fluid. Although these procedures required the cooperation of the pregnant woman, they were not as physically intrusive or potentially risky as surgery. The difficulty with fetal surgery is that treatment of the fetus can be accomplished only by violating the woman's physical integrity and invading her privacy. She must consent to surgery, not only on her unborn child but on herself. (These issues are discussed in more detail in Chapter 7, which focuses on problems in the maternal-fetal relationship.)

Many obstetricians prefer to view the mother and fetus as a single biological entity with shared interests that are furthered by proper maternal care during pregnancy. But this perception is being challenged by recent advances in fetal care that require separation of the fetus from its mother for treatment purposes (Harrison et al. 1990, 1582). Although many medical practitioners identify their concern for the patient or the fear of malpractice suits as the prime motivations for the use of these technologies, critics point to the profit motive and market interests as the major motivating factors. They argue, for instance, that the proliferation of these technologies in obstetrical practice is concurrent with the end of the baby boom and the rapid drop in fertility and reflects the desire of the profession to develop a new "patient population" to "look at and treat" (Petchesky 1988, 65).

Pressures on the pregnant woman to use available fetal therapies will likely increase when the technologies are no longer considered merely experimental and are accepted as routine therapeutic procedures. At present the immediate concern is the possible harm caused by fetal surgery to the fetus and the mother; however, the rapid advances being made in instrumentation, technique, and skills will lessen this risk and substantially increase the options available for intervening in utero to correct fetal defects surgically. Sherman Elias and George Annas view forcible medical treatment as "brutish and horrible," but they concede that when fetal surgery becomes accepted medical practice, and if the procedure can be done with minimal invasiveness and risk to the mother and significant benefit to the fetus, there is an argument to be made that the woman should not be permitted to reject it. Such rejection of therapy could be considered "fetal abuse" and, at a late stage in pregnancy, "child abuse," and an appropriate court order sought to force treatment. (1983, 811)

A society where there is widespread dependence on technological solutions, reinforced by a medical community trained in the technological imperative, often has a false degree of security as to what medicine can accomplish. Many therapies come into widespread use without adequate assessment as to their risks and benefits. Increasingly, as the demand for medical solutions increases, the line between experimentation and therapeutic application becomes a tenuous one. There is a danger in such a society that new technologies will be offered to, or even forced on, pregnant women without adequate proof of benefit. The argument that a pregnant woman has a legal duty to use "established" medical procedures must therefore be viewed critically. We cannot assume that because a procedure is accepted as routine, the anticipated benefit to the fetus warrants state intervention under force of law.

Increased Empathy for the Fetus

The rapidly developing advances being made in a variety of treatments, including fetal surgery, are evidence of a subtle but real shift toward a recognition that the fetus has an independent self. Technologies that allow us to visualize the growing organism as human, amniocentesis whose purpose is to label that entity as a "boy" or a "girl," and the prospect of developing other forms of direct surgical intervention certainly suggest recognition of the developing fetus as an individual of some importance. Although it does not seem feasible to speak of the fetus as a fully autonomous person, its assumption of human characteristics would seem to necessitate a reevaluation of parental responsibility to the "unborn" patient.

The Study of Human Genes

In recent years, the U.S. government has assigned a high priority to mapping and sequencing the human genome. Although the amount of money required to determine the sequence of the 3 billion base pairs will be less than the amount spent by the government to send an astronaut to the moon, "the implications of the Human Genome Project for human life are likely to be far greater" (Watson 1990, 44).

The Human Genome Initiative is an international research effort whose goal is to analyze the basic genetic structure of human DNA and to determine the location of the estimated 100,000 human genes. The information generated by the initiative will serve as a source book for biology and medicine in the twenty-first century and "help us to understand and eventually treat many of the more than 4,000 genetic diseases in which genetic predisposition plays an important role" (National Center for Human Genome Research 1990, vii).

This initiative is being coordinated by the National Institutes of Health and the Department of Energy. In anticipation of its leading role in the Human Genome Initiative, the National Institutes of Health established the Office of Human Genome Research in 1988. In 1989, when the budget proposal for fiscal year 1990 designated $100 million for human genome research, thus justifying an independent program, the office became the National Center for Human Genome Research. The eagerness to fund the Human Genome Initiative and the quick approval of the center reflect the strong support for this research, within both the administration and Congress. Apparently acknowledging the widespread impact the initiative was expected to have, Congress set aside up to 5 percent of the annual budget to study the ethical, legal, and social implications of increased genetic knowledge (see Langfelder and Juengst 1993, 273).

Genetic Diagnosis and Testing

In the early 1970s, genetic screening was given a place on the public policy agenda, largely because some states had instituted mandatory sickle cell screening programs targeted at black populations. These programs, many of which were well intentioned but misconceived, led to considerable stigmatization of and discrimination against individuals identified as having the sickle cell trait. In response, Congress passed the National Sickle Cell Anemia Control Act in 1972, under which states qualified for federal funding only if their program was voluntary.

Until recently, genetic diagnosis focused on screening for a handful of single-gene-recessive diseases, most prominently sickle cell anemia and Tay-Sachs disease. Once identified as carriers of the trait, individuals could be educated as to the risk of having an affected child or offered prenatal diagnosis, if it was available for that particular disease. The innovations made in carrier screening and prenatal diagnosis since the mid-1970s have been impressive. The recent development of a wide variety of molecular techniques also suggests new possibilities for human genetic intervention.

At present, two types of tests can be performed on the DNA cells taken from blood samples. When the gene responsible for a particular disease has been identified, the test constitutes a DNA probe, or a labeled segment of DNA that binds directly to the defective gene, if one is present. If the specific gene for a condition is not yet known, genetic markers are identified that are in close proximity enough to the unknown gene to be inherited with it. These restriction fragment-length polymorphisms indicate the approximate chromosomal location of an unknown gene. If overlapping polymorphisms that are related to a gene disorder are used, the actual gene can eventually be isolated. Such indirect marker tests are more expensive, complicated, and probabilistic than the DNA probes. With the use of increasingly sophisticated cloning and sequencing techniques, however, tests to detect these markers in individuals can be developed to be used either prenatally, neonatally, or in adults to determine carrier status.

Since the discovery of a molecular probe for the gene for Huntington's disease in 1983 (Hayes 1992, 1449), efforts have been initiated to identify genetic markers for Alzheimer's disease, sickle cell anemia, manic depression, malignant melanoma, and many other conditions. As a result of this research, a gene for cystic fibrosis was found in 1989 (Nishimi 1993, 1921). The identification of the retinoblastoma gene on chromosome 13 in 1986 and the discovery of its linkage to breast cancer in 1988 have aroused considerable enthusiasm in the medical community that genetic bases may be found for other types of cancer (Steel 1993, 754).

Research is now under way to identify genetic factors that might predispose a person to be an alcoholic (Gordis et al. 1990, 2094). Although no single gene or gene complement has yet been found, researchers have accumulated a great deal of information associating genetic factors with alcohol abuse. In 1991, the National Institute on Alcohol Abuse and Alcoholism launched the first systematic, multilevel study of the genetics of alcoholism, with a budget of $25 million for the first five years (Holden 1991, 163).

One particularly sensitive area of research is that aimed at discovering which genes are associated with intelligence. Work on the "fragile-X" chromosome associated with mental retardation is the first wave of this investigation (Bishop and Waldholz 1990, 316-317). The discovery of genetic markers for some forms of Alzheimer's disease on chromosome 21 (the same chromosome associated with Down syndrome) also suggests hypotheses for genetic linkages, particularly since older Down syndrome patients exhibit Alzheimer-type symptoms. Eventually, genetic tests may allow scientists not only to predict the course of genetic abnormalities but to identify traits that put certain individuals at higher risk for susceptibility to a host of environmental factors.

Table 6-3   Incidence of Cystic Fibrosis in the United States

Babies born annually with cystic fibrosis	1,700 to 2,000
Americans with cystic fibrosis	30,000
Median age of individuals with cystic fibrosis	12 years
Median life span of individual cystic fibrosis patient	28 years
Number of Americans who might be cystic fibrosis carriers	8,000,000
Frequency of cystic fibrosis carriers among white Americans of European descent	1 in 25
Frequency of cystic fibrosis carriers among Hispanic-Americans	1 in 40 to 50
Frequency of cystic fibrosis carriers among African-Americans	1 in 60 to 65
Frequency of cystic fibrosis carriers among Asian-Americans	1 in 150
Pregnancies per year that might be screened for cystic fibrosis status	6,000,000
American men and women who might be screened annually if routine screening is included in prenatal examinations	10,000,000
Number of Americans of reproductive age who theoretically could be subjects of cystic fibrosis carrier screening	125,000,000
Office of Technology Assessment estimate of the number of cystic fibrosis carrier tests in 1991	9,310
Office of Technology Assessment estimate of the number of cystic fibrosis carrier tests in 1992	63,000

Source: Adapted from Nishimi 1993, 1921

Major commercial applications of recombinant DNA (rDNA) technology center on the development of new diagnostic and therapeutic products. Various rDNA techniques are being used in the production of human insulin, human growth hormone, and new drugs for individuals with heart disease, as well as to improve a number of diagnostic tests for infectious diseases. One rapidly emerging set of applications that promises to have a large market comprises diagnostic tests for common conditions that have a genetic component, such as hypertension, heart disease, and cancer. Table 6-3 gives some idea of the potential market for the screening of cystic fibrosis.

As new diagnostic tests and genetic probes are developed, public expectations and demand for access to information derived from such research will increase. If the tests become accepted by policy makers as legitimate, legislatures and courts might recognize professional standards of care that incorporate them. Genetic probes cannot account for all the variance in the expression of the genes; but many persons are likely to interpret a positive gene probe test wrongly as an indicator of a person's biological destiny (Nelkin and Tancredi 1989, 168).

Sensitive policy problems will likely emerge as more precise and inclusive tests enable medical professionals to identify people who are at high risk for a particular disease or condition. Increasingly, policy makers will be pressured by employers and insurance companies for access to information obtained from these tests (Kass 1992). The potential use of DNA probes as a means to identify persons at risk for poor health has focused attention on the issue of how much information should be made available to third parties. A 1989 report of the American Council on Life Insurance made clear that the insurance industry will demand access to such data on persons seeking life and disability insurance (Bishop and Waldholz 1990, 299). But when, if ever, should the patient's right to privacy be sacrificed to serve the interests of the employer? Under what circumstances does the genetic counselor's or physician's responsibility to society outweigh his or her responsibility to the patient? As more knowledge is gained about specific susceptibilities related to certain genetic traits and as more accurate tests are found to identify a wide variety of these traits, debate on workplace screening will become more widespread and intense.

Medical science is in a transition period regarding genetic tests. Although advances in human molecular genetics have increased the capability to identify individuals at risk for a variety of conditions, a battery of molecular probes is not yet available. The commercial development and marketing of accurate and inexpensive genetic tests is imminent, however; such tests are likely to become as routine as the health screening indicators currently in use. Companies might consider including these tests as part of their health promotion or preventive medicine programs. For instance, a person identified as having a genetic proclivity for hypertension or a malignant melanoma could be placed in an early diagnosis program. But it should be pointed out that a company might attempt to use to the same tests to preclude such a person's employment in order to reduce its health care expenditures.

Human Gene Transfer

Although human gene transfer is still in its infancy, the increase in such research since 1991 has been "phenomenal" (Healy 1993, 567). At least forty-six studies of human gene transfer have been received by the Food and Drug Administration and the number continues to increase (Kessler et al. 1993, 1169). Using gene transfer techniques, it is possible to correct genetic defects, not by environmental manipulations but by attempting to directly affect the DNA in the patient's cells. One approach, which has been tried on some victims of thalassemia and sickle cell anemia, is to activate certain genes that would otherwise be inactive, so that they can take over the job of the defective genes. Another approach is gene therapy—the introduction of normal genes into chromosomes of cells that contain defective genes in the hope that the manipulated genes will express themselves and ultimately replace the defective ones, thus enabling the patient to be cured.

The research emphasis today is on somatic cell therapy—the insertion of genes into particular body cells other than the germ cells (sperm and egg cells, and cells that give rise to them). Because somatic cell therapy does not affect the germ line, the genes transferred in this procedure will not be transmitted to the recipient's children. A more controversial type of gene therapy consists of intervention in germ line cells that contribute to the genetic heritage of offspring (Elias and Annas 1992). Although it has been argued that germ line "genetic intervention is the *only* way in which certain couples can exercise their rights to reproductive health" (Zimmerman 1991, 593), technical difficulties, in combination with ethical concerns, make it unlikely that germ line gene therapy will have wide application in the near future, even though theoretically it may be the most effective means of therapy.

> The options of germ cell gene therapy must not be prematurely foreclosed. . . . Before germ-cell therapy is seriously considered, it must demonstrate its long-term safety beyond other standard treatments, since changes would affect not only the patient but also those progeny who inherit the chromosomes bearing the inserted genes. Benefits, however, would also be propagated in to future generations. (Fletcher and Anderson 1992, 36)

Gene therapy was first attempted at NIH in September 1990, when doctors treated a 4-year-old girl who suffered from a grave immune deficiency because she lacked the enzyme adenosine deaminase. The doctors took some of the girl's white blood cells, altered them by inserting a gene from the missing enzyme, and returned the altered cells to the girl's body. Two months after this test, the FDA gave approval for a test using genetically modified tumor-infiltrating lymphocytes to treat ten patients with advanced melanoma. This strategy, introduction of a cancer-fighting substance into the DNA of the melanoma patients' blood cells, has wide implications for the treatment of many diseases.

New applications for new tests of gene therapy continue to be developed. Some observers have already termed this the beginning of a "second generation" of gene therapy (Merz 1989, 3). A recent melanoma test is evidence of a shift away from the initial strategy of replacing defective

Table 6-4 Likely Uses of Gene Therapy

Type of disease	Treatment
Lung	Aerosol delivery of genes for alpha 1-antitrypsin to treat patients with emphysema, and of the gene for transport protein to treat patients with cystic fibrosis
Cardiovascular	Use of endothelial cells containing genes for clot-dissolving agents, vasodilators, or angiogenic factors to line surfaces of natural and prosthetic vessels
Liver	Implantation of hepatocytes carrying genes for LDL receptors in patients with familial hypocholesterolemia
Malignant tumors	Use of tumor-infiltrating lymphocytes armed with genes for tumor necrosis factor or other cytokines
AIDS	Implantation of lymphocytes with gene for soluble CD4 to secrete proteins to intercept HIV
Blood	Transfer of skin fibroblasts bearing genes for clotting factors, enzymes
Immunodeficiency	Implantation of lymphocytes carrying genes for missing enzymes

Source: Adapted from Merz 1989, 3.

genes with normal ones throughout the body, to using transferred genes as drug delivery systems to supply proteins only to the organs that need them. This development means that gene therapy is likely to be extended to the treatment of nongenetic medical problems such as emphysema, cardiovascular disease, liver failure, AIDS, malignant tumors, and blood and immune system diseases (see Table 6-4). These uses also have important implications for the practice of medicine.

The shift in emphasis, from diagnosis to therapeutic application as the goal of genetic intervention, complicates many policy issues regarding the role government ought to play in encouraging or discouraging genetic research and experimental application. It also raises new ethical questions concerning parental responsibilities to children, societal perceptions of children, the distribution of social benefits, and the definition of what it means to be a human being.

NIH Statement on Reproductive Genetic Testing: Impact on Women

Reproductive genetic testing, counseling, and other genetic services can be valuable components in the reproductive health care of women and their families. They can also have negative effects on individuals, families, and communities. These services have the potential to increase knowledge about possible pregnancy outcomes, enhance the developing relationship between the woman and her expected child, allow a woman to decide whether to continue a pregnancy in which the expected child has a birth defect or genetic disorder, and prepare the family for rearing a child with a disability. Conversely, these services have the potential to increase anxiety, place excessive responsibility, blame, and guilt on a woman for the pregnancy outcome, interfere with mother-infant bonding, and disrupt relationships among the woman, family members, and the community.

Complex individual differences among women challenge efforts to evaluate the safety and efficacy of reproductive genetic services. To reflect the function of genetic services in reproductive health care, evaluation criteria must be client centered. This understanding of genetic services has several important implications that should be considered in the development of a future research agenda.

1. Reproductive genetic services should not be used to pursue "eugenic goals," but should be aimed at increasing individuals' control over their own reproductive lives. . . .

2. Reproductive genetic services should be meticulously voluntary. The testing should not be swept in with other "routine" or "universal" reproductive interventions unless informed consent or refusal can be assured. . . .

3. Reproductive genetic services should be value sensitive. Providers should be particularly sensitive to individual differences and similarities in ethno-cultural and religious matters.

4. Standards of care for reproductive genetic services should emphasize genetic information, education, and counseling rather than testing procedures alone. . . .

5. Social, legal, and economic constraints on genetic services should be removed. Government and institutional policies have continued to influence legal and fiscal rules that limit the genetic testing choices which women have available to them. Research is needed to clarify such constraints and reduce the barriers to genetic services for women who desire them.

6. Increasing attention focused on the development and utilization of reproductive genetic testing services may further stigmatize individuals affected by a particular disorder or disability. The values that some individuals place on health and disabilities, what people may be told about disabilities, and even the use of certain language to describe the benefits of testing have the potential to devalue the worth that individuals with disabilities have in society. . . . Individuals with disabilities, who have a variety of information, experiences, and views to share, must be involved in the development and implementation of further research to be carried out in this area.

Source: National Institutes of Health 1992, 1161.

Conclusion

Innovations as rapid and numerous as those being made in human genetics and reproductive technology are bound to affect traditional social structures. If the use of these new techniques is limited to a small proportion of the population, such innovations are likely to be acceptable, despite their impact on individual children and parents. If, however, their use becomes widespread, or if they are routinely used, they are likely to have unanticipated consequences. The NIH statement (see the box on page 151) is a summary of some issues raised by reproductive genetic testing; it suggests important implications that should be considered in developing a future research agenda. The mere availability of these technologies might produce a social climate in which refusal to accept them is viewed as irresponsible behavior. Social pressure will compel use of technologies that are now largely construed as expanding procreative choice.

Furthermore, the availability of technologies for prenatal diagnosis, screening, and selection may heighten discrimination with regard to children born with congenital or genetic disorders (Miringoff 1989, 393). Leon Kass expressed concern that as societal attitudes toward such individuals are "progressively eroded," they will come to be viewed as having escaped the "net of detection and abortion" (1979, 317)—unfortunate persons who would not have been born if only someone had gotten to them in time. Parents might feel tremendous guilt or resent such a stigmatized child, especially if social pressures are directed against them. The "right to be born healthy" is misleading because it actually means that "only healthy persons have a right to be born." The choice of those affected is not between a healthy and unhealthy existence but rather between an unhealthy existence and none at all (Murphy, Chase, and Rodriguez 1978, 358).

The important policy issues raised by the technologies of prenatal intervention and human genetics require public attention. On the one hand, these innovations promise to lessen the individual and social costs of genetic disease and allow more control over the destiny of future generations. On the other hand, widespread use of these technologies increases considerably the ability to categorize individuals according to precise genetic factors. The new technologies enable prospective parents to predetermine the sex of their progeny, to select the frozen embryo that best meets their expectations, and, through DNA tests, to identify and possibly modify "undesirable" characteristics. Although they expand the range of individual choice, they also have the potential to dehumanize.

Conflict in the Maternal-Fetal Relationship

Twenty-seven-old Angela Carder had lived with cancer since the age of 13. She had had a variety of treatments including radiation, chemotherapy, and several major operations, including a leg amputation. The disease had been in remission for three years when Carder married. Shortly after her marriage she became pregnant. In June 1987, twenty-six weeks into her pregnancy, physicians at George Washington University Medical Center in the District of Columbia advised Carder that the cancer had reappeared and that she was near death. They believed that although Carder was terminal, the fetus could be saved by cesarean delivery. Carder initially agreed to palliative care to extend her life to twenty-eight weeks to allow for the possibility of the cesarean delivery, although she was equivocal about wanting to have the baby. Physicians, however, decided that the cesarean should be done quickly, and when Carder objected, the hospital obtained a court order to which she also objected. A daughter was delivered, but died within hours, and Carder died two days later.

Throughout this book it is emphasized that as a result of improved prenatal technology, the secrets of the womb have been revealed for all to see. The ability to visualize the fetus through ultrasonography and to treat the fetus in utero have led to societal recognition of the fetus as a patient, separate from the mother. When the mother and the fetus are viewed as separate patients, each with distinct needs, the potential for conflict arises. As discussed in Chapter 1, claims of positive rights by one party necessitate the assumption of duties by other parties. In cases of maternal-fetal conflict, rights claims made on behalf of the fetus may require duties on the part of the pregnant woman.

This would appear to be a simple matter. A pregnant woman, many would argue, has a duty to care for the fetus that is inside her body. But this viewpoint is, in reality, an oversimplification. Most pregnant women will make personal sacrifices in terms of medical treatment and life-style in order to deliver a healthy infant. A potential for conflict exists, however, when a pregnant woman refuses to accept recommended treatment or alterations in her life-style. This chapter concerns three such potential areas of conflict: court-ordered obstetrical intervention, maternal use of drugs during pregnancy, and fetal protection in the workplace.

Ethical Considerations during Pregnancy

The debate over the welfare of the fetus versus that of the pregnant woman is like the abortion debate in that it invariably involves a discussion of fetal rights. However, the most fundamental question in any discussion of potential conflict between fetus and pregnant woman is: how do the woman's actions during pregnancy affect the born child? In *Roe v. Wade* (1973) and *Planned Parenthood of Southeastern Pennsylvania v. Casey* (1992), the Supreme Court ruled, in essence, that the pre-viable fetus does not have a constitutional right to life. The conclusion follows, then, that it does not have a constitutional right to have its health protected. A potential for conflict thus arises when activity during pregnancy negatively affects the *born* child.

There is considerable debate among ethicists and other scholars regarding the duties that a pregnant woman owes the fetus and whether those duties should be legally enforced. It should be noted that rights to preserve bodily integrity and to make intimate family decisions have been upheld in the courts. Thus all such issues should be considered in any analysis of whether the state should intervene to coerce a pregnant woman to comply with treatment or to alter her life-style against her will.

Lawrence Nelson and Nancy Milliken argue that although a pregnant woman has ethical obligations to the fetus, those obligations should not be enforced by the state because such enforcement invades the woman's privacy; thrusts her into a confrontation with an adversarial system at a time when she is ill-prepared, both psychologically and physically, to deal with it; demonstrates the physician's willingness to use physical force against a competent adult; and violates the tradition of bodily integrity. They conclude that "society will . . . gain far more by allowing each pregnant woman to live as seems good to her, rather than by compelling each to live as seems good to the rest of us" (1988, 1066).

Dawn Johnsen points out that "by creating an adversarial relationship between the woman and her fetus, the state provides itself with a powerful means for controlling women's behavior during pregnancy, thereby threatening women's fundamental rights'' (1986, 600). Martha Field takes a similar view, arguing that ''controlling women to protect their fetuses is using pregnancy to deprive women of the most basic civil rights'' (1989, 116). The American College of Obstetricians and Gynecologists also opposes court-ordered interventions because they are destructive to the pregnant woman's autonomy, damage the physician-patient relationship, and are often utilized in emergency situations that have serious limitations and unexpected outcomes (1987).

Although these claims in support of maternal autonomy are powerful, there are also well-reasoned arguments against allowing the pregnant woman complete autonomy. Relationships create moral and legal responsibilities. Most people would agree that parents have a moral responsibility to care for their born children, and the courts have clearly established that parents also have a legal responsibility for such care. One way in which a parent discharges his or her responsibility to the born child is by caring for the fetus. The loss of some autonomy is inevitable in this relationship.

> Although the mother's right to autonomy and privacy in reproduction is fundamental, like all other constitutional rights it is not absolute. Therefore, at times she may be legally restrained from performing some action that under other circumstances would be considered a personal choice. (Blank 1986, 442)

Although it is unreasonable to force a woman to refrain from all contact that could harm the fetus, it is also unreasonable to conclude that she has no obligations to it. The more severe the harmful effect on the fetus and the higher the risk of that effect occurring, the higher should be the standard of care (Blank 1986, 444).

Norman Fost, former chair of the American Academy of Pediatrics Committee on Bioethics, argues that ''it is morally irresponsible to voluntarily bring an infant into the world but refuse to make reasonable efforts to allow that child to be born healthy'' (1989, 252). Compelling women to behave in ways that avoid fetal risk should be confined, he argues, to circumstances when there is a high probability of live birth, a high probability of serious physical harm to the ''infant to be,'' a high probability that the harm can be prevented using standard established treatment, and a low probability of serious harm to the mother.

A more forceful argument is presented by Margery Shaw, who draws an analogy between child abuse and fetal abuse:

> We should not allow children to be victimized by adult behavior either before or after birth. They need special safeguards, including legal protection. The parent's right to reproduce, even though consti-

tutionally protected, should be subordinated to the needs of the child. (1984, 102)

In general, when the courts have addressed issues concerning the fetus, they have done so in the context of a fetus becoming—or potentially becoming—a born child. In *Roe*, the Supreme Court ruled that the state has a legitimate interest in protecting potential life after the point of viability; in *Webster v. Reproductive Health Services* (1989), the Court upheld mandated viability tests, finding that their requirement ''permissibly furthers the State's interest in protecting potential human life'' (at 519-520).

In ruling on the rights of the fetus, a number of lower courts have upheld actions against the mother for her behavior during pregnancy. In *Grodin v. Grodin* (1980), a Michigan appellate court upheld the right of a child to be compensated for injuries received in utero as a result of the mother's use of tetracycline during gestation. In *Stallmann v. Youngquist* (1984), an Illinois appellate court upheld the right of a child to be compensated by her mother for automobile injuries sustained in utero.

Court-Ordered Obstetrical Intervention

Since the early 1970s, there have been some dramatic breakthroughs in the diagnosis and treatment of the fetus in utero. Breakthroughs such as in utero surgery are nearly universally applauded, but they are not without some negative consequences, particularly for the pregnant woman because the only way to treat the fetus is by invading the woman's body. As was argued in Chapter 1, if these procedures become routine, women will be increasingly pressured to submit to them.

On both ethical and legal grounds, physicians are required to obtain informed consent prior to administering treatment. Treatment without consent constitutes battery committed by the physician against the patient. A competent adult can generally refuse such treatment, even if it results in his or her death. A complex issue of rights and duties arises, however, when treatment is sought for a fetus without the mother's consent. Obviously, the fetus can give neither informed consent nor informed refusal. Since the only way to treat the fetus is by invading the body of the pregnant woman, she gives the consent or refusal both for herself and for the fetus. This creates a potential conflict of rights and duties because what is beneficial for the fetus may not be beneficial for the pregnant woman, or at least the woman's perception may be that it is not beneficial for her.

Occasionally a physician recommends a prenatal therapy or procedure and the pregnant woman refuses to comply. Such therapies and procedures vary greatly in cost, extent of inconvenience, invasiveness, and possibility of fetal or maternal harm. The consequences of refusal can be devastating for the infant and sometimes for the woman. For example, fetal sepsis (infection) can result in brain damage or death, and vaginal delivery in cases of placenta previa (blockage of the birth canal by the placenta) is almost universally fatal for the fetus and has a high rate of maternal mortality as well.

It is logical to ask why a pregnant woman would refuse a recommended treatment, since the overwhelming majority of women go to great lengths to deliver healthy babies. Some women refuse interventions on religious or cultural grounds. Jehovah's Witnesses refuse blood transfusions, and Hmongs refuse cesarean sections. In one of the earliest cases of judicial intervention (*Raleigh Fitkin-Paul Morgan Memorial Hospital v. Anderson*, 1964), a New Jersey court ordered a member of Jehovah's Witnesses to submit to blood transfusions to save her life and that of her unborn child. In 1985 a New York court ordered a blood transfusion for the benefit of a previable 18-week fetus, finding that the state's interest in protecting the fetus outweighed the patient's interest (*In the Matter of the Application of Jamaica Hospital*).

Some women disagree with the physician's diagnosis or fear the procedure will harm themselves or the fetus. Many interventions are expensive, and the poor and uninsured may simply not have the financial resources to pay for them. Even treatments that would appear to be cost free are, in reality, expensive. For example, bed rest is not a viable alternative for a pregnant woman who must work full time to support her existing children and who may lose her job, income, and possibly her employer-paid health insurance if she does not work.

Thus when a woman is asked to submit to an unwanted obstetrical intervention, she faces a complex ethical dilemma. If she ultimately refuses to consent to the intervention, the physician may seek a court order forcing her to submit. Although physicians have rarely resorted to such action, with improving prenatal technologies it is to be expected that the number of these cases will increase.

Unwanted Cesarean Sections

Much of the controversy over prenatal diagnosis or treatment concerns court-ordered cesarean sections. There are at least two considerations, aside from the basic issues of bodily integrity and informed consent, to be weighed in this debate. First, the rate of delivery by cesarean section is much higher in the United States than in other countries, even those with equally sophisticated perinatal care systems; there has been much discussion about the number of unnecessary surgical deliveries. Second, delivery by cesarean section is highly invasive, carries a greater risk of maternal mortality than does vaginal delivery (although the risk is still quite low), and typically requires a lengthy and usually uncomfortable recovery period. Moreover, diagnoses sometimes prove to be inaccurate.

In a number of cases reported in the literature, court orders were issued requiring delivery by cesarean section, but healthy babies were subsequently delivered vaginally. In 1981, Griffin Spaulding County Hospital obtained a court order requiring Jessie May Jefferson to submit to a cesarean delivery if she had herself admitted to the hospital. Physicians had diagnosed her as having placenta previa, but she opposed the surgery on religious grounds. In ordering the cesarean section, the Superior Court stated that there was a 99 percent certainty that the child would die during delivery and a 50 percent chance that Jefferson would die as well (*Jefferson v. Griffin Spaulding County Hospital*). Despite these predictions, Jefferson had a normal vaginal delivery and a healthy baby. The following year a Michigan woman was also diagnosed with placenta previa and also refused a cesarean delivery on religious grounds; rather than submit to the surgery, she went into hiding. Police were authorized to search for her, but their search proved unsuccessful. Newspapers later reported that she had a normal vaginal delivery at another hospital (Rhoden 1986a, 2009).

Other cases are also noteworthy. In 1986, Georgetown University Hospital obtained a court order when Ayesha Madyun refused to comply with the recommendation for delivery by cesarean section. The physician was concerned about the possibility of fetal infection, but Madyun disagreed with the diagnosis. She attended a hearing that was convened at the hospital even though she was already in labor. In *In re Madyun* (1986), the Superior Court of the District of Columbia ordered the surgery, stating that ''parents may not make a martyr of their unborn infant.'' The trial court's decision was upheld by a late-night call to two appellate justices. Madyun's son was delivered by cesarean section and showed no signs of infection. He and his mother recovered without complication.

A similar case, *Unborn Child of Chao Lee* (1990), concerned a Hmong immigrant living in LaCrosse, Wisconsin, who had been diagnosed with placenta previa but refused to consent to a cesarean delivery. It is believed that she objected because her cultural values did not sanction surgery, she was pressured by influential members of her clan, and she disagreed with the diagnosis. The physician sought and obtained a court order, which required a cesarean section if Chao Lee arrived voluntarily at the hospital, and if the procedure was deemed necessary to save her life (personal correspondence with the author, September 22, 1992).

Shortly before the hearing a public defender was appointed to represent Chao Lee. Due to the emergency nature of the hearing, he was not given adequate time to prepare a defense. He had never met or even talked with his client, and did not know the facts of the case. Moreover, the issues were outside his normal practice of law. Chao Lee did not attend the hearing. It is not known whether she was ever informed about it or even understood the American judicial process. Chao Lee consulted another physician, who testified at a subsequent hearing that vaginal delivery could be safely accomplished. The initial order was rescinded, and a healthy child was subsequently delivered vaginally without complication.

Callian Bricci was also delivered vaginally in a healthy condition at Northwestern Memorial Hospital in Chicago in December 1993. Tabita Bricci, a Pentecostal, had refused to submit to a cesarean section recommended by physicians at St. Joseph Hospital, also in Chicago, who believed that because of problems with the placenta, the child would be born brain-damaged or might die if delivered vaginally. The hospital then sought a court order. The order was denied by the trial court, and the denial was upheld by the Illinois Appellate Court. The Illinois Supreme Court and the United States Supreme Court refused to hear the case. (See Table 7-1 for a summary of cases.)

As related in the beginning of this chapter, Angela Carder was diagnosed with cancer as an adolescent, received various treatments, and was in remission when she married and became pregnant. When Carder was advised that her case was terminal, she agreed to palliative care in order to extend her pregnancy to twenty-eight weeks so that the baby could be delivered by cesarean section.

Doctors at George Washington University Medical Center, however, wanted to perform the cesarean section at twenty-six weeks gestation, which she opposed. The hospital then sought a court order to force the surgery. The trial court convened at the hospital and separate counsel were appointed for both Carder and the fetus. The District of Columbia intervened as *parens patriae.* The events leading up to the court's hearing had transpired so quickly that Carder's attorney had been unable to meet with her; Carder could not attend the hearing because she was heavily sedated; and her personal physician had not been advised that the surgery was planned or that a court hearing had been scheduled. (He later indicated that he would have opposed the surgery had he known about it.) Despite the fact that Carder's mother testified in opposition to the surgery, an order authorizing it was issued. When Carder was advised of the order she objected; the court was advised of her objection, but it again ordered the surgery. Her counsel sought a stay from the Court of Appeals of the District of Columbia, but it was denied by a hastily assembled panel of three judges. Surgery was performed, and both mother and daughter died.

Several months later, the Court of Appeals for the District of Columbia reversed its order denying Carder's attorney's motion for a stay. In 1990, sitting *en banc,* the same court reversed the trial court's order to perform

Table 7-1 Cases on Issue of Court-Ordered Obstetrical Intervention

Raleigh Fitkin-Paul Morgan Memorial Hospital v. Anderson (1964)

New Jersey court orders a member of Jehovah's Witnesses to submit to blood transfusions to save her life and that of her unborn child.

Jefferson v. Griffin Spaulding County Hospital (1981)

Georgia court issues an order requiring pregnant woman diagnosed as having placenta previa to submit to delivery by cesarean section if she seeks delivery at the hospital. Jefferson delivers a healthy baby through an uncomplicated vaginal delivery.

In the Matter of the Application of Jamaica Hospital (1985)

New York court orders blood transfusion for the pregnant woman for the benefit of a pre-viable fetus, finding that the state's interest in protecting the fetus outweighed the pregnant woman's interest.

In re Madyun (July 25, 1986)

Superior Court of the District of Columbia orders delivery by cesarean section after diagnosis of potential fetal sepsis. Child is delivered by cesarean section but with no signs of fetal sepsis.

In re A. C. (April 26, 1990)

In 1987 a District of Columbia trial court orders cesarean delivery for Angela Carder, who has terminal cancer and is twenty-six weeks pregnant, despite her objections and those of her family. The District of Columbia Court of Appeals affirms the order. Both mother and newborn daughter die shortly after delivery. In 1990, the District of Columbia Court of Appeals, sitting *en banc*, reverses the trial court's order to perform the cesarean.

Unborn Child of Chao Lee (1990)

Hmong immigrant refuses delivery by cesarean section after diagnosis of placenta previa. Court orders delivery by cesarean section if Chao Lee presents herself at the hospital voluntarily and if delivery by cesarean is considered necessary to save her life. The order is rescinded after a second hearing in which a different physician testifies that vaginal delivery can be safely accomplished. A healthy baby is subsequently delivered in an uncomplicated vaginal delivery.

---

the surgery. It also made a strong statement supporting the right of all patients, particularly pregnant patients, to make decisions concerning their own medical care. Regarding cesarean deliveries, it found that "in virtually all cases the question of what is to be done is to be decided by the patient—the pregnant woman—on behalf of herself and the fetus" (*In re A. C.,* 1990 at 1110). The notion of a maternal obligation to "rescue" the fetus was clearly ruled out:

[The] courts do not compel one person to permit a significant intrusion upon his or her bodily integrity for the benefit of another person's health. . . . Surely . . . a fetus cannot have rights in this respect superior to those of a person who has already been born. (at 1123)

The Angela Carder case is a tragic example of perceived conflict between the rights of the pregnant woman and those of the fetus. Decisions were made quickly, the prognosis that the infant could be saved was inaccurate, Carder's life was most certainly shortened, and she died with the knowledge that her daughter had preceded her in death. Carder's rights were clearly trampled upon by the court.

Patterns in Court-Ordered Intervention

An analysis of these cases reveals several recurrent patterns. First, a number of the women were nonwhite. The conclusion that there is a greater likelihood that court orders for obstetrical interventions (including cesarean sections, hospital detentions, and intrauterine transfusions) will be sought for minority women than for white women is borne out by a 1986 survey of obstetricians. Of twenty-one cases reported, 81 percent involved black, Asian, or Hispanic women, and 24 percent involved women whose native language was not English (Kolder, Gallagher, and Parsons 1987, 1193).

Second, in all these cases the physicians and courts rushed to judgment. Court hearings were scheduled with little notice and some were held without the pregnant woman in attendance. Defendants had inadequate opportunity to retain counsel, and if retained, counsel had little opportunity to prepare arguments. Judges were under pressure to make decisions quickly because of the perception that an unborn infant's life was threatened.

This pattern is also substantiated by the 1986 survey. In 70 percent of the cases studied, hospital administrators and lawyers were aware of the situation for a day or less before an order was sought. In 88 percent of the cases, court orders were obtained in less than six hours, and in 19 percent of the cases, the orders were issued in less than one hour. Often, the speed at which these orders are sought is ironic, since the diagnoses sometimes prove inaccurate. In six of the sixteen cases in which orders were sought requiring cesarean deliveries, the diagnosis of harm to the fetus was inaccurate (Kolder, Gallagher, and Parsons 1987, 1195).

The cases discussed in this chapter illustrate the complexities involved in utilizing the courts to force unwanted medical intervention on pregnant women. Patients are sometimes misdiagnosed and unnecessary treatments are given. Yet failure to treat some conditions can result in serious harm to the newborn that might have been prevented. The potential for conflict is great, and the conflict is not easily resolved. Another potential area of maternal-fetal conflict is maternal substance abuse during pregnancy.

Maternal Substance Abuse during Pregnancy

In recent years, there have been many reports in the news media of problems associated with maternal substance abuse during pregnancy and the consequences of that abuse for the newborn. It is difficult to characterize this as a case of conflict between the rights of the mother and those of the fetus (or born child) because most of the substances utilized (except alcohol) are illegal, and therefore no constitutional claim can be made concerning the pregnant woman's right to use them. A claim can legitimately be made, however, that the legal system can and should be used to prosecute a pregnant woman for injuring the fetus (or the born child).

A nationwide hospital study conducted in 1988 revealed that 11 percent of the pregnant women in the United States used chemical substances (Chasnoff 1989, 208). This suggests that as many as 375,000 infants per year may be exposed to such substances in utero. It is also estimated that as many as 8,000 of the infants born each year manifest the effects of fetal alcohol syndrome (Nolan 1990, 15), a leading cause of mental retardation in the United States.

Not all newborns are affected by their mothers' substance abuse during their gestation periods; however, 60 percent to 90 percent of the infants born to women with recent histories of narcotic use do show clinical signs of withdrawal. Other effects vary depending on the substance of choice, but common effects include increased rates of perinatal morbidity and mortality, premature delivery, premature separation of the placenta, neonatal meconium aspiration, and infections such as venereal diseases and hepatitis, as well as signs of withdrawal after delivery (Chasnoff 1988, 275). A New York study revealed that mortality rates of infants born to substance abusers was nearly 2.5 times the citywide rate and that three-fourths of the HIV-positive newborns were born to intravenous drug users (Chavkin, Driver and Forman 1989, 659-660).

Measuring the long-term impact of substance abuse during pregnancy is complicated by a number of factors. The population group itself is difficult to study because of its transient nature. Many substance-abusing women lack adequate nutrition and prenatal care; in the same study, only 42 percent of the substance-abusing mothers reported having received prenatal care (Chavkin, Driver, and Forman 1989, 660). Although long-term data are limited, the National Association for Perinatal Addiction Research and

Education reports that intrauterine drug exposure may place infants at risk for developmental outcome (Chasnoff et al. 1992, 284).

If utilization of chemical substances during pregnancy were a conscious choice, resolution of the rights issue would be simple. If able to choose, a pregnant woman should choose not to use drugs during pregnancy, not only because they affect the child after birth but because they are detrimental to the woman's health and are illegal. However, the underlying causes of maternal substance abuse have not been determined, and the question of "disease versus morality" continues to be debated in the United States. Nevertheless, attempts have been made to criminalize maternal substance abuse. The Center for Reproductive Law and Policy reported that as of April 1992, at least 167 women in twenty-four states had been arrested on criminal charges related to their pregnancies (1992). As of February 1995, however, no conviction for substance abuse during pregnancy had been upheld on appeal.

A well-publicized case is *Florida v. Johnson* (1989), in which Jennifer Johnson was convicted in July 1989 in Seminole County, Florida, of illegally delivering a controlled substance (cocaine) to her two children through the umbilical cord during the birth process. Although both children tested positive at birth for the presence of cocaine, neither was born addicted or was disabled. In finding her guilty, the judge took the position that her cocaine addiction was a conscious choice:

> [T]he fact that the defendant was addicted to cocaine at the time of these offenses is not a defense. The choice to use or not use cocaine is just that—a choice. Once the defendant made that choice she assumed the responsibility for the natural consequences of it. The defendant also made a choice to become pregnant and to allow those pregnancies to come to term. Upon making those choices the defendant assumed that responsibility to deliver children who were not being delivered cocaine or a derivative of it into their bodies. Children, like all persons, have the right to be free from having cocaine introduced into their systems by others.

Johnson's conviction was upheld by Florida's Fifth District Court of Appeals but reversed by the unanimous decision of the Florida Supreme Court in 1992 on the grounds that the intent of the state legislature was to treat drug-dependent mothers and newborns as public health problems, not as criminal problems. Moreover, there was insufficient evidence to support the trial court's findings that delivery of cocaine had occurred during the birth process.

The Supreme Court of Ohio reached a similar verdict in *State v. Gray* (1992); it upheld the trial court's dismissal of a grand jury indictment of child endangerment, finding that the statute did not apply to the maternal use of drugs during pregnancy. Similar decisions have been reached by state appellate courts. In Michigan, Kim Hardy was charged in 1989 with child abuse and delivery of cocaine through the umbilical cord during the birth process. The trial court dismissed the child abuse charge on grounds of insufficient evidence that Hardy's use of cocaine during pregnancy had harmed the newborn, and the Michigan Court of Appeals, in *People v. Hardy* (1991), dismissed the delivery of a controlled substance charge, finding that the legislature had not intended for the controlled substance law to be used in cases in which cocaine was transferred through the umbilical cord. In *State v. Gethers* (1991), the Fourth District Court of Appeals in Florida dismissed charges of child abuse because the statute did not apply to the fetus, and in *Welch v. Commonwealth* (1992), the Kentucky Court of Appeals reversed a criminal abuse conviction on the ground that the statute did not apply to the fetus or unborn child.

A number of lower court actions are also noteworthy, such as the 1986 California case of Pamela Ray Stewart, who did not seek prenatal care until she was seven months pregnant. Her physician advised her at that time that she had placenta previa and should not use drugs or have intercourse, and if bleeding began, she should seek prompt medical attention. Contrary to the physician's instructions, she took amphetamines and smoked marijuana, had intercourse, and did not seek prompt medical attention when she began to bleed. The prosecutor filed charges under a criminal statute requiring parents to provide medical support for their children. The trial court dismissed the charge, finding that the legislature had not intended that statute to be used to prosecute pregnant women for failing to seek prenatal care or for not following a physician's advice.

In 1988, Brenda Vaughn pleaded guilty to second-degree theft in the District of Columbia Superior Court and as part of her probation was ordered to submit to drug testing. She tested positive for cocaine, and when it was learned that she was six months pregnant, the judge ordered that she be incarcerated in order to protect the unborn child ("Criminal Law and Procedure" 1989). Prior to the theft incident, her employer had paid for inpatient drug treatment (Churchill 1989, A1). In Illinois in 1989, Melanie Green was charged with involuntary manslaughter and delivery of a controlled substance through the umbilical cord after the death of her two-day-old daughter. Both mother and infant tested positive for cocaine. Charges were later dropped when the county grand jury refused to indict (Logli 1990, 24). In 1990, Diane Pfannenstiel was charged with felony child abuse in Albany County, Wyoming, because she was intoxicated while pregnant (*Wyoming v. Pfannenstiel*). She had contacted a victim's advocacy group after an incident of family violence and was taken to a hospital (Galvan 1990), where she was arrested by police for being intoxicated. Charges were later dropped because the prosecution failed to prove the existence of an actual injury since the child had not yet been born.

There are a number of problems with attempting to criminalize maternal substance abuse. First, there are no appropriate statutes. As of April 1992, no states had established criminal penalties for giving birth to substance-exposed infants (Center for Reproductive Law and Policy 1992b). Therefore, prosecutors have attempted to utilize statutes aimed at child abuse, delivery of controlled substances, failure to provide medical support, or manslaughter. Even when successful at the trial court level, these arguments have failed at the court of appeals level.

Second, criminalization is an extremely expensive alternative; if prosecution were aggressively pursued, more prison facilities would probably be needed. In 1989, a total of 40,556 women were incarcerated nationwide in state and federal correctional facilities (U.S. Dept. of Justice 1991). Since it is estimated that in an average year more than 375,000 infants are exposed to harmful substances in utero, pursuing a large number of these cases would be extraordinarily expensive.

Third, evidentiary problems arise because not all infants exposed to such substances will suffer negative effects, and there is thus no proof of injury prior to delivery. Proof of injury after delivery, caused by maternal substance abuse during pregnancy rather than by some other factor, is also problematic.

Fourth, racial discrimination looms as a problem because minority women are more likely to be reported and charged with substance abuse than are white women. A 1989 study conducted in Pinellas County, Florida, indicated that although black women and white women had similar rates of substance abuse, black women were reported to authorities at a rate approximately ten times higher than the rate for white women (Chasnoff, Landress, and Barrett 1990, 1202). The American Civil Liberties Union reported that in 1990, more than one-half of all arrests nationwide for maternal substance abuse during pregnancy were made in South Carolina; all of these women were poor and the vast majority were black (American Civil Liberties Union Reproductive Freedom Project 1990).

Fifth, legal proceedings may create an adversarial relationship between the pregnant woman and her physician and cause the pregnant woman to resent the fetus (or born child). Both can have unfortunate consequences. Women, especially those with chemical dependency problems, should be able to seek medical care in an atmosphere of trust. Treatment of addicts is frequently difficult because they deny existence of the problem. The threat of criminal prosecution may deter women who might otherwise seek chemical dependency treatment; some may also avoid prenatal care. Moreover, removal of the infant from the mother's custody because of her detention or incarceration may interrupt the bonding process.

Sixth, there is a lack of adequate treatment facilities. Data on nationwide drug treatment programs for pregnant women are not readily available, but regional studies indicate that there are few programs that serve their needs. In New York City, 54 percent of the treatment programs categorically exclude pregnant women, and 67 percent reject pregnant Medicaid patients (Chavkin 1990, 485). An amicus curiae brief filed in the *Florida v. Johnson* appeal indicated that although 3,500 pregnant addicts were reported in the state of Florida (and an estimated 10,425 were not reported), only 135 residential beds were available for pregnant addicts in the entire state (Am. Pub. Health Ass'n. 1991).

The foregoing analysis suggests that prosecution of pregnant women for substance abuse will not ameliorate that abuse. If the aim is to protect the rights of newborns and pregnant women, prenatal care combined with maternal substance abuse treatment will be far more effective than criminalization of substance abuse. Studies indicate that prenatal care can make a significant and positive contribution to a healthy pregnancy (Torres and Kenney 1989; Witwer 1990). It is also cost effective. The Institute of Medicine estimates that increased use of general prenatal care will reduce the rate of low birth weight infants and that every $1.00 spent for prenatal care will result in a savings of $3.38 for medical care after delivery (1985, 232). Prenatal care also increases the likelihood that problems associated with maternal substance abuse can be medically managed. Another area in which maternal (as well as paternal) behavior during pregnancy has become controversial is the workplace.

Protection of the Fetus in the Workplace

One of the most volatile policy issues related to fetal health is the existence (or potential existence) of hazards in the workplace. This issue contrasts the right of the pregnant woman to control her life with the interests of the fetus in having as risk-free an environment as possible. Does the fetus have an independent right, superior to that of the mother, to require a workplace free of environmental hazards? Should a fertile woman be allowed to work in an environment that might endanger the health of her offspring? If so, how much risk and of what type should be allowable before such employment is precluded? Does evidence ever support treating men and women differently in the workplace because of potential adverse effects on their children? Although the societal interest in preventing fetal injury demands that some accommodation be made so that the mother can be removed from work environments that are known to be dangerous, society has also made a commitment to remove barriers to women's choice of careers. Because these two goals conflict, the issue has become an important public policy concern.

The threat of workplace hazards to the developing fetus came to public attention in 1975 with the publication of a federal government-sponsored report on the occupational health problems of pregnant women (Hunt 1975). This report detailed the increasing scientific evidence that occupational exposure to some chemicals can affect a woman's capacity to produce normal children. In response to the public concern aroused by this report about workplace risks to the pregnant woman, many American companies, including Dow Chemical, Du Pont, Exxon, Shell Oil, Monsanto, and General Motors, established "fetal protection policies" that exclude all fertile women from positions in which workers are exposed to high levels of toxicants or potential toxicants. Since the early 1980s, an estimated 100,000 jobs have been closed to women because of the existence of reproductive hazards, and 20,000,000 other positions are subject to closure (Becker 1986, 1226).

The controversy over exclusionary policies should be viewed in the context of women's struggle to overcome overt job discrimination, in many instances rationalized by a woman's pregnancy. Companies that enforce such policies have justified their actions by arguing that the developing fetus has a right to be protected from injuries that might result if the mother is exposed to workplace toxicants. Employers are also attempting to avoid possible tort liability in cases that might be brought as the result of the birth of a child affected by a toxicant. These policies have raised serious concerns about the right of women to equal employment opportunity, however. Critics of exclusionary policies argue they encroach on women's civil rights and that fertile women, not employers, must make decisions that are best for themselves and for their fetuses.

Scientific Evidence of Fetal Harm

It is extremely difficult to prove any linkage between environmental hazards and harm to the fetus. One reason is that a combination of and interaction between two or more agents is often the cause, but they are very difficult to isolate. Also, much of the data are necessarily based on case reports or epidemiological studies, which yield statistical evidence but do not determine cause. Statistical data are amenable to varying interpretation depending on the perspective of the user, and thus can lead to conflicting conclusions. Toxic substances can harm the fetus either indirectly, by altering the mother's or father's genetic material or reproductive system, or directly, by affecting the developing fetus in utero. Mutagenic agents alter the chromosomal structure of the parent's genetic material; teratogenic agents operate directly on the fetus, causing developmental malformations.

Table 7-2   Potential Fetal Health Hazards in Selected Occupations

Occupation/field	Female employment (in thousands, 1988 est.)	Potential risk factors
Health care (nurse, nurses' aide, dental assistant, laboratory technician)	3,500	Ionizing radiation, infection, mercury vapor, anesthetic gases, disinfectants and sterilizing agents, phenolic compounds
Clothing and textiles, laundry and dry-cleaning	1,350	Benzidene-type dyes, formaldehyde, solvents, carbon disulfide
Office worker	14,500	Benzene in rubber cement, cleaning compounds, and solvents; ozone or methanol and ammonia from duplicating machines; air contaminants
Hairdresser, cosmetologist	750	Bleaches, hair dyes, nail varnishes (acetone, toluene, xylene, plasticizers)
Janitorial maid; cleaning, household jobs	1,750	Cleaning substances, disinfectants, bleach/ammonia, organic solvents
Child care	1,185	Infections

Source: Adapted from Bureau of Labor Statistics, *Employment and Earnings,* January 1989.

In addition, transplacental carcinogenic agents (such as diethylstilbestrol) have been identified that are capable of acting on the cells of the fetus and can eventually cause cancer to develop in their offspring (Sor 1986-1987, 156). Table 7-2 illustrates potential hazards in occupations which employ large numbers of women.

Although the precise mechanisms by which chemicals affect the fetus are unknown, there is mounting evidence that a number of substances can have a devastating impact on the fetus. The registry of the National Institute for Occupational Safety and Health lists more than 79,000 chemical substances known to have toxic effects. Although only 30 to 40 of these agents are proven human teratogens, more than 1,000 have exhibited some teratogenic potential in animal studies (1988, 2).

Of the tens of thousands of chemicals and chemical substances commonly present in the workplace, the substance with the most well-documented link to fetal damage is lead. Lead rapidly crosses the placental barrier early in gestation, when the fetus is most vulnerable to its effects (Crocetti, Mushak, and Schwartz 1990). Preganant female workers exposed to high levels of lead are at abnormally high risk for spontaneous abortion and stillbirth. Maternal exposure to elevated levels of lead during pregnancy has been correlated with mental retardation, intrauterine growth retardation, and neurological disorders in the offspring. Inorganic and organic mercury have also been found to cross the placental barrier in experimental animals and humans and to cause damage to the central nervous system of the fetus, resulting in mental retardation, cerebral palsy, seizures, and blindness, as well as heightened rates of stillbirth (Smith 1977).

Many other substances widely used in industry are known or suspected to have adverse effects on the reproductive systems of exposed female workers. Chromosomal damage has been reported in workers exposed to the solvent benzene, an element in paint strippers, rubber cement, nylon, and detergents. Anesthetic gases have produced miscarriages, as well as birth defects in the progeny of both male and female operating room and dental personnel. Exposure to pesticides and chlorinated hydrocarbons, used in the manufacture of dry-cleaning fluid and other general solvents, has caused serious fetal damage. Female workers exposed to vinyl chloride risk severe impairment of their reproductive systems; exposure has been linked to abnormal rates of miscarriage and chromosomal damage to fetuses.

Today more than 75 percent of the workers making semiconductors and printed wiring circuit boards are women (Quinn and Woskie 1988, 489). They are exposed on a daily basis, and often under conditions of inadequate ventilation, to a wide variety of hazardous agents, including solvents, acids, resins, adhesives, sealants, rubber, and plastics. Furthermore, soldering and welding operations result in the formation of toxic gases and may involve solders such as cadmium and lead (Hunt 1979, 135). Other agents have also been linked to fetal harm. Women in the health industry are exposed to ionizing radiation, which can cause substantial fetal damage. Such women may also contract infections that can cross the placental barrier and cause spontaneous abortion, fetal infection, or fetal abnormalities.

The Paternal Contribution to Fetal Damage

With a few exceptions, male and female animals of the same species differ little in susceptibility to the toxic effects of chemicals. Age, weight, and developmental maturity are more important determinants than sex. Toxic chemicals thus affect both male and female reproductive systems;

both eggs and sperm are susceptible to damage from radiation, viral infection, and chemical insult. But because male and female reproductive systems differ, there are significant differences in the ways they are affected by toxic agents.

Only recently has research on workplace hazards focused on the male human; however, extensive research on experimental animals and a few of the studies done on humans suggest that reproductive harm to fertile males can be manifested in birth defects in the worker's offspring. For instance, there is evidence that males exposed to lead have a decreased ability to produce normal sperm. The mates of such males might have abnormal pregnancies. The mates of males exposed to vinyl chloride have a significantly higher than normal rate of fetal loss. Moreover, the children of these males, and children born in communities located near vinyl chloride-processing facilities, have an increased incidence of congenital birth defects. The herbicides DBCP; Kepone; 2, 4, 5-T; DDT; 2, 4-D; and Agent Orange may have teratogenic effects on the progeny of exposed males, although the findings are far from conclusive (Office of Technology Assessment 1985, 74-78). Recent findings that sperm may transport cocaine to the ovum might explain why cocaine use in males is linked to abnormal development in their offspring; this might be one mechanism for the transmission of a broad range of toxicants to male progeny (Yazigi, Odem, and Polakoski 1991, 1956).

Despite the evidence of a male contribution to fetal damage, most employer policy initiatives continue to focus attention on female workers. According to the Council on Environmental Quality, however, the potential adverse effect of the fetus is not a valid scientific reason for treating men and women unequally. The fairness of an employer policy cannot be judged until more research is done on the potential contribution to fetal damage of male workers who have been exposed to teratogens or mutagens. The factual evidence that harm is transmitted primarily by women can then be a valid basis for excluding women of childbearing age from employment because of possible effects of toxicants on the fetus. Clearly, if a substance harms both men and women and their offspring, any policy that excludes only women discriminates on the basis of sex. If a workplace toxicant puts both women and men employees at risk but only women are excluded, then the men are also discriminated against because they are allowed to work in jobs that endanger their reproductive capacities (Clement et al. 1987, 522).

Government Response to Employer Fetal Protection Policies

In October 1978, Congress passed the Pregnancy Discrimination Act, which includes the Pregnancy Amendment to Title VII of the 1964 Civil

Rights Act. This amendment left no doubt that Congress considered discrimination on the basis of pregnancy to be a case of sex discrimination. The amendment states that ''women affected by pregnancy, childbirth, or related medical conditions shall be treated the same for all employment-related purposes . . . as other persons not so affected.'' A clash was virtually ensured between two interest groups: employers intent on excluding pregnant women from certain jobs, and pregnant employees who wished to be temporarily excused from certain jobs.

While the Pregnancy Discrimination Act put pregnancy on a par with other forms of sex discrimination under Title VII, it must be understood that Title VII provides exceptions to prohibition against discrimination. In each case, however, the burden of proof is on the employer to defend the exception. There are two defenses available to employers in Title VII challenges. The first, the Bona Fide Occupational Qualification (BFOQ) can be advanced only if two conditions are met: (1) invocation of the qualification must be reasonably necessary to the conduct of the employer's business; and (2) the employer must have a reasonable factual basis for believing that virtually all women would be unable to perform the duties of the job safely and efficiently. The second defense for making such employment distinctions is ''business necessity'': the business purpose must be ''sufficiently compelling'' to override any discriminatory impact.

In the 1980s, the courts issued a series of confusing and contradictory decisions that concerned employers' fetal protection policies. In *Wright v. Olin* (1982), the Fourth Circuit Court of Appeals attempted to balance the requirements of Title VII and evidence of fetal vulnerability to workplace hazards. Although the court found the Olin Corporation's exclusionary policy to be in violation of Title VII, it rejected the argument that all classifications based on pregnancy constitute disparate treatment of women. The court said, however, that in order to use the business necessity defense, Olin must prove that protection of the fetus requires restrictions only on female employees. In *Hayes v. Shelby Memorial Hospital* (1984) the Eleventh Circuit Court of Appeals found that the hospital's policy of firing a pregnant X-ray technician violated Title VII and concluded that in order to avoid liability, ''an employer must adopt the most effective policy available with the least discriminatory impact possible'' (at 1553).

The key court decisions that led to action by the Supreme Court on exclusionary policies centered on the fetal protection policy of Johnson Controls, a manufacturer of automotive batteries. In 1989 the U.S. Court of Appeals for the Seventh District (*United Automotive Workers v. Johnson Controls*) reaffirmed the district court ruling that Johnson Controls's policy was reasonably necessary to industrial safety. According to the Appeals Court, available scientific data indicate that the risk of transmission of harm to the fetus as a result of lead exposure is confined to fertile female employees (at 889). The employer's fetal protection policy was based on real differences between men and women relating to childbearing capacity and was consistent with Title VII.

In a conflicting state ruling, however, the California Court of Appeals, Fourth District (*Johnson Controls v. California Fair Employment and Housing Commission,* 1990), reversed a superior court decision and found that Johnson Controls's policy violated the California Fair Employment and Housing Act. The appellate court held that the fetal protection program "unquestionably discriminates against women" because only women are affected by its terms (at 160). It concluded that categorical discrimination against a subclass of women such as all women of childbearing capacity violates the California statute prohibiting discrimination on the basis of sex. Contrary to the U.S. Court of Appeals in *United Automotive Workers,* the California court held that Johnson Controls could not defend its fetal protection program as a Bona Fide Occupational Qualification.

On March 20, 1991, the Court issued its ruling on *United Automotive Workers v. Johnson Controls,* on an appeal from the Court of Appeals for the Seventh Circuit. In a 9-0 decision (with four concurring opinions), the Court reversed the lower court's decision and remanded the case to the Seventh Circuit. The Court stated that the bias in Johnson Controls' fetal protection policy was obvious because fertile men, but not fertile women, were given a choice as to whether they wanted to risk their reproductive health by holding a particular job (at 7). Justice Blackmun, who wrote the majority opinion, held that the company's fetal protection policy represented disparate treatment and thus required the more difficult BFOQ defense. The Johnson Controls policy classified on the basis of gender and child-bearing capacity rather than fertility alone, said the Court, because it did not seek to protect the unconceived children of its male employees, despite "evidence in the record about the debilitating effect of lead exposure on the male reproductive system" (at 9). Johnson Controls chose to treat all its female employees as potentially pregnant; that choice "evinces discrimination on the basis of sex" in clear violation of Title VII (at 10). Furthermore, the absence of a malevolent motive did not convert an overtly discriminatory policy into a neutral policy that simply happens to have a disparate impact on men and women.

In the Pregnancy Discrimination Act, Congress had made clear that the decision to become pregnant or to work while being either pregnant or capable of becoming pregnant was reserved for an individual woman to make for herself. The Court concluded that the language of both the BFOQ provisions and the Pregnancy Discrimination Act that amended it, as well as the legislative history and the case law, prohibited an employer from discriminating against a woman because of her capacity to become pregnant unless her reproductive potential prevented her from performing the duties of her job. The BFOQ defense thus did not apply because the fetus to be protected was not part of the workplace environment, nor did the fetus qualify for a special "third party" exception. The Court therefore had "no difficulty concluding that Johnson Controls could not establish a BFOQ" (at 17).

Although the Court was divided on whether fetal protection policies could ever conceivably be justified under the BFOQ defense (in concurring opinions, White, Rehnquist, Kennedy, and Scalia did not rule such policies out), all nine justices agreed that the Johnson Controls policy could not. No matter how sincere Johnson Controls was in its concern about prenatal injury, the company did not "begin to show that substantially all of its fertile women employees are incapable of doing their jobs" (at 18).

State and federal regulatory agencies have also taken action regarding employer fetal protection policies. Because of the various and often confusing standards that have been established in case law, it was thought that government regulation of workplace reproductive hazards would provide an effective solution. Reproductive hazards can be regulated by a variety of federal agencies, but confusion has been created because of the jurisdictional conflict among them. Regulatory action is based on the 1970 Occupational Safety and Health Act and the 1976 Toxic Substances Control Act. The purpose of the first act is "to assure so far as possible every working man and woman in the Nation safe and healthful working conditions" (29 U.S.C. 6516, 970). The act provides the secretary of labor with various mechanisms for regulating workplace safety and health, including a "general duty" clause stipulating that each employer "shall furnish to each of his employees employment and a place of employment which are free from recognized hazards that are causing or are likely to cause death or serious physical harm to his employees" (29 U.S.C. 654(1)).

In 1980, the Occupational Safety and Health Administration concluded that exclusionary policies such as those aimed at pregnant women undermine the principle that the workplace should be a safe environment for all persons. Instead of discriminating against women of childbearing age or raising the possibility that they might wish to end their fertility, employers should establish exposure standards that take such vulnerability into account. High-risk industries should not be able to reduce their liability for damage awards by excluding classes of workers. Moreover, no worker should be forced to sacrifice her reproductive right to privacy in order to hold her job.

In 1988, after what Rep. August Hawkins (D-Calif.) termed a decade of "abdication of enforcement activities" by the Equal Employment Opportunity Commission (U.S. Congress, House 1990, 12), the EEOC issued its first policy guideline on reproductive and fetal hazards, which states that any practice that denies employment opportunities to one sex because of reproductive or fetal hazard, without similarly barring the other sex, is unlawful under Title VII. The EEOC recognized the application of the less difficult business necessity defense in fetal liability cases but stated that employers invoking that defense must demonstrate that there is a substantial risk of harm to the fetus, that the risk is transmitted only through women, and that there are no less restrictive alternatives to exclusion of women from the workplace. Any such denial of employment must be justified by objective, scientific evidence of substantial harm, which the EEOC admitted would be difficult to supply, given the inconclusiveness of much of the research on fetal hazards. Although the 1988 policy guideline does not declare every fetal protection policy unlawful, it is designed to prevent unnecessary restrictions on women's employment opportunities.

In January 1990, the EEOC published an additional policy guideline in response to the decision of the Seventh Circuit Court of Appeals in *Johnson Controls.* The EEOC rejected the court's ruling because it placed the burden of proof on the employee. Because fetal protection cases involve overtly discriminatory policies, the burden of proof must be on the employer to prove that its fetal protection policy is a business necessity rather than on the plaintiff to prove that it is not. Therefore, in cases the EEOC handles, it will require employers to prove that protection of fetuses from risk is reasonably necessary to the normal operation of their businesses and that the exclusionary policy is reasonably necessary to implement the protections. The employer must supply objective, scientific evidence of substantial harm in order to restrict access to jobs. A subjective judgment or a good faith belief that an exclusionary policy is necessary to protect employees or to minimize liability is not a valid defense of exclusionary policies.

Balancing Interests in the Workplace

Given the growing evidence of potential harm to fetal health resulting from workplace hazards, some balance must be found between the competing claims of employers and women, and the interests of unborn children. As in cases of coerced obstetrical intervention and maternal substance abuse, the burden of proof that potential harm exists must be borne by those who would constrain the rights and choices of pregnant and fertile women. Employers' exclusionary policies that result in the differential treatment of male and female employees and the failure to protect pregnant women in workplaces heavily dependent on female employees raise critical questions concerning the motivation behind fetal protection policies.

Unfortunately, the debate over fetal protection policies in the 1980s did not emphasize the wide range of reproductive hazards that face both women and men in the workplace. The reduction of these hazards and the establishment of comprehensive preventive health measures will do more in the long run to maximize fetal health than have the exclusionary policies instituted in traditionally male-dominated industries. Guaranteed access to prenatal care, pregnancy leave with job security, and expanded employment opportunities for all women should be the priorities if the goal of healthy children is to be realized (Blank 1993, 1828-1829).

Conclusion

In the areas of court-ordered obstetrical intervention, maternal substance abuse, and workplace hazards, the rights of the born child would appear to be paramount. Many would argue that the born child is entitled to a positive right of a healthy environment during gestation and that the pregnant woman has a duty to protect the health of the fetus. This argument is not as straightforward as it would seem, however. Because technology is available to diagnose and treat the fetus in utero, does it follow that women must submit to such procedures even though they might contradict the woman's religious, moral, or cultural values? Should pregnant women be required to follow the advice of physicians or judges who are third-party participants in the reproductive process? Should women be prosecuted for their behavior during pregnancy if they were chemically addicted and unable to make rational choices? Finally, should women be required to undergo sterilization or face losing their jobs because of reproductive hazards in the workplace if the defects caused by the same or similar hazards can be transmitted to the fetus from its father as well as from its mother?

Such complex questions make it is difficult to find a balance. Both pregnant women and their partners have moral obligations to protect the fetus. This does not necessarily mean that such protection should be ordered by the court, or that the courts should never intervene. In the cases discussed in this chapter, the courts had an unenviable track record in predicting pregnancy outcome. In cases of maternal substance abuse, the rights of both the born child and the pregnant women are best served by treatment rather than prosecution. And with regard to reproductive hazards in the workplace, it is clear that fetal protection policies have been discriminatory against women. Most potential parents will make every effort to ensure the birth of a healthy child. For the most part, pregnant women and their partners should be allowed to make their own judgments about their personal activities relative to their reproductive capacities.

C H A P T E R   8

Issues in Fetal and Embryo Research

An extension of the debate over reproductive rights and of the conflict among various interests in human reproduction centers on the utilization of human embryos and fetuses for research and as sources of cells, tissues, and organs. (The term embryo generally refers to the stages of development until about the eighth week after conception while the fetal period extends from nine weeks to term.) All of the reproductive technologies discussed in earlier chapters are dependent at some stage on research on human organisms. Therefore, the regulation and funding of fetal and embryo research are critical for the development and transmission of knowledge about such technologies, ranging from fertility control to diagnostic techniques.

The political controversy over fetal and embryo research is basically a disagreement about its moral and legal status. There is evidence that abortion politics have had a stifling effect on many areas of this research (Gold and Lehrman 1989, 6). The issue of abortion ''looms heavily in the background of any discussion of policies regarding research on conceptuses [embryos and fetuses]'' (Andrews 1993, 26). Because federal funding of basic research, largely through the National Institutes of Health, is so important, recent restrictions on the funding of specific types of fetal and embryo research have raised questions concerning the long-term impact of such policies on reproductive science and health (Donovan 1990, 224).

Because the fetus is unable to consent to being a research subject, concern has been expressed about whose consent is necessary and what type of consent is sufficient. Questions also arise as to the types of fetal research that ought to be pursued, the proper ends of such research, and how research needs can be balanced with the interests of the pregnant woman.

The issue of fetal research has appeared on the political agenda sporadically since the mid-1970s and has been addressed by national and presidential commissions, Congress, and many state legislatures.

Although there are various degrees of support for and opposition to particular applications of fetal research, in general there are two sides in the debate. On one side are the research community and its supporters, who argue that research using the human fetus and embryo materials is critical for progress in many areas of medicine. The general sources of fetal material include tissue from dead fetuses; pre-viable or nonviable fetuses in utero generally prior to an elective abortion; nonviable living fetuses ex utero; tissue from dead fetuses used in fetal tissue transplantation research; and embryos, in vitro and preimplantation. By and large the research community recognizes no moral objections to the use of fetal tissues from electively aborted fetuses for basic research and transplantation, and they cite a wide range of areas where significant contributions can be made.

On the other side are anti-abortion groups, who claim that the use of aborted fetuses for research will give abortion greater legitimacy and will encourage its use to further research efforts or for therapy for individual patients. They contend that use of embryos and fetuses for research exploits them as the means to another person's ends and dehumanizes them. Other interests not totally opposed to such research also express concern about potential commercialization of and payment for fetal tissues, and raise questions regarding the ownership of fetal tissues and the definition of acceptable uses of such material.

This chapter begins with a summary of the types of fetal and embryo research and their major applications. It then looks in more depth at neural grafting of fetal tissues, which extends the issue of rights beyond reproduction toward therapy for adult patients. After discussing the current state of neural grafting research, attention is shifted to the emerging political framework for fetal and embryo research at the federal and state levels. The chapter returns to the policy controversy surrounding neural fetal tissue transplantation and the political conflict over funding which has accompanied it since its development in 1988. It traces the regulatory and funding priorities of the Reagan and Bush administrations and the policy shift instituted by President Bill Clinton immediately upon taking office.

Types of Fetal and Embryo Research

It is difficult to generalize about fetal and embryo research because there are many types of research, conducted in many different areas. One important distinction is that between investigational research, which is not beneficial to the fetus, and therapeutic research, which may be beneficial to

Table 8-1   Areas of Fetal and Embryo Research

Fetal research (postimplantation)

Investigational: When and how is HIV transmitted in utero? Can the rubella vaccine pass through the placenta? Is first-trimester chorionic villi sampling as safe and as accurate a method of prenatal diagnosis as mid-trimester amniocentisis?

Therapeutic: Is in utero surgery an effective treatment for fetal diaphragmatic hernia? Will dexamethasone prevent the harmful effects of fetal adrenal hyperplasia?

Fetal tissue research (dead fetuses)

Includes testing vaccines in fetal cell lines, growing cell cultures using fetal cells, and testing fetal cells for expression of DNA.

Fetal tissue transplant research (dead fetuses)

Can fetal neural cells replace dopamine in Parkinsonism? Can fetal pancreatic islet cells treat juvenile diabetes? Can fetal bone marrow or live cells be used in treatment of fetal genetic disorders?

Embryo research (in vitro and preimplantation)

Can karyotypes be made of the cell nucleii of human embryos? Can DNA from one cell taken from several embryos be analyzed prior to transfer to the uterus? Can the pregnancy rate of in vitro fertilization be increased?

RU-486

Is mifepristone an effective ''contragestive''? Contraceptive? The ''contragestive'' research involves expulsion of the postimplantation embryo in an unwanted pregnancy.

Source: Adapted from Fletcher 1993, 202.

the fetus but is more likely to be beneficial to potential future fetuses. Another key variable is the stage of development of the human organism when the research is conducted, from preimplantation to the late fetal stages. The variety of potential uses of fetal tissue is virtually unlimited; five important areas are summarized in Table 8-1.

Fetal Development Studies

The purpose of studying fetal development and physiology is to increase scientific knowledge about normal fetal development in order to provide a basis for identifying and understanding abnormal processes and, ultimately, to eliminate birth deformities. Most fetal development studies involve autopsies of dead fetuses; the development of fetal behavior can also be studied in utero by monitoring fetal breathing movements. Fetal hearing, vision, and taste capabilities have been documented following the application of various stimuli to the live fetus in utero. Studies of fetal physiology utilize the fetus in utero as well as organs and tissues removed from the dead fetus. This research sometimes requires the administration of drugs to the woman prior to abortion or delivery by caesarean section, followed by analysis to detect the presence of the substance or its metabolic effects in a sample of umbilical cord blood or in the fetal tissue. Most controversial are the physiological studies that include observation of nonviable but live fetuses outside the uterus to test for response to touch and to detect the presence of swallowing movements.

Diagnostic Research

Diagnostic research focuses on the development of techniques (such as amniocentesis) to diagnose fetal problems. Initially, such research was conducted primarily on amniotic samples withdrawn as a routine part of induced abortion to determine the normal values for enzymes known to be defective in genetic diseases. Once it had been demonstrated that the particular enzyme was expressed in fetal cells and the normal values were known, this information was used in the diagnosis of the abnormal condition in the fetus at risk. Prenatal diagnostic research on fetuses has concentrated on the extension of these diagnostic capacities to other genetic diseases, the development of chorionic villus sampling, and the detection of fetal cells in maternal blood samples.

Diagnostic research has also been directed at the identification of physical defects in the developing fetus. Accomplishments in the last two decades include such procedures as ultrasonography, alpha-fetoprotein tests, amniography, tests to determine fetal lung capacity, and a variety of techniques for monitoring fetal well-being and detecting distress. In each case, animal studies were first undertaken to establish the safety and efficacy of the procedure; human fetal research was then conducted in a variety of settings. Fetoscopy, for example, because of its potential risk to the fetus, was developed selectively in women undergoing elective abortion. The procedure was performed prior to abortion and an autopsy was performed afterward to determine its technical success.

Pharmacological Studies

Studies to determine the effects of drugs on the developing fetus are largely retrospective. All studies of oral contraceptives or other drugs as a possible cause of multiple births or congenital abnormalities, and most studies of the effects on the fetus of drugs administered to treat maternal illness during pregnancy, have been retrospective. The fetus or infant is examined after an accidental exposure to a drug and is never intentionally exposed to it for research purposes. However, substances are sometimes intentionally administered to pregnant women prior to abortion in order to compare quantitative movement of these agents across the placenta as well as their absolute levels achieved in fetal tissues. These studies serve as guidelines for drug selection in the treatment of intrauterine infections such as syphilis; dead fetuses are examined after abortion to assess the superiority of one drug over another.

Embryo Research

The availability of human embryos for research purposes was a result of the development of in vitro fertilization. In 1982, Patrick Steptoe and Robert Edwards, who four years earlier had reported the first birth made possible by IVF, announced plans to freeze "spare" (untransferred) embryos for possible clinical or laboratory use. Theoretically, the number of spare embryos could be increased by the deliberate creation of embryos for research, if donors consented to having their gametes or embryos used in this way. Another potential source of human embryos for research is harvesting by means of embryo lavage. However, there is considerable hesitancy to initiate the deliberate production of embryos for research, even though that might be the only way to satisfy expanding research needs.

Although all assisted reproduction technologies are experimental at some stage and thus might be described as research, there are many nonclinical uses of human embryos that more clearly fit the research paradigm. They can be used in (1) the development and testing of oral contraceptives; (2) the investigation of abnormal cell growth; (3) analysis of the development of chromosomal abnormalities; (4) implantation studies; and (5) cancer and AIDS research. Potential genetic uses of the embryos include (1) experimental alteration of gene structures; (2) preimplantational screening for chromosomal anomalies and genetic diseases; (3) preimplantation therapy to treat genetic defects; and (4) the development of characteristic selection techniques, including sex preselection. Research on artificial placentas is also dependent on the availability of human embryos at some stage.

Fetal Tissue Transplantation

In many areas of fetal research, the tissue is used to develop a treatment that might be beneficial to future fetuses. In fetal transplantation research, the tissue *is* the treatment used for the possible benefit of an identifiable adult patient. Many contend that the use of fetal tissue to benefit individual recipients is ethically questionable because, unlike the transplantation of adult organs, there are no possible benefits to particular fetuses or to future fetuses (Nolan 1988, 13).

Despite the ethical controversy surrounding the use of fetal tissue, many scientists consider it especially well suited for grafting (Weiss 1989; Lindvall et al. 1990). Fetal tissue cells replicate more rapidly than those of adult tissue and have the capacity to differentiate into functioning mature cells. This capacity is maximal in the early stages of fetal development and diminishes gradually throughout gestation. Moreover, unlike mature tissue, fetal tissue has been found to have considerable potential for growth and restoration when transplanted to a host organism. Nutritional support provided by blood vessels from the host is readily accepted and likely promoted by fetal tissue (Auerbach 1988).

In animal experiments, fetal tissue has displayed a considerable capacity for survival within the graft recipient. Fetal cells also appear to have the ability to resist oxygen deprivation, which makes them especially useful for transplantation (Mullen 1992, 5). Furthermore, fetal cells are easily cultured in the laboratory, thus allowing the development of specific cell lines. They are also amenable to cryopreservation, and because of their immunological immaturity, fetal cells are less likely than adult cells to provoke an immune response leading to rejection by the host organism (Office of Technology Assessment 1990, 43).

Although fetal tissue transplantation is still largely experimental, it has many potential uses (see Table 8-2). Only one treatment is proven to be effective: fetal thymus transplants have been the standard treatment for the rare DiGeorge's syndrome for more than twenty years (Office of Technology Assessment 1990, 151). Despite less than encouraging success, fetal pancreatic tissue transplants are seen as promising for the treatment of juvenile diabetes. Fetal liver cells have been transplanted with reasonable success to patients with aplastic anemia, but clinical trials and more research are needed to ascertain the responsible mechanism for the recovery of these patients. Potential applications of fetal liver tissue transplants include treatment of bone marrow diseases such as severe combined immunodeficiency and acute leukemia when HLA-matched donors are not available, inherited metabolic storage disorders, and radiation accidents.

Neural Grafting Research

The grafting of fetal neural tissue has already stimulated considerable policy debate. The Office of Technology Assessment noted in 1990 that many neurological disorders, including Parkinson's disease, Huntington's disease, Alzheimer's disease, stroke, epilepsy, multiple sclerosis, and amyotrophic lateral sclerosis, as well as brain and spinal cord injuries, are

Table 8-2 **Potentially Treatable Clinical Conditions and Types of Human Fetal Tissue Transplanted**

Condition	Tissue
Acute leukemia	Liver
Addison's disease	Adrenal
Aplastic anemia	Liver
Bare lymphocyte syndrome	Liver
DiGeorge's syndrome	Thymus
Huntington's disease	Neural
Juvenile diabetes	Pancreas
Metabolic storage disorders	
Fabry's disease	Liver
Fucosidosis	Liver
Gaucher's disease	Liver
Glycogenosis	Liver
Hunter's disease	Liver, fibroblasts
Hurler's disease	Liver, fibroblasts
Metachromatic leukodystrophy	Liver
Morquio's syndrome, type B	Liver
Niemann-Pick disease, types A, B, C	Liver
Sanfilippo's syndrome, type B	Liver
Parkinson's disease	Neural, adrenal
Radiation accidents	Liver
Schizophrenia	Neural
Severe combined immunodeficiency	Liver and thymus

Source: Vawter 1993, 80

potentially amenable to the grafting of fetal central nervous system (CNS) cells. (Table 8-3 illustrates the large numbers of persons who might be candidates for such procedures.) It emphasized, however, that at best only a subset of the patients suffering from a particular disorder is likely to benefit from neural grafting (1990, 93). To date, the controversy has centered on neural grafting to treat Parkinson's patients.

In 1988 announcement was made of the successful grafting of human fetal neural tissue in the brains of Parkinson's patients in Mexico (Madrazo et al. 1988) and Sweden (Lindvall et al. 1988). Clinical trials using fetal neural tissue were subsequently begun in many countries, including Great Britain and the United States. By 1992 at least two dozen Parkinson's patients in the United States had had fetal tissue grafts. The first American patient to undergo the procedure showed improvement in movement and motor coordination after fifteen months (Freed et al. 1990, 505). Forty-six months after the procedure, this American patient was still doing well. Six other Parkinson's patients with fetal tissue grafts showed similar improvement, leading some to conclude that "fetal tissue implants appear to offer

Table 8-3 Prevalence of Neurological Disorders in the United States

Neurological disorder	Prevalence
Alzheimer's disease	1 to 5 million
Stroke	2.8 million
Epilepsy	1.5 million
Parkinson's disease	500,000 to 650,000
Multiple sclerosis	250,000
Spinal cord injury	180,000
Brain injury	70,000 to 90,000
Huntington's disease	25,000
Amyotrophic lateral sclerosis	15,000

Source: Office of Technology Assessment 1990, 93.

long-term clinical benefit to some patients with advanced Parkinson's disease'' (Freed, Breeze, and Rosenberg 1992, 1549). Although patients continued to be disabled by their disease, the symptoms of Parkinson's were found to be diminished during eighteen months of evaluation (Spencer et al. 1992, 1541).

Despite such reports of success, many researchers remain skeptical of fetal neural tissue grafting and argue that additional basic animal research is needed, coupled with limited human experimentation. Don Gash and John Sladek believe that

> too many questions remain unanswered about the use of embryonic nerve cells to propose anything more than limited fetal grafting in humans . . . . Although scientifically it seems logical to proceed, considerable information is needed before therapeutic success may be predicted. (1989, 366)

In addition to a number of potential risks, there are questions of policy concerning informed consent, the blurred boundaries between experimentation and therapy, and the ethics and politics of using human fetal tissue.

One risk factor is possible immune system rejection. Although fetal neural tissue grafts do not appear to be immediately rejected, long-term rejection is a possibility, which would create a need for immunosuppressants. Also, research to date has centered on testing the ability of grafts to provide relief from symptoms and reduced disability; it has not addressed the question of whether grafts can achieve cessation or reversal of the degenerative process. The grafted tissue might be susceptible to the same pathological processes that characterize the disorder being treated.

Furthermore, the assessment of fetal neural tissue grafts in Parkinson's patients has revealed unwanted psychological effects such as hallucinations, confusion, and somnolence (Goetz et al. 1989). Invasive graft placements in the brain might cause excessive bleeding or injury to the brain tissue. Surgery also temporarily disrupts the protective blood-brain barrier near the graft site, posing a further threat to the patient's health. Another risk is that fetal neural tissue, some nonneuronal tissue, and continuous cell lines can continue to replicate, thus presenting the possibility of excessive graft enlargement. This expanding mass of tissue might itself compress and permanently damage the host brain tissue, obstruct the flow of cerebrospinal fluid (dangerously increasing pressure on the brain), and result in tumor formation (Office of Technology Assessment 1990, 53).

The Politics of Fetal Research

Establishment of a National Commission

Fetal research appeared on the national policy agenda for the first time in the early 1970s, following widely publicized reports of gruesome experiments conducted on live fetuses. In response, Congress in 1974 passed the National Research Act (Public Law 93-345), which established the National Commission for the Protection of Human Subjects of Biomedical and Behavioral Research, charged with investigating the scientific, legal, and ethical aspects of fetal research. The statute prohibited the conduct of any federally funded research on fetuses prior to or subsequent to abortion until the commission made its recommendations and regulations were adopted.

In 1975 the commission issued its recommendations, which established a framework for the conduct of fetal research; regulations concerning the federal funding of such research were promulgated in 1976 (45 CFR 46.201-211). Under these regulations, certain types of fetal research are fundable; constraints are based on parental consent and minimization of risk to the pregnant woman and the fetus. With respect to use of cadaver fetuses, the regulations defer to state and local laws in accordance with the provisions of the Uniform Anatomical Gift Act. This act was drafted by the Commissioners on Uniform State Laws and adopted in all fifty states. It provides guidelines for the donation and receipt of cadavers for research, education, therapy, and transplantation. Although the act includes stillborn infants and fetal cadavers, some states have excluded fetuses from their provisions of the law. In general, fetal cadaver tissue is to be treated the same as any other part of a human cadaver.

The regulations stipulate that appropriate studies on animal fetuses must precede research on live fetuses. The consent of the pregnant woman and the prospective father (if reasonably possible to obtain) are required and the research must not alter the pregnancy termination procedure in a way that would cause greater than "minimal risk" to either the pregnant woman or the fetus. Moreover, researchers must not have a role in determining the abortion procedure or assessing fetal viability. If it is unclear whether an ex utero fetus is viable, that fetus cannot be the subject of research unless the purpose of the research is to enhance its chances of survival *or* the research subjects the fetus to no additional risk and its purpose is to develop important, otherwise unobtainable, knowledge. Research on living, nonviable fetuses ex utero is allowed if the vital functions of the fetus are not artificially maintained. Finally, fetal research in utero is permissible if (1) it is designed to be therapeutic for the particular fetus and subjects the fetus to the minimal risk necessary to meet its health needs, or (2) it imposes minimal risks and promises to produce important knowledge unobtainable by other means.

Federal Regulation of Fetal Research

In 1985, Congress passed a law (42 U.S.C. 289) forbidding federal sponsorship or funding of research on viable fetuses ex utero, with the exception of therapeutic research or research that poses no added risk of suffering, injury, or death to the fetus *and* may lead to important knowledge unobtainable by other means. Research on living fetuses in utero is still permitted, but the standard of risk for fetuses to be aborted is required to be the same as for fetuses that will be carried to term.

Congress also passed legislation in 1985 (42 U.S.C. 275) creating a Biomedical Ethics Board whose first order of business was to study the issue of fetal research. In 1988, Congress suspended the power of the secretary of the Department of Health and Human Services to authorize waivers of the risk provisions of existing federal regulations in cases of individual need and cases that had significant scientific benefit until the Biomedical Ethics Board Advisory Committee had conducted a study of the nature, advisability, and implications of the exercise of such a waiver. In 1989, however, the activities of the committee itself were suspended, leaving the question of waivers unresolved.

Federal regulations thus seem to be quite clear in allowing the funding of fetal research within the stated boundaries. But, in the critical areas of embryo research and fetal tissue transplantation research, federal funding has in effect been prohibited. A de facto moratorium on the funding of human embryo research has existed since 1980. A provision of the 1976 regulations prohibits the federal funding of research posing more than minimal risk to the embryo unless an Ethics Advisory Board recommends a waiver of this provision on grounds of scientific importance. The board was chartered in 1977, convened for the first time in 1978, and in May 1979 recommended federal funding of a study of spare, untransferred embryos. Interestingly, since then no secretary of the Department of Health, Education, and Welfare or of its successor, the Department of Health and Human Services, has approved the board's recommendation of that study; in September 1980, HEW Secretary Patricia Harris allowed the charter of the Ethics Advisory Board to expire. Some observers have speculated that she did so to avoid overlap with a planned presidential commission to study ethical issues in medicine. John Fletcher concludes that she did so because of her opposition to federal funding of IVF research; she was probably fully aware that the board was the only lawfully constituted body that could recommend waiver of the minimal risk provision in embryo research (1993, 212).

Throughout the 1980s, NIH directors called for a recharter of the Ethics Advisory Board, but no action was taken until 1988. Under pressure from Congress, Robert Windom, assistant secretary for Health, Department of Health and Human Services, announced that a new charter was to be drafted and a new board appointed. The draft charter was published in the *Federal Register,* as required by law, and the charter was approved by HHS Secretary Otis Bowen shortly before he left office. The incoming Bush administration never acted to implement the charter, however, and the Ethics Advisory Board was not reestablished. As a result, the 1980 moratorium on federal funding of all human embryo research, including IVF and other assisted reproduction techniques, continues, and, according to the Institute of Medicine, has severely hampered progress in medically assisted reproduction.

State Regulation of Fetal Research

State regulation of fetal research, like federal regulatory activity, was largely a response to the increase in research involving legally aborted fetuses after *Roe v. Wade* (1973). State statutes restricting fetal research are described in Table 8-4. Many of these laws were enacted by conservative legislatures as an effort to prevent the granting of social benefits that might be viewed as lending support to abortion. Of the twenty-six statutes that specifically regulate fetal research, twelve apply only to research with fetuses prior or subsequent to an elective abortion; most of the statutes are either part of or attached to abortion legislation. Moreover, of the thirteen statutes that apply to fetuses more generally, five impose stringent restrictions on fetal research conducted in conjunction with an elective abortion (Office of Technology Assessment 1990, 135-136).

Research on fetal cadavers is regulated by the Uniform Anatomical Gift Act, which has been adopted by all fifty states. Some states have excluded fetuses from the act's provisions, however, and in others such research is regulated by fetal research statutes. Forty-five states permit the use of fetal

Table 8-4 State Statutes Regulating Fetal Research

State	Regulate use of fetal cadavers	Prohibit nontherapeutic research on fetus		Prohibit sale of fetal tissue	May restrict pre-embryo research
		Live ex utero	Live in utero		
Arizona	x	x			x
Arkansas		x		x	x
California		x		x	x
Florida		x	x	x	x
Illinois	x			x	x
Indiana	x	x			
Kentucky		x		x	x
Louisiana		x[a]	x	x	x
Maine		x	x	x	x
Massachusetts	x	x	x	x	x
Michigan	x	x	x	x	x
Minnesota		x	x	x	x
Missouri		x	x	x	
Montana		x			
Nebraska		x		x	
Nevada				x	
New Mexico		x	x	x	
North Dakota	x	x	x	x	x
Ohio	x	x		x	x
Oklahoma	x	x	x	x	x
Pennsylvania	x	x	x	x	x
Rhode Island	x	x	x	x	x
South Dakota	x[b]	x[b]	x		
Tennessee	x[b]	x[b]			
Utah			x	x	x
Wyoming		x		x	x

Source: Adapted from Office of Technology Assessment 1990, 133-134.

[a] Found unconstitutional by the U.S. Court of Appeals for the Fifth Circuit in *Margaret S. v. Edwards* (1986).
[b] Requires mother's consent.

tissue from elective abortions; fourteen states have regulations that differ from the Uniform Anatomical Gift Act in that they impose either consent requirements for the use of fetal cadaver tissue in research or specific prohibitions on the use of such tissue. Five states prohibit any research on fetal cadavers with the exception of pathological examinations and autopsies. The statutes of these four states apply to electively aborted fetuses.

State laws regulating research on live fetuses (either in utero or ex utero) generally prohibit research that is not therapeutic to the fetus itself. Because these state laws were adopted in the context of the abortion debate, the primary focus is on research performed on the fetus ex utero (Andrews 1993, 30): twenty-three states regulate research on fetuses ex utero; fourteen states regulate research on fetuses in utero. Although the specifics of the prohibitions and sanctions differ by state, most states would appear to prohibit research involving transplantation, nontherapeutic research, and pre-embryo research.

Another restriction imposed by some of the statutes regulating fetal research concerns remuneration for use of fetal materials or for participation in such research. At least twenty-one states prohibit the sale of fetal tissue; seven prohibit its sale for any purpose and nine prohibit its sale specifically for research purposes. In some states, these prohibitions apply only to elective abortions, not to spontaneous abortions or ectopic pregnancies. In some states the penalties for violation are very stiff. In Wyoming, for instance, the selling of a viable fetus for purposes of research is punishable by a fine of not less than $10,000 and imprisonment for terms ranging from one to fourteen years (Office of Technology Assessment 1990, 135).

The Controversy over Fetal Tissue Transplantation

Fetal and embryo research has been the subject of controversy since the mid-1970s; more recently, however, the national debate has focused on the use of fetal tissue for transplantation research. As noted earlier, whereas fetal research in general has yielded knowledge concerning treatment that may benefit future fetuses, the transplantation of fetal tissue benefits primarily adult patients, and the tissue is the treatment. Transplantation has important implications for public policy and raises questions of consent and rights. This section explores the political context of the debate concerning this area of fetal research.

The Source of Fetal Tissue

The major political issue surrounding the use of fetal neural tissue in neural grafting is not the protection of experimental subjects or the establishment of funding priorities but rather the use of fetal tissue in transplantation research. There are four possible sources of fetal tissue: (1) spontaneous abortions; (2) induced abortions in cases of unintended pregnancy; (3) induced abortions of fetuses conceived specifically for research or therapy; and (4) embryos produced in vitro.

A dependence on spontaneously aborted fetuses for research purposes is impractical because of the limited number available, the inability to control the timing, and the fragility of fetal tissue, which deteriorates quickly after the death of the fetus (Office of Technology Assessment 1990, 152-154). Most fetal tissue, therefore, is likely to come from induced abortions in unintended pregnancies; it is reserved for research or transplantation rather than discarded or destroyed. Fetuses from the 1.5 million induced abortions performed in the United States each year would appear to be more than adequate to meet most research needs (Robertson 1988, 5). Each year approximately 90,000 fetuses could be available for the transplantation of brain cells. This estimate is based on the percentage of abortions performed between weeks six and twelve, the percentage performed by the safest method, and the fraction of fetuses in which the midbrain can be identified (Fine 1988, 6).

A dependence on elective abortions as the primary source has aroused vehement objections by groups opposed to abortion on moral grounds. Serious questions are also raised when the research or therapy needs affect the timing and method of abortion, or when the women undergoing the abortion are pressured to consent to donation.

Even more controversial is the induced abortion of a human fetus conceived specifically for the purpose of aborting it for use in research or therapy. There have been several cases in which individual women have attempted to produce tissue or organs for a relative or friend. The daughter of an Alzheimer's patient asked to be inseminated with the sperm of her father and, at the appropriate stage, to be allowed to abort the fetus to provide her father with fetal neural tissue for transplantation (Krimsky, Hubbard, and Gracey 1988, 9). Although there is at present no evidence that this would be technically possible, and the woman's request was denied, this case suggests the potential demand for such applications. A woman with severe diabetes wanted to conceive and then abort in order to use the pancreatic cells from the fetus for transplants to ameliorate her condition (Kimbrell 1993, 49). These two women may have been making decisions freely on their own, but situations are bound to arise in which family members exert implicit or explicit coercion on a woman to undergo this process. There is also concern that increased demand for fetal tissue may create a market for this scarce resource and lead to the exploitation of poor women (in the United States or elsewhere) who are paid to conceive solely to provide fetal materials.

The production of embryos by means of IVF to obtain fetal tissue raises questions of consent, ownership, and payment. A distinction must be made between those embryos deliberately created for research purposes and the spare, untransferred embryos remaining after the IVF of multiple ova. Those who believe that life starts at conception oppose any use of human embryos for research purposes, but many supporters of the use of spare embryos object only to the production of human embryos specifically for research.

The Moratorium on Funding of Fetal Tissue Transplantation Research

On March 22, 1988, in response to the growing political controversy stimulated by the publicity surrounding the successful grafting of fetal neural tissue to treat Parkinson's patients in Mexico and Sweden, Robert Windom, assistant secretary for Health, announced imposition of a moratorium on federal support for fetal tissue transplantation research, pending a report by a special panel he directed the NIH to convene in order to answer the ethical and legal questions posed by a proposal for the transplantion of fetal brain tissue to treat patients with Parkinson's disease. A similar project, involving the implantation of fetal pancreatic tissue to treat patients with juvenile diabetes, had previously been funded. The principal investigator had decided not to proceed with studies until receipt of the NIH panel's report, however.

In September 1988, the Human Fetal Tissue Transplantation Research Panel recommended that funding for such research be restored (NIH 1988b). By a vote of 17-4, the panel concluded that such research is "acceptable public policy." Seeking to protect the interests of the various parties, the panel recommended the establishment of guidelines to prohibit financial inducements to women; prohibit the sale of fetal tissue; prevent donations of fetal tissue specifically to relatives; differentiate between the decision to abort and the decision to donate; and require consent of the women and the nonobjection of the father.

The panel was chaired by retired federal Judge Arlin Adams, who is a known opponent of abortion but who was not adverse to discussion of the use of fetal tissue for research. Membership on the panel, nomination to which required White House approval, included persons who espoused a pro-life, anti-abortion philosophy that included opposition to the use of any tissue obtained by means of what they view as an immoral act. The pro-life lobby claimed that the panel's membership was stacked in favor of the research community, but there was considerable consensus among the various interests represented on the panel concerning the appropriateness of fetal tissue transplantation research.

In December 1988, the NIH director's Advisory Committee unanimously approved the special panel's report without making any change and recommended that the moratorium be lifted (NIH 1988a). The committee concluded that existing procedures governing human research and organ donation were sufficient to regulate fetal tissue transplantation. On January 19, 1989, James B. Wyngaarden, director of NIH, issued a memorandum stating that he concurred with the position of the Advisory Committee and transmitted it to the assistant secretary for Health. The report languished in the department without action until November 2, 1989, when Secretary of the Department of Health and Human Services Louis B. Sullivan, under pressure from Sen. Gordon Humphrey (R-N.H.), Rep. William Dannemeyer (R-Calif.), and other pro-life members of Congress, announced an indefinite extension of the moratorium on fetal research funding. His statement was in in direct conflict with the committee's recommendations:

> I am persuaded that one must accept the likelihood that permitting the human fetal research at issue will increase the incidence of abortion across the country. Providing the additional rationalization of directly advancing the cause of human therapeutics cannot help but tilt some already vulnerable women toward a decision to have an abortion.

This action was challenged by Rep. Ted Weiss (D-N.Y.) on technical grounds. He warned that a simple announcement by the administration making the moratorium permanent could be construed legally as a rule and should thus be made subject to the formal rule-making process (Hilts 1990).

Congressional Action on Fetal Tissue Research

In April 1990, the Subcommittee on Health and the Environment of the House of Representatives Committee on Energy and Commerce held hearings on human fetal tissue transplantation research. The House passed the Research Freedom Act (H.R. 2507) in July 1991, which limited the authority of executive branch officials, such as the secretary of HHS, to ban federal funds for an entire field of research without the support of an ethics advisory board. In May 1992, the House voted to approve the version of the House-Senate conference committee, which included privacy and consent provisions added by the Senate, and sent the bill to the president, whose veto was certain. In anticipation of a congressional override of his veto, President George Bush issued an executive order directing the NIH to establish a fetal tissue bank dependent on spontaneously aborted fetuses and ectopic pregnancies, even though there was little evidence that such a bank could provide sufficient amounts of high-quality tissue for transplantation (Vawter 1993, 82).

The political controversy continued, and in June 1992 a compromise bill was introduced in both houses. In effect, it gave the administration one year to demonstrate that the tissue bank would work. If researchers were unable to obtain suitable tissue from the bank within two weeks of their request, they could obtain it from other sources, including elective abortions. In October 1992, a Senate filibuster by opponents of fetal research ended attempts to pass legislation concerning it. Majority leader George Mitchell of Maine vowed that consideration of such a bill would be the first order of business when the Senate reconvened in 1993. On January 23,

1993, on his second day in office, President Clinton, as expected, issued an executive order that removed the moratorium on the funding of fetal tissue transplantation research.

Unresolved Policy Issues

Although President Clinton opened the way for public funding of fetal tissue transplantation research, many legal and ethical issues remain. They include:

1. The method of determining fetal death
2. Whether a distinction should be made between viable and nonviable fetuses as a tissue source
3. The suitability of federal and state regulations and guidelines concerning the use of fetal tissue
4. Determination of who should consent to the procurement of fetal tissue and who can seek consent, the procedures for obtaining consent, the timing of consent, and what information must be disclosed
5. The permissibility of altering routine abortion methods or timing in the interest of increasing the yield and quality of fetal tissue suitable for research or transplantation
6. Standards for quality control of fetal tissue, including screening of tissue and storage procedures
7. Clarification of the distribution system, including financial arrangements between physicians performing abortions and researchers using tissues, payment for cell lines (whether they can be treated as property), and the legality of recipients designated by the tissue donors

Concern regarding these issues is bound to intensify as the amount of transplantation research, and the corresponding need for fetal tissue, increases. Because of the importance of the questions of consent and procedural modification, they are discussed in detail in the remainder of this section.

Consent for the Use of Fetal Tissue

The question of rights is basic in the debate over the procurement of fetal tissue: Does a woman who decides to abort a fetus have any rights concerning the disposal of the fetal cadaver? In those states that include fetal cadavers under Uniform Anatomical Gift Act, proxy consent is required. The most logical proxy is the pregnant woman. Not only is she the next of kin but, as suggested by the privacy argument, she has a right to control her own body and its products. Some observers argue that to deny the woman the opportunity to veto the use of fetal remains for transplantation research or therapy is to deny her autonomy (Robertson 1988, 9). Consent should be obtained not because the fetus has interests to be protected but in consideration of the interests of the woman. Following this reasoning, the NIH Human Fetal Tissue Transplantation Research Panel in 1988 recommended that maternal consent be obtained prior to the use of fetal cadavers for research.

Others argue that in having an abortion, the woman abdicates responsibility for the fetus, and as a result, there is no basis for a requirement that her consent be obtained concerning its disposition. Once abortion has taken place, the tissue is no longer part of the woman's body; therefore, her claim to bodily property carries little weight (Burtchaell 1988). Furthermore, since the woman clearly does not intend to protect the fetus, it is inappropriate for her to act as a proxy. "If she withholds permission, we must ask what gives her the right to decide that others should not benefit from the research or from transplantation" (Harris 1985, 122).

Another argument against requiring maternal consent is that such a requirement may be an unwelcome intrusion for a woman already facing a tortuous decision about whether to have an abortion. In *Margaret S. v. Edwards* (1986) the United States Court of Appeals for the Fifth Circuit struck down a Louisiana regulation that required a woman's consent as to the disposal of the dead fetus. The court noted that informing a woman of the burial or cremation of the fetus would intimidate pregnant women and prevent them from exercising their constitutional right to abortion or would create unjustified anxiety in the exercise of that right (at 1004). In the interest of reducing a woman's emotional burden and thus preventing harm to her, the court ruled that the woman need not be informed of, or have to consent to, the disposal of the fetus. The question arises whether informing a woman that her aborted fetus may be donated for research is also potentially unwelcome information. Some women might find it an intrusion; others may welcome the opportunity to specify donation for that purpose. Both the Uniform Anatomical Gift Act and many state statutes require the woman's informed consent in order for her fetus to be a legal donation. But the decision in *Margaret S. v. Edwards* suggests that this requirement may be construed as an intrusion on her in making an abortion decision and thus is unconstitutional.

But there are some who argue that all fetal tissue from elective abortions should be routinely harvested without the necessity of obtaining maternal consent:

Routine salvaging of foetal [sic] tissue would not only provide more material, it would remove fears that women had been pressured into unwanted pregnancies in order to produce foetal tissue . . . and also remove the burden of extra decisions at a difficult time during the contemplation of abortion. (Lamb 1990, 80)

Those who advocate this position believe that denying a pregnant woman control over disposal of a dead fetus may be the price that has to be paid to maintain the distinction between the ethics of abortion and the use of fetal tissues.

This argument may seem attractive, but using fetal tissue without the consent of the pregnant woman would create more problems than it would solve. Maternal consent as to the disposition of the fetus should therefore be required as recommended by the NIH panel and other bodies (American Medical Association 1990). Although information about fetal disposition might trouble some women, denying women knowledge of the facts and freedom of choice in making the decision is clearly paternalistic and a violation of basic principles of informed consent underlying the conduct of research.

Bambi Robinson (1993, 23) raises an interesting question about the woman's decision regarding abortion once she has consented to research on the fetus in utero. Should the woman be able to change her mind about the planned abortion once the experiment with the fetus has begun? If the answer is yes, the woman's autonomy is assured at the cost of potentially serious harm to the fetus. If the answer is no, limits on her autonomy are accepted in order to prevent possible harm to the fetus. Robinson argues that in this situation, the woman should not be permitted to change her mind about the abortion once she has begun to participate in the experiment. The woman freely chooses to limit her own autonomy when she consents to experimentation in utero and should understand that she is making an irrevocable decision. Robinson notes that in any abortion, there is a point of no return; in the case of research in utero, this point simply comes earlier in the process—when the experiment starts. Whether the woman is allowed to change her mind or not, even if the fetus were to survive, it would likely have suffered considerable harm needlessly. Irrespective of the validity of Robinson's conclusion, the debate on this issue emphasizes the need for full and informed maternal consent prior to any experimentation on the fetus.

Modification of the Abortion Procedure

In fetal research, and especially in grafting procedures, for which the tissue must be of the appropriate gestational age and in optimal condition for transplantation, an important issue is whether the pregnant woman's medical care can be altered to meet research needs (Mahowald, Silver, and Ratcheson 1987, 11). Some observers approve of modifications in the abortion procedure if they pose little risk for the woman, and if she is adequately informed and consents (Robertson 1988); no one has publicly advocated changing abortion procedures so that they significantly increase the probability of harm or discomfort to the woman (Vawter et al. 1990, 147). At this stage in the debate there is general agreement that the means and timing of abortion should be determined by the pregnant woman's medical needs, not by the needs of research (Office of Technology Assessment 1990, 158). In 1988, the Human Fetal Tissue Transplantation Research Panel (1988) made this requirement a high priority for implementation.

But there is still disagreement as to what alterations can be made that pose acceptable risks, particularly if grafting becomes standard procedure and progresses from experimentation to therapeutic application. The following alterations have reportedly been made in the abortion technique in order to increase the yield and quality of fetal tissue (Vawter et al. 1990, 197):

1. Use of ultrasonography to more accurately determine the placement of the fetus
2. Reduction in the pressure of the suction used to remove the contents of the uterus
3. Performing a suction abortion under general anesthesia
4. Variation of suction abortion to allow extraction of the fetus intact
5. Unusual procurement practices such as removal of fetal tissue with forceps before vacuum aspiration is used

Although there is no evidence that these alterations present more than minimal risk to the woman, it has been reported that some modifications in the abortion technique dictated by tissue procurement needs may lengthen the procedure from less than ten minutes to thirty minutes (Kolata 1989).

The possibility that abortion clinics and obstetricians may not cooperate in making fetal tissue available for research, in part because of their reluctance or inability to meet the additional time and resource requirements, raises concern about maintenance of an adequate supply. Moreover, the availability of RU-486 and other abortifacients in the near future will diminish the supply of usable fetal tissue at a time when demand might increase, should fetal tissue prove to be a successful treatment for a common disease (Vawter et al. 1990, 200). Despite a near consensus that fetal tissue procurement should not pose a significant risk for the pregnant woman and widespread support for procedural protections, continual vigilance will be necessary to minimize the abuses that are certain to occur as the demand for usable fetal tissue increases.

Fetal Research and Abortion

It is unlikely that the debate over whether the use of fetal tissue from elective abortion encourages or legitimizes abortion will soon be resolved. Those opposed to abortion will no doubt continue to oppose the use of all fetal tissue except that obtained from spontaneous abortions and ectopic pregnancies. The argument that fetal research devalues the fetus and uses it as the means to achieve others' ends is strongly rooted in the anti-abortion position. Arguments emphasizing the benefits derived from such research are unlikely to sway strong opponents. There is no evidence that the use of fetal tissue has increased the number of abortions because it has encouraged women who were ambivalent about the abortion decision, and most experts believe it will not do so (Vawter 1993, 84).

It is incumbent upon policy makers, however, to establish procurement procedures that minimize the likelihood of pressure on women to abort in order to provide fetuses for research or transplantation. Precautions to this end include separating the abortion choice from the consent to use the fetus for research by prohibiting abortion clinic personnel from even discussing donation until after the woman has formally consented to abortion. If possible, consent for fetal donation might be requested after the abortion procedure. Specification of tissue recipients, including the woman herself, should be prohibited. The woman should also be fully informed of any risks to her privacy or well-being that may result from donation of the fetal tissue, and of any financial or research interest the abortion provider might have in her donation. Payments to women who abort, including compensation for the cost of the abortion procedure, should be prohibited. To further reduce the profit motive with regard to the disposition of fetal remains, payments to doctors, clinics, and other parties involved in the abortion procedure should be prohibited. Public registries should be established to distribute, on a non-profit basis, fetal materials to be used for research. Dorothy Vawter points out that

> appropriate guidelines for fetal tissue procurement are necessary to replace the inadequate practices currently in widespread use so that fetuses and the women asked to donate tissue after elective abortion receive the respect and protection owed them. (1993, 84)

The Impact of Governmental Limits on Funding Fetal Research

The moratoriums on the federal funding of human embryo research (de facto by the elimination of the Ethics Advisory Board) and fetal tissue transplantation research (imposed by HHS directly) do not prohibit such research. Researchers at the University of Colorado and Yale University have relied on private funding for the study of fetal tissue transplants in the treatment of diabetes and Parkinson's disease, respectively. They are bound by regulations protecting human subjects if their institution receives any funding from the NIH for other projects. Moreover, private funding makes possible the embryo research that continues to be conducted using IVF and other techniques.

One of the dangers of eliminating federal funding is that public control of the research will be limited. When private funds are used exclusively, the peer review process that is a concomitant to federal funding is circumvented. For instance, the failure of the NIH to fund IVF research has placed it outside the traditional boundaries of public control. Second, the line between fetal tissue transplantation experimentation and its clinical applications is easily blurred when there is no public oversight. Third, unlike pharmaceuticals, for which the FDA mandates a rigid testing protocol, medical procedures have no corresponding regulation of testing protocol. Without the controls that accompany public funding, it is possible that such procedures will not follow proper testing protocol.

Fourth, research priorities are being driven increasingly by the marketplace. Research areas that are potentially more lucrative or have more immediate applications are pursued at the expense of basic research that, in the long run, is likely to be scientifically more important. For example, IVF research has focused on clinical applications, but research on the potential deleterious effects of some of these applications has received little attention.

A shift from governmental to private funding of embryo and fetal research would severely limit the public debate of the legal, ethical, and scientific issues surrounding specific applications. Research financed by government funds is conducted openly, in the public domain; thus its implications can be debated while the work is in progress. But information about ongoing research financed by the private sector is often carefully guarded so as to protect the proprietary interests of the corporate sponsors. By claiming exclusive patent rights for the products of this research and receiving royalty payments on their use, the companies can recoup their investment. Private sources provide funds for research using human fetal tissue only when such research is viewed as yielding a near-term financial payoff. This not only alters the type of research conducted but tends to restrict communication concerning the various research initiatives until there is certainty that the proprietary interests have been protected.

Conclusion

Progress in some critical areas of research has been constrained on political, not scientific, grounds. Long-term scientific goals have been compromised because of immediate, pragmatic political objectives. Abortion politics continues to exert a strong influence on research funded by the government in a wide range of substantive areas. Given the sensitive issues surrounding human embryo research and fetal research and their interdependence with abortion, this should not be surprising. Because such research elicits intense opposition and support, it will continue to have a place on the political agenda. Fetal research raises moral red flags for many people. Yet research on human embryos and fetal tissue transplantation promise to contribute significantly to scientific knowledge about the human condition and may yield revolutionary treatment options.

C H A P T E R 9

Reproductive Rights and Neonatal Care

On April 9, 1982, an infant boy was born in Bloomington, Indiana. Baby Doe, as he came to be known, could not eat or drink because he was born with a defective esophagus. This condition could be easily corrected with routine surgery, however. But Baby Doe was also born with Down syndrome, a form of mental retardation, and his parents would not consent to the surgery. A legal battle between the hospital and parents ensued, but in the end, surgery was not performed, and Baby Doe died.

The role of the physician is to preserve life. In few settings is that role more evident than in neonatal intensive-care units (NICUs), where physicians provide emergency care to newborns with life-threatening conditions. The nation's 750 NICUs are a relatively recent addition to high-technology medicine; most were founded in the 1960s and 1970s as pediatricians became more knowledgeable and more skillful in treating newborns. Neonatology was established as a subspecialty of pediatrics in the mid-1970s.

NICUs are structured according to the same principles as adult and pediatric intensive-care units. Care is provided by a team of staff and consulting physicians, nurses, and other care givers such as respiratory therapists. Hospital ethics committees may also be consulted. The units are generally located at regional research and teaching hospitals, to which critically ill newborns are transferred from the community hospitals where they were born. The units are equipped with complex, sophisticated monitoring and life-support equipment and have low nurse-to-patient ratios. Medical teams tend to be highly aggressive; for to them, ''death in the [NICU] is always a defeat'' (Guillemin and Holmstrom 1990, 139).

NICU patients fall into several categories. A large number are in intensive care due to low birth weight (less than 2,500 grams or 5.5 pounds) or very low birth weight (less than 1,500 grams or less than 3.3 pounds) due to premature delivery. The National Association of Children's Hospitals and Related Institutions has reported that in the early 1990s, approximately 7 percent of all babies born in the United States were low birth weight, yet they accounted for more than half (57 percent) of the hospital costs of all newborns. In 1992, low birth weight babies averaged nearly sixteen days in the hospital at an average per patient cost of approximately $39,280, or an annual nationwide cost of $4.25 billion. The costs for each infant weighing less than 1.6 pounds at birth ranged from $150,000 to $200,000 (National Association of Children's Hospitals and Related Institutions 1994, 45). Mortality rates among low birth weight babies are extremely high. In general, the more premature the delivery, the higher the incidence of neonatal complications. Data published in the *New England Journal of Medicine* in late 1993 indicated that the mortality rate for infants born at twenty-two weeks was 100 percent; the rate for those born at twenty-five weeks was 21 percent (Allen, Donohue, and Dusman 1993, 1597).

Babies born too soon are afflicted with a variety of life-threatening conditions. Because their lungs are inadequately developed, they often suffer from respiratory distress syndrome and must be placed on mechanical ventilators. Sometimes the infants become ventilator-dependent, and it is difficult to wean them from the support system. Many are not able to suck or swallow; thus they cannot take nutrition and hydration orally. This necessitates intravenous feeding, which is not only painful for the newborn but may overtax its heart and kidneys. Intracranial hemorrhaging with resulting neurological damage is also common. Low birth weight deliveries are most prevalent among young, low-income women who are poorly educated and have not had prenatal care (President's Commission 1983, 201). Many such babies would probably be carried full term if their mothers had had access to and utilized prenatal care.

The first few hours after the birth of a premature infant are the most important for viability. But this is also the time when the medical staff knows the least about the infant's condition and the prognosis. No one can predict whether infants born prematurely will die, develop normally, or survive with profound retardation or other severe impairments. Life-and-death decisions thus must be made in the absence of the information necessary to predict or evaluate the results of those decisions (Rhoden 1986b).

Other patients in the NICU include those with life-threatening anomalies due to genetic defects, chromosomal abnormalities, paternal exposure to or ingestion of chemical substances prior to pregnancy, or maternal exposure or ingestion of chemical substances before or during pregnancy.

The diagnostic techniques and rates of prognostic accuracy are higher for most congenital anomalies than for low birth weight babies, but still the realm of uncertainty is great. Finally, some babies are admitted to NICUs because they suffer withdrawal symptoms due to maternal use of drugs during pregnancy or because they are injured during labor or delivery.

These crises involve many parties with potentially conflicting rights. The infant has the most to gain and the most to lose, for its life hangs in the balance. Yet it cannot speak for itself so others must speak on its behalf. Traditionally, parents have spoken for minor children in medical decision making. But parents, despite their presumed love and concern for their children, sometimes have needs that are incompatible with the needs of the newborn, and this conflict can be problematic.

The hospital staff also help to determine the infant's future. Physicians are trained to save lives. To do otherwise is to fail. They are also acutely aware of the possibility of malpractice litigation. Nurses provide the daily care, which can include tasks that are painful to the patient, such as needle insertion. Government child protective services agencies may intervene to ensure that infants are not victims of medical neglect. With such diversity and passion, conflict of rights is a likely scenario. We turn now to a discussion of how such conflicts are played out in the arena of public policy.

Developing the Policy Agenda for Critically Ill Newborns

It is generally agreed in the United States that children are vulnerable and in need of care and protection. It is also assumed that parents will provide that care and protection; thus government intervention in parental decision making is avoided in most cases unless it can be shown that parental choices injure the child in some way. In *Prince v. Massachusetts* (1944), the Supreme Court concluded that

> parents may be free to become martyrs themselves. But it does not follow they are free, in identical circumstances, to make martyrs of their children before they have reached the age of full and legal discretion when they can make that choice for themselves. (at 444)

Given the capabilities of high-technology medicine, the widespread perception that physicians can cure most serious injuries and illnesses, and a pervasive societal bias against individuals with mental or physical disabilities, it is reasonable to assume that critically ill newborns will receive all that medicine has to offer. Not all newborns are destined to be discharged from the NICU, however, nor is discharge predictive of future health. Some will inevitably die. Others will "graduate" to less intensive units and will either be discharged or become "boarder babies," unable to leave the hospital because their parents cannot or will not care for them at home.

Since the early 1970s there has been a debate among bioethicists and clinicians regarding decisions in the treatment of critically ill newborns (Duff and Campbell 1973; Shaw 1973, 1977; Jonsen and Garland 1976; Fost 1982; Weir 1984; Murray and Caplan 1985; Kuhse and Singer 1985). The medical community was rife with rumors about physicians and parents who refused treatment—and sometimes food and water—for newborns with disabilities. This debate was brought to public attention in the early 1970s with the publication of articles by noted physicians who openly admitted to withholding care—including food and water—and with the well-publicized deaths of disabled newborns in some of the nation's most prestigious medical centers.

The catalyst for public debate concerning the treatment of disabled newborns was the slow death of an infant with Down syndrome at Johns Hopkins University Hospital in Baltimore in 1971. The child had been born with an intestinal blockage, easily repairable with routine surgery. The parents, however, had refused consent for the surgery even though it had been strongly recommended by the medical staff. The hospital did not seek a court order to coerce treatment, and a note specifying that the child was not to be fed was attached to his bassinet as he lay dying for fifteen days in an isolated section of the hospital nursery. The situation had a demoralizing effect on the medical staff, particularly the nurses. Public debate was fueled by a documentary filmed by the Joseph P. Kennedy Foundation about the case.

In 1973, Yale University pediatricians Raymond Duff and A. G. M. Campbell openly admitted to withholding treatment from some newborns, and thereby causing their deaths. In discussing the complexity of ethical decision making in the nursery, Duff and Campbell argued that

> since families primarily must live with and are most affected by the decisions, it therefore appears that society and the health professions should provide only general guidelines for decision making. Moreover, since variations between situations are so great, and the situations themselves so complex, it follows that much latitude in decision making should be expected and tolerated. (1973, 894)

They concluded that if it was in fact illegal to withhold treatment despite parental wishes, then the law should be changed.

Shortly after publication of this article, a number of surveys were conducted to asses the extent to which treatment had been withheld. In a survey of San Francisco area obstetricians and pediatricians, 22 percent of the respondents favored active or passive euthanasia for Down syndrome infants who had no complications, and 50 percent favored euthanasia if the

Down syndrome infant had an intestinal blockage (Treating the Defective Newborn 1976, 2). A significant majority (79.6 percent) of Massachusetts pediatricians responding to another survey believed that informed consent should include the right of parents to withhold consent for surgery, but only 46.3 percent would recommend surgery in the case of a Down syndrome infant with a duodenal atresia whose parents would not consent to surgery. Less than half (40.2 percent) of those recommending surgery in such a case would pursue a court order (Todres et al. 1977, 198-199).

In a nationwide study conducted in 1977 and headed by Dr. Anthony Shaw, a pediatric surgeon, 50 percent of the pediatricians and 77 percent of the pediatric surgeons surveyed would not operate on a Down syndrome infant with an intestinal atresia if parental consent was not given (Shaw, Randolph, and Manard 1977, 590). In the same year, Shaw published a formula in which he urged physicians and others to consider the contributions of the family and society, as well as the infant's physical and intellectual endowment, in determining the infant's quality of life. He clearly did not, however, advocate using the formula as a method of calculating the value of human life, defining personhood, or determining when to withhold treatment (Shaw 1977, 11). These events—the death of the Down syndrome child at Johns Hopkins; the articles by Duff, Campbell, and Shaw; the surveys indicating that most physicians would not favor operating on Down syndrome children when parental consent was not given— were publicized in the press and thus were major agenda-setting events in the public debate about the care and treatment of newborns with disabilities.

This ethical discussion received front-page coverage in newspapers throughout the United States in 1982, when treatment was withheld from a Down syndrome infant in Bloomington, Indiana. Like the Down syndrome infant at Johns Hopkins a decade earlier, Baby Doe (as the news media nicknamed the Bloomington infant) was born with a life-threatening but surgically correctable anomaly—in this case a blocked esophagus. The father had worked with mentally disabled children, and the parents felt they could not raise a mentally disabled child in their home. The obstetrician advised them that the prognosis for the child's mental development was not good. The child's pediatrician felt otherwise and strongly advocated the surgery. Ultimately, the parents refused to give consent for the surgery and also refused consent for the intravenous feedings that were necessary for nutrition and hydration.

The hospital petitioned the Circuit Court of Monroe County, Indiana, to determine the legality of the parents' position. The court upheld the parents' position and ordered the hospital to comply with nontreatment (*Doe v. Bloomington Hospital*, 1983). The hospital appealed to the Indiana Supreme Court, which refused to hear the case, and it was appealed to the

U.S. Supreme Court. Members of the news media camped on the hospital's doorstep throughout the ordeal. Other couples came forward, offering to adopt Baby Doe. Private attorneys and county prosecutors sought unsuccessfully to deprive the parents of custody. Nurses in the NICU refused to participate in the withholding of treatment, so the parents hired private nurses, and Baby Doe was transferred to another unit in the hospital.

Hours before arguments were to be heard by Supreme Court Justice John Paul Stevens and while attorneys were en route to the nation's capital to present them, Baby Doe died. Pro-life and disability rights groups— among others—expressed outrage. Columnist George Will, a friend of President Ronald Reagan and father of a Down syndrome child, editorialized that it was murder: "The baby was killed because it was retarded. . . . Such homicides in hospitals are common and will become more so now that a state's courts have given them an imprimatur" (Will 1982, 64).

Public concern for the plight of disabled newborns intensified a year later with the publication of an article detailing the treatment used at Oklahoma Children's Memorial Hospital. In this article, physicians acknowledged that they had been "influenced" by Shaw's formula and that "treatment for babies with identical [medical] 'selection criteria' could be quite different depending on the contribution from home and society" (Gross et al. 1983, 456). According to Norman Fost, former chair of the American Academy of Pediatrics Bioethics Committee, this rate of nontreatment was much higher than had been reported elsewhere in the United States. The research thus stimulated widespread controversy (Fost 1986, 151).

The news media focused on the Oklahoma treatment methods; an investigative report entitled "Who Lives, Who Dies?" aired on the Cable News Network in February 1984. The "camera captured the picture of Carlton Johnson, a black baby born with spina bifida to an unmarried mother receiving welfare" (U.S. Commission on Civil Rights 1989, 136). The report indicated that the child had not been given surgery and that the mother had been told he was terminally ill (Cable News Network transcript, *Who Lives, Who Dies?* 3 (February 21, 22, and 24, 1984), cited in U.S. Commission on Civil Rights 1989, 136). Some alleged that the selection process at the University of Oklahoma constituted racial and socioeconomic discrimination. Disability rights organizations filed formal complaints with the Department of Health and Human Services and the Department of Justice in February 1984, and the American Civil Liberties Union, in conjunction with the National Center for the Medically Dependent and Disabled, filed suit against the physicians in October 1985 (U. S. Commission on Civil Rights 1989, 136-138).*

---

* Oklahoma Children's Memorial Hospital subsequently denied that the quality of life formula had been a part of the selection process or that there had been racial or socioeconomic discrimina-

Government Regulations and the Critically III Newborn

With all the publicity surrounding the events in Indiana, it was only a matter of time before government officials would become involved in the debate. (See Table 9-1 for a chronology of policy events.) The Reagan administration was under strong pressure from the pro-life movement to take a stand against the withholding of treatment. Realizing that it could not succeed alone, the pro-life movement began to forge alliances with disability rights organizations, which had become politically active in the 1970s. In the spring of 1982, representatives of such disparate groups as the Christian Action Council and the American Life Lobby met with officials of the Spina Bifida Association and the Association for Retarded Citizens to discuss Baby Doe issues. These alliances seemingly brought together odd bedfellows since most disability rights organizations were pro-choice on abortion. Nevertheless, they developed a common strategy of publicizing cases in which they believed treatment was being withheld and instituting litigation in an attempt to force treatment (Paige and Karnofsky 1986).

The alliance's strategy proved effective, for in May 1982 HHS sent a letter to all hospitals receiving federal aid stating that denial of benefits to handicapped persons was a violation of their civil rights under section 504 of the 1973 Rehabilitation Act. The letter made it appear that the Reagan administration strongly supported civil rights for citizens with disabilities, but it should be noted that only weeks earlier, President Reagan had proposed a 30 percent reduction in funds for education of the handicapped and the administration was in the process of drafting guidelines to limit federal enforcement of section 504 with regards to adults with disabilities (*Washington Post*, March 4, 1982).

The letter was followed by a series of rules, also based on the civil rights provisions of section 504. The first rule (called the Interim Final Rule), published on March 7, 1983, required that all hospitals receiving federal aid post large signs in maternity and pediatric units and in delivery rooms advising that the withholding of medical care from newborns with handicaps was a violation of federal law. The signs included a toll-free "hotline" telephone number so that possible violators (most likely physicians and nurses) could be reported to federal authorities. The rule permitted on-site inspection of newborn units by medical

---

tion as some had alleged. Data from the Gross et al. research group bear out the latter. Treatment records indicate that all of the children on public assistance without insurance and 69 percent of the children qualifying for medical assistance were aggressively treated, whereas 58 percent of the patients with private insurance were aggressively treated. Moreover, all of the black children and 83 percent of the Hispanic children were aggressively treated, compared with 57 percent of the white children (U.S. Commission on Civil Rights 1989, 356, 367).

Table 9-1   Events in the Development of Baby Doe Policy, 1982-1991

April 9, 1982
Baby Doe is born in Bloomington, Indiana, suffering from Down syndrome and
having an esophageal atresia and a tracheoesophageal fistula.

May 18, 1982
HHS publishes a Notice to Health Care Providers, "Discriminating Against Handicapped by Withholding Treatment or Nourishment." (*Federal Register*, vol. 47, no.
116)

May 26, 1982
Rep. John Erlenborn introduces legislation in Congress to prevent denial of treatment to children with disabilities. This legislation is later modified and eventually becomes the Child Abuse Amendments of 1984.

March 7, 1983
HHS publishes its Interim Final Rule, "Nondiscrimination on the Basis of Handicap." (*Federal Register*, vol. 48, no. 45)

April 14, 1983
In *American Academy of Pediatrics v. Heckler*, the U.S. District Court for the District of Columbia invalidates the HHS Interim Final Rule on the grounds that the department had not followed appropriate procedural requirements in that the rule had not
been published for public comment.

representatives from HHS. The response by the medical community was
quick and forceful. The American Academy of Pediatrics, in conjunction
with the National Association of Children's Hospitals and Related
Institutions and the Children's Hospital National Medical Center, filed
suit in federal district court and, in *American Academy of Pediatrics
v. Heckler* (1983), the Interim Final Rule was invalidated on procedural
grounds.

In the spring of 1983, representatives of the Reagan administration attempted to negotiate a compromise between the pro-life and disability
rights movement and the major medical associations. In urging compromise, Surgeon General C. Everett Koop played a pivotal role. As a well-
respected pediatric surgeon and outspoken pro-life supporter, he could
view the issue both from the medical and the pro-life perspectives. The
medical community argued that care for disabled newborns should be
monitored by hospital review committees. The pro-life and disability rights
movement wanted stricter federal regulations. By the fall of 1983, a modi-
cum of cooperation had developed. The American Academy of Pediatrics

---

October 11, 1983
Baby Jane Doe is born in Port Jefferson, New York, suffering from spina bifida, hydrocephalus, microcephaly, and related complications.

January 12, 1984
HHS publishes its Final Rule, "Nondiscrimination on the Basis of Handicap; Procedures and Guidelines Relating to Health Care for Handicapped Infants." (*Federal Register*, vol. 49, no. 8)

October 9, 1984
President Reagan signs Public Law 98-457, the Child Abuse Amendments of 1984.

April 15, 1985
HHS issues the Final Rule to Implement the Child Abuse Amendments of 1984: "Child Abuse and Neglect Prevention and Treatment Program." (*Federal Register*, vol. 50, No. 72)

June 9, 1986
In *Bowen v. American Hospital Association*, the Supreme Court upholds a federal court decision invalidating the HHS Final Rule, "Nondiscrimination on the Basis of Handicap; Procedures and Guidelines Relating to Health Care for Handicapped Infants, " dated January 12, 1984.

October 25, 1991
President Bush signs Public Law 101-126, reauthorizing the Child Abuse Amendments of 1984.

Source: Adapted from Caplan, Blank, and Merrick 1992, Appendix.

joined with a number of medical and disability rights organizations in issuing a statement, usually referred to as the "Joint Statement," that read in part:

> Discrimination of any type against any individual with a disability/ disabilities, regardless of the nature or severity of the disability, is morally and legally indefensible. . . . Consideration such as anticipated or actual limited potential of an individual and present or future lack of available community resources are irrelevant and must not determine the decision concerning medical care. . . . The individual's medical condition should be the sole focus of the decision. (Joint Policy Statement 1984)

The political controversy over who should control treatment decision making for critically ill newborns was soon complicated by another case that made the front pages of the newspapers. On October 11, 1983, Baby Jane Doe was born in Port Jefferson, New York, suffering from spina bifida, hydrocephalus, microcephaly, and related complications. Her parents, after consultation with physicians, chose a ''conservative'' treatment involving antibiotics and dressing rather than surgery.

While the young parents struggled to deal with the medical crises surrounding the birth of their first child, a pro-life attorney who had worked for a New York branch of the National Right to Life Committee filed suit seeking to force surgery. The parents' rights to determine their daughter's medical treatment were thus being challenged by a third party, unrelated to the child and unknown to the child's family, claiming to advocate the rights of their daughter. The state trial court authorized the surgery but its appellate division reversed that decision, arguing that the parents had made reasonable choices from among the various medical options available to them and had had the best interests of their daughter in mind (*Weber v. Stony Brook Hospital*, 1983). The New York State Court of Appeals subsequently found that the trial court had erred in allowing a party with no relationship to the child, family, or medical staff to bring suit (*Weber v. Stony Brook Hospital* Ct. App. 1983).

HHS also filed suit in federal court, demanding access to Baby Jane Doe's medical records, which the hospital had refused to release. The court upheld the hospital's refusal to release the records, since that refusal was based on parental unwillingness to authorize the release. Moreover, the court found that the hospital had failed to perform the surgery because the parents had refused to consent to it, and that the parental refusal was a reasonable choice based on treatment methods (*United States v. University Hospital of the State University of New York at Stony Brook*, 1983). The trial court decision was affirmed on appeal (*United States v. University Hospital, State University of New York at Stony Brook*, 1984).

In January 1984, HHS promulgated its Final Rule based on section 504. Its provisions were essentially the same as those of the interim final rule, with a few modifications. The hospital sign was to be smaller and to be placed only in areas where hospital staff, not parents, would see it. On-site inspections would still be permitted. State child protective services agencies receiving federal aid for their child abuse programs were required to establish procedures for reporting medical neglect. Infant care review committees were encouraged but not mandated. Most important, health care workers were allowed to use reasonable medical judgment in selecting courses of treatment; the rule specifically stated that treatment that merely prolonged the dying process was not to be considered medically beneficial.

Although the American Academy of Pediatrics and the National Association of Children's Hospitals and Related Institutions had endorsed the Joint Statement, the American Medical Association and the American Hospital Association did not. They took on HHS in the courts and won. In *Bowen v. American Hospital Association* (1986), the U.S. Supreme Court invalidated the Final Rule on the grounds that withholding treatment when parents had not given consent for it did not violate section 504; the requirements for posting signs and providing on-site access to patient medical records were not founded on evidence of discrimination and were foreign to the authority conferred on HHS; and HHS could not use federal resources without regard to whether or not handicapped newborns were victims of discrimination.

The 1984 Child Abuse Amendments

While the battle over the right to control medical decision making about infants was being fought in the courts, Congress became involved as well. Where the HHS rules were based on civil rights clauses in section 504, Congress enacted legislation in 1984 (and reauthorized it in 1991) making failure to treat handicapped newborns a form of child neglect. The pro-life and disability rights movement and the American Academy of Pediatrics, joined by several other medical groups, continued to negotiate to try to reach a compromise. In the end, the fragile coalition supported amendments to the Child Abuse Prevention and Treatment Act. The amendments define medical neglect as

> failure to respond to the infant's life-threatening conditions by providing treatment (including appropriate nutrition, hydration, and medication) which, in the treating physician's reasonable medical judgment, will be most likely to be effective in ameliorating or correcting all such conditions. (at 1752)

The amendments provided for three exceptions (that is, situations in which treatment is not medically indicated):

a. the infant is chronically and irreversibly comatose;
b. the providing of (medical) treatment would (i) merely prolong dying, (ii) not be effective in ameliorating or correcting all of the infant's life-threatening conditions, or (iii) otherwise be futile in terms of the survival of the infant; or
c. the provision of such treatment would be virtually futile in terms of the survival of the infant, and the treatment itself under such circumstances would be inhumane. (at 1752)

The scale for weighing the rights of interested parties was clearly tipped against parents and, to a large extent, against physicians. The latter were free to make the diagnosis but could develop the treatment plan only within the framework of the law. They could not withhold treatment unless the child was irreversibly comatose or would die regardless of treatment. They could not make treatment determinations on the basis of quality of life prognoses.

The first legal test of the Child Abuse Amendments of 1984 involved a five-week-old Minnesota infant who lapsed into a coma in April 1986 after having been beaten by his father. All the treating physicians agreed that there was no possibility that Baby Lance would recover and had virtually no expectation that he would regain consciousness. After consultation with the hospital's ethics committee, Lance's mother decided to pursue a program of "comfort care," including food and water but excluding antibiotics, resuscitation, or ventilator support. The father opposed the comfort care approach and, invoking the Child Abuse Amendments, argued for aggressive treatment. (It should be noted that shortly after the beating, the father pleaded guilty to assault, and under Minnesota law he would have been charged with third-degree homicide if Lance had died prior to sentencing on the assault charge.) The mother and the hospital obtained a court order forcing termination of treatment except to provide nutrition, hydration, and medication (*In the Matter of Lance Steinhaus*, 1986). Lance's father was sentenced on the assault charge and subsequently agreed to abide by a "do not resuscitate" order ("Agreement Ends Legal Fight" 1986). Lance died in February 1987 of the injuries received in the beating.

This case indicates the complexity of conflicts that can arise between parties involved with critically ill or injured newborns. One wonders what position Lance's father would have taken had his own incarceration not hinged on whether Lance would die before his assault plea could be heard by the court. The case also points to the potential misuse of the intent of the Child Abuse Amendments.

Whether the amendments should apply to extremely low birth weight babies is also debatable because NICU care may not improve their chances of survival. Maureen Hack and Avroy Fanaroff report that the mortality rates of babies born at less than twenty-five weeks' gestation or with birth weights below 750 grams were not improved despite aggressive treatment (1989, 1642). They question the utility of treating these tiny infants:

> These results have ethical, economic, and medicolegal implications. Extremely-low-birth-weight infants who require prolonged, often futile sojourns in neonatal intensive care units or who have poor long-term outcomes have become major consumers of health care resources and in some cases a major drain on health maintenance organizations. The allocation of limited resources may in the future mean denying care to some of these infants. At present, the prevailing moral and medicolegal climate dictates active intervention even when the prospects for survival are minimal and those for survival without severe impairment still smaller. (1646)

Another consideration with regard to resource allocation is that money expended on intensive care for extremely low birth weight babies could be utilized for prenatal care, thus increasing the number of babies born full term and reducing the number of babies admitted to NICUs. As mentioned in Chapter 7, the Institute of Medicine estimates that for every $1.00 spent on prenatal care, approximately $3.00 is saved in infants' medical costs (1985, 232).

An interesting paradox is that the 1984 Child Abuse Amendments took away from some parents what it had seemingly given to others. Whereas it is illegal for parents to refuse to treat a child because they do not want it to endure a life of pain and suffering, it is legal for parents to refuse conventional medical treatment and to rely instead on prayer as a means of spiritual healing regardless of whether the child suffers or dies. The exemption is the result of the Department of Health Education and Welfare rules for implementing the 1974 Child Abuse Neglect Prevention and Treatment Act, which was amended in 1984 to require medical treatment of critically ill newborns with disabilities (Merrick 1994).

While most of the public policy debate regarding critically ill newborns with disabilities has centered on those cases where parents have sought to withdraw treatment, there are also cases where parents have attempted to force treatment in seemingly futile circumstances. Such is the case of Baby K, an anencephalic infant born in October 1992 at Fairfax Hospital in Falls Church, Virginia. Standard medical treatment for anencephalics is comfort care only (warmth, nutrition, and hydration). But Baby K's mother insisted that she be intubated and placed on a mechanical ventilator as needed. Fairfax Hospital initiated action in federal district court for the Eastern District of Virginia, seeking a ruling that would allow the hospital to discontinue what it considered to be futile treatment.

The district court, however, ruled in the mother's favor on several grounds (*In re Baby K*, 1993). First, it found that the Emergency Medical Treatment and Active Labor Act (federal legislation designed to prevent hospitals from refusing emergency medical care to indigent patients) required hospitals to stabilize patients to prevent their deterioration. Thus Baby K should be placed on mechanical ventilation when needed to stabilize her condition. Second, the district court found that Baby K was a "disabled" person within the guidelines of the 1973 Rehabilitation Act, and therefore she could not be denied mechanical ventilation because of her anencephalic disability. Third, the district court found that the Americans with Disabilities Act "does not permit the denial of ventilator services that would keep alive an anencephalic baby when those life-saving services would otherwise be provided to a baby without disabilities at the parent's request" (*In re Baby K*, 1993, 1029).

On appeal to the United States Court of Appeals for the Fourth District, only arguments relative to the Emergency Medical Treatment and Active Labor Act were considered. The appeals court found for the mother, concluding that the hospital could not deny mechanical ventilation for Baby K because it would not deny ventilation to other infants without anencephaly. It also found that the hospital had a duty to stabilize Baby K (provide mechanical ventilation) because the Act required the stabilization of patients who cannot be transferred to other medical facilities—Baby K could not be transferred because her mother refused to approve the transfer, the hospital had not shown that the benefits of the transfer outweighed the risks, and no other appropriate medical facility would accept the transfer (*In re Baby K,* 1994). This is another paradox in the treatment of critically ill newborns because conflict regarding their care is possible both when parents want to withdraw treatment and also when parents want to pursue aggressive treatment. Neither situation is easily resolved.

Conclusion

The controversy about caring for newborns with life-threatening disabilities centers on some of the same rights issues that have pervaded the other areas of reproductive rights discussed in this book. A number of parties play key roles in determining the care for such children. Newborns, whose continued existence and quality of life are the focus of this debate, obviously cannot give either informed consent or informed refusal for medical care. But that does not diminish the importance of the fact that they have rights. Important issues have been raised concerning newborns' rights and the impact of the NICU on these newborns:

> It is ironic that the [Child Abuse Amendments], which supposedly protect infants from child abuse, may in some cases actually be the instrument for child abuse in the form of prolonging dying under conditions of a brutal intensive care from which there is no escape. . . . There is both deprivation of the usual tender, need-fulfilling 'mothering' of the infant during the NICU stay, and the experience of over stimulation of noxious or painful invasive stimuli—emergency needle thoracentesis, uncountable heel sticks, numerous insertions of needles to start intravenous lines, prolonged periods of sleep interruption, periods of anxiety caused by acute air hunger, and other discomforts. The sicker the infant, the longer the NICU stay, the more damaging the physical and emotional cumulative effect of these experiences. (Penticuff 1992, 273)

Moreover, some have argued that the child has a right not to be victimized by medical experimentation: "To say that medical treatment must be given to a 450-gram neonate on the grounds that to deny care is to neglect an infant because it is disabled or may become disabled is simply to waffle the distinction between experimentation and treatment'' (Caplan 1992, 118).

The proponents of the Child Abuse Amendments in the 1980s were primarily concerned about babies with Down Syndrome and spina bifida. But such infants are not the typical patients in today's NICU; thus outdated legislation constitutes the legal framework for current decision making. The Baby Doe of today

> is likely to be a 500-700 gram premature baby on ventilatory support, an infant with short-bowel syndrome resulting from volvulus or necrotizing enterocolitis . . . an infant with multiple complex physical anomalies coupled with severe brain damage, or an infant in a persistent vegetative state requiring tube feeding and gastric fundoplication to prevent death from aspiration pneumonia. (Shaw 1992, 200)

Parental rights have clearly been diminished by passage of the 1984 Child Abuse Amendments. There is a long-standing legal precedent guaranteeing couples the right to have children; parents do not, however, always have the legal right to determine the treatment for those children. Specifically, they do not have the right to refuse consent for potentially life-saving care unless the child is permanently unconscious or unless the care would merely prolong dying, or would be ineffective in ameliorating all life-threatening conditions, or would be a futile attempt to ensure the survival of the infant.

The law gives physicians—clearly third parties in this struggle—more power than parents, although most physician respondents in surveys conducted in the aftermath of enactment of the Baby Doe legislation believed that the legislation interferes with parental rights to determine what medical care is in the best interests of their children (Kopelman, Irons, and Kopelman 1988). It is reasonable to assume that physicians want to consider parental preferences in determining care. Moreover, physicians and families typically do not welcome the intrusion of government agencies. Donald Shapiro and Paul Rosenberg point to the negative impact that the early HHS Baby Doe regulations had on the medical staff and family. After an HHS on-site investigation involving critically ill conjoined twins, family, physicians, and staff felt ''demeaned'' and ''under suspicion''; the family's private tragedy became a news media event as a result of sensationalized reporting. Other parents who had infants in the same unit were also emotionally affected. The cost of the twins' care increased, and hospital administrators, legal counsel, physicians, and family members had to spend much of their time responding to the investigators (Shapiro and Rosenberg 1984).

The state holds the trump card in this struggle, yet rarely has it exercised its authority (Civil Rights 1989, 149). The lack of state action may be fortunate—not because treatment should be withheld from vulnerable infants but because the final decisions in disputed cases will be made by the courts. As has been discussed earlier, however, generally the courts are not the appropriate arena for determination of medical care.

Medical decisions, particularly those made in the NICU, are typically made in an atmosphere of emergency medicine. Babies are in the NICU because they have life-threatening conditions that require immediate attention. The parties, especially the parents who may already be suffering from shock and grief, usually do not have adequate time to retain counsel, and counsel, if retained, usually does not have adequate time to prepare arguments. Judges, who have no training in medicine, must rush to judgment, pressured by the thought that a baby is dying. Resorting to the courts to determine treatment for newborns is part of the gradual erosion of parental rights in nearly all aspects of reproduction, from conception to care of newborns, and is premised on the misconception that the state cares more for the welfare of children than do the parents. The courtroom is clearly not an atmosphere conducive to thoughtful decision making regarding the rights of the state, hospital staff, parents, or newborns. Injecting the state into the volatile circumstances of treatment for a critically ill newborn divides rather than unifies the parties who have the most to gain or lose in the struggle to determine who shall decide treatment.

C H A P T E R   10

Changing Reproductive Rights: Technology and Policy

Many aspects of human reproduction are undergoing major change as more sophisticated technologies emerge. Each of the substantive areas discussed in earlier chapters contributes a unique element to the public policy debate over reproductive rights, yet all have certain features in common. First, they are being modified by rapid developments in technological intervention capabilities. Long-standing reproductive issues are being complicated by new knowledge and innovations, which include RU-486, Norplant, and IVF, as well as intensive medical interventions for seriously ill newborns.

Second, these areas are affected by the increasing presence of a large number and wide variety of participants in the procreative process: medical clinicians and technicians, entrepreneurs, attorneys, researchers, donors of sperm and ova, and surrogate mothers. Although these parties may have common objectives, such as the production of healthy children, conflicts often develop among them. These conflicts are often defined in terms of rights and many are assigned a high priority on the public policy agenda.

This chapter suggests some key elements to consider in re-evaluating the contribution of reproductive rights and discusses the need to take the vigorous steps necessary to shape and channel these technologies in socially acceptable directions. It also demonstrates why the constitution of the opposition to reproductive interventions makes for such difficult politics. It concludes by arguing that while prohibition of any reproductive technology would be dangerous, we must better anticipate the long-term social implications and introduce regulations where necessary to protect those parties which are most vulnerable to abuses of the new reproduction.

Table 10-1   Reproductive Rights and Types of Medical Intervention

	Reproductive right		
Intervention	Not to have	To have	To control characteristics, quality
Abortion	x		
Fertility control	x		
Assisted reproduction		x	
Surrogate motherhood		x	
Prenatal intervention			x
Genetic screening, therapy			x
Maternal intervention			x
Fetal and embryo research			x
Neonatal care			x

Redefining the Concept of Reproductive Rights

Reproductive rights have expanded from a right not to have children, to a right to have children, to a right to attempt to control the characteristics and quality of progeny. The major reproductive rights impacted by each form of medical intervention are listed in Table 10-1. Abortion and fertility control raise issues concerning the right to decide whether or not to have children, assisted reproduction and surrogate motherhood, the right to have children, and to some degree other interventions, to control progeny characteristics and quality.

Reality, of course, is more complex, given the wide range of uses of intervention techniques, depending on who controls them and the motivation for each application. For instance, although the primary rights issue raised by abortion and sterilization centers on legal and effective access to these services, coerced use of these procedures interferes with the right to have children. Similarly, although the primary issue raised by assisted reproduction is the right to have children by having access to DI, IVF, and other techniques, extensions of their direct clinical applications (DI with sex preselection or IVF with preimplantation testing) concern the right to control the quality of progeny. And surrogate motherhood contracts can lead to legal disputes over who has the right to the potential child.

Prenatal intervention, genetic screening, and attempts to provide a safe fetal environment presumably facilitate the production of healthy children, but if coercion is used, the result may be conflict with the right to have children. This becomes particularly relevant when society deems irresponsible the decisions of parents who refuse, for whatever reason, to make use of available technologies or who act in ways that might be injurious to the potential child. As discussed in Chapter 8, yet other issues are raised when the benefits of fetal research go not to fetuses but to third parties.

Abortion and fertility control, the issues that are most firmly established on the policy agenda, concern primarily the right not to have children—the right that has the most solid moral and constitutional basis. Because the issues discussed in Chapters 4 through 9 concern rights that are less solidly grounded in either ethics or law, they are more complex than the contentious issues of abortion and sterilization, and their resolution poses a significant challenge for policy makers.

Government Involvement in Human Reproduction

Government involvement in human reproduction is as varied as the applications themselves. This variation is understandable, given that reproductive innovations are continually creating new policy dilemmas. The pace of change means that the efforts of policy makers to address each issue as it develops are likely to be futile. Keeping pace is especially difficult for legislators, for whom policy making is a deliberative and generally slow process of negotiation and compromise. Moreover, most of the issues discussed in this book are not amenable to the bargaining process because reproductive rights are often nonnegotiable.

Agenda setting in a context of rapid technological change is also problematic. What is new and controversial today may be of little public interest tomorrow. Even though cases pertaining to human reproduction make dramatic headlines, there seems to be little sustained interest on the part of the news media in specific procedures, events, and legal cases. For example, although in vitro fertilization dominated the headlines in 1978 and Baby M was the issue in 1988, both were soon superseded by other newsworthy reproductive issues. As a result, the public, as well as its representatives in Congress and the state legislatures, have a difficult time comprehending the underlying issues.

Table 10-2 summarizes the government institutions that have been involved in each area of policy making. The table does not indicate degree of activity, however, which varies both by institution and across the states. In general, the most active involvement in reproductive issues has been that of the courts; legislatures and federal agencies are sometimes able to avoid becoming embroiled in the conflicts, and the possible political controversy, precipitated by such issues. But state legislatures are increasingly finding reproductive issues on their agenda, sometimes because the courts request policy guidance in a highly publicized case. Conflicts on issues such as

Table 10-2 Government Policy Making on Issues of Human Reproduction

Policy area	Courts	Congress	Federal agency	State legislatures
Abortion	x	x	x	x
Fertility control	x		x	x
Assisted reproduction	x		x	x
Surrogate motherhood	x			x
Prenatal diagnosis	x			x
Genetic screening	x	x		
Human genome initiative		x	x	
Conflict in maternal-fetal relationship				
Medical intervention	x			
Substance abuse	x			x
Workplace hazards	x	x	x	x
Fetal and embryo research	x	x	x	x
Neonatal care	x	x	x	x

neonatal intensive care, abortion, and genetic intervention have also found their way to the congressional agenda; disputes over issues such as workplace hazards and fetal research have triggered considerable activity on the part of federal agencies. Many of these issues have also been the subject of study by national and presidential commissions, the Office of Technology Assessment, and other government committees and task forces.

The existence of an issue on the public policy agenda does not guarantee that the problem will be adequately addressed, much less resolved; government intervention may even hinder efforts to find a solution. As discussed in Chapter 9, some of the actions of the Reagan administration and Congress regarding the treatment of ill newborns were at best symbolic and at worst counterproductive. There may be some areas of reproductive policy that should be primarily the concern of the private sector. Some areas, however, have public dimensions and will still require public-sector involvement.

Although a strong case can be made for federal or state legislation in certain areas (such as genetic screening, surrogate motherhood, and nonconsensual sterilization) in order to ensure consistent standards and protections, other areas might require continued judicial involvement because every situation is different. The problem, then, is not the absence of a comprehensive national policy on issues of human reproduction, which may not be feasible in any case, but rather the absence of a national debate on what the priorities of such a policy should be.

A major problem is that the political system in the United States is reactive rather than anticipatory. The courts respond to the cases before them and decide on the basis of the facts in each case. Although legislatures in theory select their agendas, lawmakers tend to react to immediate political pressures and sometimes take action only after an issue has reached the crisis stage. Legislatures also tend to work within a limited time frame and do not always adopt a long-term perspective. This helps explain why preventive measures, whose costs are imposed in the present but whose benefits usually accrue in the future, frequently lose out to potentially curative measures in the competition for scarce resources.

Reproductive Rights: A Reevaluation

The preceding chapters have focused on some of the policy issues created by new technological capabilities and knowledge, especially those regarding the rights of the many parties involved in technologically mediated procreation. The issues of the commercialization and the medicalization of reproduction, and the inclusion of many third parties in the process of producing children have intensified conflicts over reproductive rights to the point that many are questioning the usefulness of a rights approach to reproduction.

The issues surrounding rights in this technological context have become increasingly complex. As difficult as it is to resolve conflicts about rights, however, rights are but one, albeit an important, element in the policy equation. Although protection of rights and preservation of human dignity have been central to reproductive policy in the United States, there are competing goals, which include maximization of societal and community welfare, scientific and technological progress, efficiency, societal stability, and social justice. Attitudes toward particular reproductive innovations and applications, as well as reproductive technology in general, depend in part on which goals are viewed as most important in each cultural setting. Historically, there always has been friction in western political thought between theories of societal good and theories of individual rights.

Although the concept of rights is the cornerstone of American political and legal theory and is central to American politics, the issues that have been raised in this book illustrate how problematic its application to reproduction has become. The cumulative policy impact of reproductive intervention has been so great as to suggest the need for a reassessment and clarification of the basic questions regarding rights that were raised in Chapter 1. Who has rights? What do they entail? What should be done in cases of conflict? Without such a reassessment of these questions at this stage, the emerging issues surrounding reproductive rights promise to become increasingly impenetrable.

The concept of reproductive rights is attractive to supporters of women's autonomy in procreative matters. Before the 1970s, the emphasis was on the right of women not to reproduce; in the 1980s, the emphasis shifted to the right to have children and, as a result of improved technological capabilities and increased knowledge, the right of the fetus (and the born child) to have a sound mind and body. Also, applications such as contract surrogacy combined with IVF have frequently led to a conflict between the rights of the genetic mother and father and those of the gestational mother. The danger in taking a rights approach is that the balance among rights can easily be altered, either subtly or overtly, to either the detriment or benefit of particular parties, as social values and technological capacities change. The advantages gained by one group in terms of rights, therefore, are not necessarily permanent. The rights approach is a clearly volatile one.

Establishing Societal Goals and Priorities

There are difficulties in using reproductive rights as the framework for analyzing reproductive technologies and for distributing the benefits and risks of the parties involved. The problems raised at all stages of reproduction, from preconception to the prenatal and neonatal stages, suggest the need for a thorough reevaluation of whether reproductive rights should continue to be the defining factor in specific cases:

> Conceptualizing and debating issues in a competing individual rights model is destined to be divisive and unproductive in a sphere of life in which community, common shared interest, and social well-being are of paramount importance. (Ruzek 1991, 83)

It is important at this juncture to analyze human reproduction in a much broader social context with a view to maximizing the freedom and the health of all individuals concerned. If such an approach is impossible, social goals and priorities should be analyzed in order to define with more precision the balance of goals that is most appropriate. Critical and objective assessment is needed to clarify where the rights model is taking society in light of the changes that have been taking place.

There is a need for creation of a national commission to provide a forum for the discussion of national goals and priorities in human reproduction and to facilitate a comprehensive analysis of the policy issues raised by reproductive technologies. This body should be responsible for clarifying the issues in debate and raising the level of public awareness. It could be included as part of a Presidential Bioethics Commission (Hanna, Cook-Degan, and Nishimi 1993), or it could be an autonomous commission concerned specifically with issues of human reproduction.

One useful role of such a commission would be to determine which areas covered in this book would be best served by active government participation. If Table 10-2 is assumed to be an accurate representation of government involvement, what would be the best mix of judicial, legislative, and executive action, and which areas, if any, should be the concern of the private sector?

Another option that ought to be given consideration is the establishment of a special governmental unit designed to provide society with a better understanding of where it is headed and what steps should be taken to get it where it wants to go. To this end, Lester Milbrath proposes establishing, as part of the federal government, a Council for Long-Range Societal Guidance, whose primary purpose would be to analyze the long-range consequences of governmental action (or nonaction) and to provide guidance to leaders and citizens. It would monitor conditions and changes in society, facilitate social learning, stimulate debate and exchange of ideas about the issues, and make policy recommendations. As a result of the council's work, the public interest would be "given a greater chance to become defined by careful, intellectual, holistic, long-term analysis, instead of by simplistic, sloganized appeals to short-term interests" (Milbrath 1989, 294).

Milbrath's proposal may or may not be feasible or desirable, but the concept of a governmental mechanism to facilitate a future-oriented debate about the issues surrounding human reproduction is a useful one. As long as the existing institutions are unable or unwilling to set reasonable priorities and goals for society and to provide a framework in which the public can have some input, the long-term resolution of the core issues is not likely to be forthcoming.

The Allocation of Scarce Resources

Although the questions concerning societal goals for the future should be placed on the policy agenda, a more immediate question is whether society can afford to define reproductive rights as positive rights. As the range of reproductive interventions widens and their costs escalate, questions of access will increase. Pressures for containment of health care costs and for more specific allocation and rationing mechanisms will increasingly place reproductive technologies in competition with other areas of health care spending such as AIDS (Ingram 1993, 105). The United States, unlike most other western nations, largely rejects the notion of a positive right or entitlement to government subsidized health care and has opted instead for a private insurance system that minimizes the role of the government (Blank 1988). This situation might be modified with adoption of some type of universal health insurance coverage, but such changes are

Table 10-3   Causes and Prevention of Infertility

Factors predisposing an individual toward infertility and available preventive measures

Sexually transmitted diseases and pelvic inflammatory disease
Ensure that adequate health education is available to discourage unpro-
tected sexual encounters; practice monogamy; conduct forthright inquiry; carefully select and check possible sexual partners for risk of sexually transmitted diseases.

Practice contraception by means of condoms; use condoms routinely with each
new sex partner; media campaign to encourage condom use.

Have periodic screenings for sexually transmitted diseases if sexually active; such
diseases in both males and females are commonly asymptomatic.

Pelvic infections after birth, abortion, surgery, or invasive diagnostic testing
Ensure that optimally safe birth and surgical services are available.

Use prophylactic antibiotics in high-risk situations to prevent infection.

Exercise, poor nutrition, and stress
Avoid regular strenuous exercise (exceeding 60 minutes daily), rapid weight loss,
low body fat, and stress, which may cause decreased fertility. Women are at higher risk
than men.

Smoking, environmental toxins, and drugs
Avoid smoking and substance abuse, which reduce reproductive potential. (Environmental exposures have not been adequately studied.)

likely to be accompanied by limits on coverage for the most expensive
types of reproductive technologies.

The economic realities of scarce resources and constrained health bud-
gets, then, make it unlikely that reproduction will be defined as a positive
right in terms of access to all technologies that guarantee the individual a
capacity to have children and to attempt to control their quality. This means
that the right to have children will likely be considered at best a negative
right. To do so, however, means that many infertile individuals, as well as
those who cannot afford reproductive services or who do not have adequate
third-party coverage, will be denied the means to exercise that right. Such a
policy discriminates against the poor and the members of minority groups
who want to have children. When Secretary of the Department of Health,
Education, and Welfare Patricia Harris allowed the charter of the Ethics
Advisory Board to expire in 1980, thus ending federal support for IVF
research, she said she failed to see how such research would benefit the
health of the poor and disadvantaged, which was for her the highest priori-

Endometriosis
   If there is a family history of endometriosis, consider oral contraception and possible specific endometriosis suppression. Oral contraceptives may suppress endometriosis even in those not at risk. Seek early diagnosis and treatment if symptoms persist.

Cryoptochidism and variococele
   Treat undescended, especially intra-abdominal, testes as promptly as possible. (Benefits of surveillance and treatment of varicocele are controversial.)

Chemotherapy and radiation
   Risks of gonadal damage should be considered; gamete collection or protection of the gonads should be performed if appropriate.

Intercurrent illnesses
   Seek treatment of the acute and chronic diseases that cause anovulation or decreased spermatogenesis.

Inadequate knowledge of reproduction
   Ensure that information on reproduction is available from parents, schools, clergy, and other sources.

Inadequate medical treatment
   If having difficulty conceiving, seek information about fertility and seek specialized care to avoid prolonging infertility.

Lack of perspective about reproduction
   Discuss family life with parents, peers, and professionals. Formulate life plan that allows adequate time for reproductive goals.

Source: Adapted from Office of Technology Assessment 1988b, 7.

ty: ''I need greater justification for such research. Whether the research will take place with or without government support is not really relevant. Why should the government support such an area as this?'' (quoted in Fletcher 1993, 212).

   One of the dangers of an overdependence on technological solutions to reproductive problems is that resources are diverted from research aimed at finding the causes of infertility and the means to prevent them. Effective means of prevention already exist for most of the factors predisposing a person to infertility (see Table 10-3). Allocating more resources to establishing preventive measures for the known causes of infertility, continued with a research priority of determining unknown causes, would ultimately benefit poor women and minority women more than would the allocation of significantly more resources for IVF and other innovations. Similarly, although some women and their potential children might benefit from sophisticated prenatal screening, fetal surgery, and gene therapy, current priorities seem misguided at a time when many women lack basic knowledge about reproduction and adequate prenatal care and nutrition.

The development of new technological capabilities, therefore, has created a paradox with regard to reproductive rights. Although individuals can now choose from among a wide range of technologies promising fertility control, infertility treatment, and characteristic selection capabilities, or seek diagnostics and therapy for fetuses and neonates, many individuals encounter problems of access. To provide these technologies to all persons as a positive right is financially prohibitive and would divert resources from other areas of health care. To deny them to individuals who desire them and need them to exercise their reproductive autonomy, however, negates their right to reproduce in any meaningful sense. Even in the absence of any legal restrictions or exclusions, persons without significant resources would be excluded de facto. But once the technologies become widely available in the marketplace, any attempts to deny their use to individuals who can afford them would conflict with their negative rights to reproduce. This dilemma illustrates the inability of a rights approach to resolve problems concerning the distribution of the impressive new technological capabilities in society.

The Future of Reproductive Technologies

Despite the medical and legal trends regarding the technologies described here, it is indeed possible to influence the boundaries and future direction of reproductive technologies. The rapidity and scope of technological change might lead one to assume that its momentum is so powerful that it denies society the capacity to manage and direct its development. It is unlikely that political decisions can fully control technological development, but theories of ''autonomous technology'' or ''uncontrolled technological determination'' also fail to explain the complicated relationship between technology and society (Street 1992, 23-45). History has shown that the control of technology is difficult, but if society so desires, significant control is possible.

Although technologies can alter values and the way people think about things, the relationship between values and technology is reciprocal—values also shape the boundaries of technology (as discussed in Chapter 1). For example, surrogate motherhood became an issue in the 1980s not because of some dramatic breakthrough in technology but because of a change in the way people thought about reproduction. Donor insemination, the procedure that is widely used today in conjunction with surrogacy contracts, has been in existence for more than a century, but surrogacy contracts became common only in the last decade, when many childless couples found adoption difficult. Also contributing to the demand were a renewed emphasis on ascertaining genetic roots and an increase in the number of young professionals whose incomes enabled them to afford expensive fertility interventions.

There is also evidence that, technically, IVF could have been practiced considerably earlier than 1978. Human eggs were fertilized ex utero as early as the 1940s, but research was phased out because of the hostile social climate existing at that time (Lorber 1987). Value changes that may have set the stage for today's reproductive technologies were influenced by the "me-centered" cultural orientation of the 1980s, which demanded immediate gratification of desires through technology.

The quest for more control over the products of reproduction—the increased acceptance of, and demand for, prenatal diagnosis, genetic screening, and characteristic selection—reflects the trend toward smaller (two children) families, which, in turn, reflects a recognition of the economic realities of raising children, a concern for population control, and altered lifestyles. The "perfect child" mentality has been encouraged by advances in technology, but it has also been a powerful force in the dispersion of technological advances.

It should be pointed out that medical advances can be used for many different ends and can affect different persons differently. These technologies are controversial because they "crystallize issues at the heart of contemporary controversies over sexuality, parenthood, reproduction, and the family" (Stanworth 1988, 18). The debate over these innovations should focus not on whether they should continue to be developed but on which uses are acceptable and which are not. "The technology is underway, but how we as a species choose to use it, where we allow it to be used, and when we draw limits are critical issues for all of us, but especially for women" (Harrison 1987, 2).

The technologies that enable the selection of children's characteristics do not necessarily result in the denigration of women or the invasion of their reproductive privacy, but given the prevalence of a male-dominated value system sympathetic to these ends and in the absence of conscious attempts to influence the use of such technologies, the danger clearly exists. A thorough policy assessment with regard to these technologies, therefore, should focus on their cumulative impact on women and on women's experiences as reproductive beings (Overall 1987). In view of the trends that have been discussed here, however, those persons who firmly reject any notion of fetal interests, and thus any constraint on pregnant women, face an uphill battle in attempting to limit advances in medical technology.

Moreover, there is increasing medical evidence that many actions by the pregnant woman can be harmful to the developing fetus. But there is a danger that efforts to protect the interests of the unborn child and to deter

Table 10-4   A Continuum of Groups Opposed to Reproductive Technology

	Women's health groups	Civil liberties groups	Minority groups	Advocates of rights of the disabled	Religious leaders	Right to life organizations	
Left							Right

Source: Blank 1990, 220.

harmful parental behavior will compromise the autonomy and the physical integrity of pregnant women. As a result of the rapid dispersion of reproductive technologies and their increased acceptance by society, however, the courts might decide to require adoption of stricter standards of care for pregnant women. Requirements might be established that dictate not only life-style choice during pregnancy but the use of prenatal diagnostic tests, genetic screening, and other appropriate medical innovations. Again, this tendency for stricter standards of care for pregnant women can be traced to a rights-oriented approach and an adversarial legal framework that requires decisions to be based on injury, proximate cause, and standards of duty. Although pitting the fetal right to have a sound mind and body against the pregnant woman's right to reproduction is ultimately counterproductive, it follows from this adversarial environment.

Technological change can progress without restriction, but only if there is a positive social climate. Just as the climate of the 1960s was ripe for the contraceptive revolution, that of the 1980s was receptive to technological change. The initial, almost unbridled, enthusiasm for reproductive innovations, however, has been moderated by the realization on the part of many that reproductive technologies can bring problems as well as benefits. Not surprisingly, the result has been widespread opposition to many applications of reproductive technology. Groups that perceive a threat to their interests have mobilized against these technologies. Resistance is as likely to come from women's health groups and minority groups as it is from religious leaders and right to life organizations (see Table 10-4). Advocates of the rights of disabled persons and civil liberties groups have expressed concern about the implications of certain applications. Although the reasons for opposition vary, the arguments often center on rights, including those of women, children, and fetuses. Although the dangers are sometimes exaggerated and the rhetoric frequently obscures a rational debate concerning reproductive innovations, the breadth and intensity of these concerns and the fact that they cut across ideological lines give some indication of the dilemmas faced by policy makers and explain why they frequently defer to the courts.

Regulating the Application of Reproductive Technologies

Despite the conflicts among rights that reproductive interventions have produced and the difficult policy issues they create, the prohibition of such interventions is both undesirable and unfeasible. First, prohibition of a particular application would be problematic, given the constitutionally based emphasis on procreative freedom. Second, banning the use of a reproductive technology in one jurisdiction, whether state or federal, is unlikely to deter its use in other jurisdictions, as evidenced by the history of abortion prior to *Roe v. Wade* (1973) and the more recent experience with prohibiting surrogacy contracts. The primary effect of prohibiting a particular application would be to widen the gap between those who have the funds to go elsewhere for the procedure and those who do not. Third, prohibiting a particular application of a technology out of concern for its undesirable consequences could foreclose the possibility that its other applications would have beneficial consequences.

Although prohibition of reproductive interventions is unfeasible, regulation—public, private, or some combination of the two—coupled with a comprehensive education program, could ensure that these technologies are used for socially acceptable purposes. Administrative mechanisms have been established to protect those persons or groups most vulnerable to exploitation in the application of fertility control technologies, especially sterilization, although there are still instances of involuntary sterilization. Sterilization for most persons represents an expansion of individual choice. The newer technological developments, such as long-term subdermal implants, also require oversight to prevent abuse.

A major policy objective should be the creation of public mechanisms to protect the interests of all parties, especially those most vulnerable to exploitation and abuse. Feminists, minority group leaders, and civil libertarians have voiced legitimate concerns about abuses in the application of these technologies and about the way access to such technologies is determined. Reproductive technologies expand the procreative choices of affluent middle-class (largely white) couples, who are free to give informed consent for their use; but there is a danger that the same freedom will be denied to the less affluent, who have access to such technologies only when approved by welfare workers. Poor women, who are largely dependent on the state for financial support, are particularly vulnerable to abuse.

There is a need for more public awareness of such abuse. The commercialization of reproductive services threatens to exacerbate social inequities and undermine efforts to ensure adequate regulation of these technologies. The answer is not simply to ban their use but rather to ensure that proper standards are enforced to protect all parties.

Conclusion

The rapid development of new interventions in human procreation and the increase in knowledge about fetal development make the issues surrounding them important matters of public policy. The new reproductive technologies promise benefits for many people, but certain applications threaten the values held by many others, thus generating what has often been intense opposition by a wide range of interests. This combination of a growing demand for reproductive services on the one hand, and condemnation of certain applications on the other, virtually ensures that interest in such policy issues will intensify and that they will increasingly require a clear response by the makers of public policy.

Innovations in human reproductive technology have made necessary a reexamination of prevailing views concerning what it means to be a human being and of social relationships. These innovations also challenge traditional notions of individual rights and arouse concern that human life may be treated as a commodity. Serious consideration should be given to changing the policy process to allow flexible societal responses to future technological developments. There is a need to clarify societal priorities and to increase public awareness about the potential impact of issues and innovations. Public mechanisms should be established so that these technological advances can be assessed and monitored on a continuing basis, rather than on an ad hoc basis as they currently are. It is essential that the potential benefits and risks associated with each technique be defined and evaluated as soon as is feasible in the developmental process, to avoid undue risks and forfeited benefits.

As the range of reproductive intervention techniques and procedures expands, public expectations concerning the availability of reproductive choice will increase. One result will be increased pressure for more widespread access, thus creating more problems with regard to the allocation of medical resources at a time when there are increasing demands to set limits on health care expenditures. The problem of determining how reproductive rights should be defined in light of the issues presented in this book will likely create new and similarly challenging policy problems. The powers that these technologies confer on potential parents to select the characteristics of their progeny carry with them a responsibility to make the right choices. Determining what the right choices are will require considerable effort by policy makers and an informed public.

Bibliography

Abel, Ernest L., and Robert Sokol. 1987. "Incidence of Fetal Alcohol Syndrome and Economic Impact of FAS-Related Anomalies." *Drug and Alcohol Dependence* 19: 51-70.

"Abortion Fueling Health Plan Battle." *Sarasota Herald-Tribune* (February 12, 1994), 5A.

"Agreement Ends Legal Fight over Baby's Life." *St. Paul Pioneer Press* (October 24, 1986), 1A.

Allen, Marilee G., Pamela K. Donohue, and Amy E. Dusman. 1993. "The Limit of Viability: Neonatal Outcome of Infants Born at 22 to 25 Weeks Gestation." *New England Journal of Medicine* 329 (22): 1597-1601.

American Academy of Pediatrics. Committee on Bioethics. 1983. "Treatment of Critically Ill Newborns." *Pediatrics* 72: 565-566.

American Civil Liberties Union Reproductive Freedom Project. 1990. "Initial Report on RFP's South Carolina Investigation." Memorandum (February 1).

American College of Obstetricians and Gynecologists. 1987. "Patient Choice: Maternal-Fetal Conflict," no. 55 (October).

American Fertility Society. 1988a. "Revised New Guidelines for the Use of Semen-Donor Insemination." *Fertility and Sterility* 49 (2): 211.

___. 1988b. "Minimal Standards for Gamete Intrafallopian Transfer (GIFT)." *Fertility and Sterility* 50 (1): 20.

___. 1993a. "Guidelines for Oocyte Donation." *Fertility and Sterility* 59 (2): 5s-7s.

___. 1993b. "Guidelines for Therapeutic Donor Insemination: Sperm." *Fertility and Sterility* 59 (2): 1s-4s.

___. 1993c. "Minimum Genetic Screening for Gamete Donors." *Fertility and Sterility* 59 (2): 9s.

American Medical Association. Council on Scientific Affairs and Council on Ethical and Judicial Affairs. 1990. "Medical Applications of Fetal Tissue Transplantation." *Journal of the American Medical Association* 263 (4): 565-570.

Anderson, James E. 1990. *Public Policy-Making: An Introduction.* Boston: Houghton Mifflin.

Andrews, Lori B. 1988. "Feminism Revisited: Fallacies and Policies in the Surrogacy Debate." *Logos* 9: 81-96.

___. 1989. *Between Strangers: Surrogate Mothers, Expectant Fathers, and Brave New Babies.* New York: Harper and Row.

___. 1993. "Regulation of Experimentation on the Unborn." *Journal of Legal Medicine* 14 (1): 25-56.

Annas, George J. 1980. "Fathers Anonymous: Beyond the Best Interests of the Donor." *Family Law Quarterly* 14 (1): 1-13.

___. 1986a. "The Baby Broker Boom." *Hastings Center Report* 16 (3): 30-31.

___. 1986b. "Checkmating the Baby Doe Regulations." *Hastings Center Report* 16 (4): 29-31.

___. June 1987. "Baby M: Babies (and Justice) for Sale." *Hastings Center Report* 17 (3): 13-15.

Arditti, Rita. 1985. "Review Essay: Reducing Women to Matter." *Women's Studies International Forum* 8 (6): 577-582.

___. 1987. "The Surrogacy Business," *Social Policy* 18 (2): 42-46.

Asch, Adrienne, and Michelle Fine. 1990. "Shared Dreams: A Left Perspective on Disability Rights and Reproductive Rights." In *From Abortion to Reproductive Freedom: Transforming a Movement,* ed. Marlene Gerber Fried. Boston: South End Press, 233-240.

Association for Voluntary Surgical Contraception. 1988. "Current Status of Sterilization Laws Regarding Retarded Persons."

"Baby Doe Task Force Hits Snag." *Washington Post* (May 23, 1983).

Bayles, Michael D. 1976. "Harm to the Unconceived." *Philosophy and Public Affairs* 5 (3): 292-304.

___. 1984. *Reproductive Ethics.* Englewood Cliffs, N.J.: Prentice-Hall.

Beauchamp, Dan E. 1988. *The Health of the Republic: Epidemics, Medicine, and Moralism as Challenges to Democracy.* Philadelphia: Temple University Press.

Beauchamp, Tom L., and James F. Childress. 1989. *Principles of Biomedical Ethics.* 3d ed. New York: Oxford University Press.

Becker, Mary E. 1986. "From *Muller v. Oregon* to Fetal Vulnerability Policies." *University of Chicago Law Review* 53 (4): 1219-1273.

Berkowitz, Richard L. 1993. "Should Every Pregnant Woman Undergo Ultrasonography?" *New England Journal of Medicine* 329 (12): 874-875.

Berkowitz, Richard L., Lauren Lynch, Robert Lapinski, and Paul Bergh. 1992. "First-Trimester Transabdominal Multifetal Pregnancy Reduction: A Report of Two Hundred Completed Cases." *American Journal of Obstetrics and Gynecology* 169 (1): 17-21.

Berry, Jeffrey M. 1984. *The Interest Group Society.* Boston: Little, Brown.

Bishop, Jerry E., and Michael Waldholz. 1990. *Genome.* New York: Simon and Schuster.

Blank, Robert H. 1986. "Emerging Notions of Women's Rights and Responsibilities during Gestation." *Journal of Legal Medicine* 7 (4): 441-469.

___. 1988. *Rationing Medicine.* New York: Columbia University Press.

___. 1990. *Regulating Reproduction.* New York: Columbia University Press.

___. 1992a. "The Limits of Biomedical Technology Assessment: Values, Time, and Public Expectations." In *Science, Technology, and Politics: Policy Analysis in Congress,* ed. Gary C. Bryner. Boulder, Colo.: Westview Press, 107-122.

___. 1992b. *Mother and Fetus: Changing Notions of Maternal Responsibility.* Westport, Conn.: Greenwood Press.

___. 1993. *Fetal Protection in the Workplace: Women's Rights, Business Interests, and the Unborn.* New York: Columbia University Press.

Blank, Robert H., and Andrea L. Bonnicksen. 1992. "General Introduction to Emerging Issues in Biomedical Policy: An Annual Review." In *Emerging Issues in Biomedical Policy, vol. 1,* ed. Robert H. Blank and Andrea L. Bonnicksen. New York: Columbia University Press, vii-xv.

Boldt, Jeffrey. 1988. "Micromanipulation in Human Reproductive Technology." *Fertility and Sterility* 50 (2): 213-215.

Bonnicksen, Andrea L. 1989. *In Vitro Fertilization: Building Policy from Laboratories to Legislatures.* New York: Columbia University Press.

___. 1992. "Human Embryos and Genetic Testing: A Private Policy Model." *Politics and the Life Sciences* 11 (1): 53-62.

Boone, Sarah S. 1992. "Slavery and Contract Motherhood: A Radicalized Objection to Autonomy Arguments." In *Issues in Reproductive Technology I: An Anthology,* ed. Helen Bequaert Holmes. New York: Garland, 349-366.

Born, Mary Ann. 1986-1987. "Baby Doe's New Guardians: Federal Policy Brings Nontreatment Decisions Out of Hiding." *Kentucky Law Journal* 75 (Spring): 659-675.

Bowes, Watson A., and Brad Selgestad. 1981. "Fetal versus Maternal Rights: Medical and Legal Perspectives." *Obstetrics and Gynecology* 58 (2): 209-214.

Bowie, Norman E., and Robert L. Simon. 1977. *The Individual and the Political Order.* Englewood Cliffs, N.J.: Prentice-Hall.

Brandenburg, Helen, Coen G. Gho, Milena G. J. Jahoda et al. 1992. "Effect of Chorionic Villus Sampling on Utilization of Prenatal Diagnosis in Women of Advanced Maternal Age." *Clinical Genetics* 41: 239-244.

Braverman, Andrea Mechanick. 1993. "Survey Results on the Current Practice of Ovum Donation." *Fertility and Sterility* 59 (6): 1216-1220.

Brigham, John, Janet Rifkin, and Christine G. Solt. 1993. "Birth Technologies: Prenatal Diagnosis and Abortion Policy." *Politics and the Life Sciences* 12 (1): 31-44.

"British 'Femshield' May Soon Enter Full-Scale Efficacy Trials." 1988. *Contraceptive Technology Update* (February): 21-22.

Brodribb, Somer. 1984. "Reproductive Technologies, Masculine Dominance, and the Canadian State." Occasional Papers in Social Policy Analysis. Toronto: Ontario Institute for Studies in Education.

Bronshtein, M., E. Z. Zimmer, L. M. Gerlis, A. Lorber, and A. Drugan. 1993. "Early Ultrasound Diagnosis of Fetal Congenital Heart Defects in High-Risk and Low-Risk Pregnancies." *Obstetrics and Gynecology* 82 (2): 225-229.

Brown, Lawrence D. 1986. "Civil Rights and Regulatory Wrongs: The Reagan Administration and the Medical Treatment of Handicapped Infants." *Journal of Health Politics, Policy, and Law* 11 (Summer): 231-254.

Bumpass, Larry L. 1987. "The Risk of an Unwanted Birth: The Changing Context of Contraceptive Sterilization in the U.S." *Population Studies* 41 (3): 347-363.

Burt, Martha R. 1986. "Estimating the Public Costs of Teenage Childbearing." *Family Planning Perspectives* 18 (5): 221-226.

Burtchaell, J. T. 1988. "University Policy on Experimental Use of Aborted Fetal Tissue." *IRB: A Review of Human Subjects Research* 10: 7-11.

Callahan, Tamara L., Janet E. Hall, Susan L. Ettner, et al. 1994. "The Economic Impact of Multiple-Gestation Pregnancies and the Contribution of Assisted-Reproduction Techniques to Their Incidence." *New England Journal of Medicine* 331 (4): 244-249.

Caplan, Arthur. 1992. "Hard Cases Make Bad Law: The Legacy of the Baby Doe Controversy." In *Compelled Compassion: Government Intervention in the Treatment of Critically Ill Newborns*, ed. Arthur Caplan, Robert Blank, and Janna Merrick. Totowa, N.J.: Humana, 105-122.

Caplan, Arthur, and Cynthia B. Cohen. 1987. "Imperiled Newborns." *Hastings Center Report* 17 (6): 5-32.

Caplan, Arthur L., Robert H. Blank, and Janna C. Merrick. 1992. *Compelled Compassion: Government Intervention in the Treatment of Critically Ill Newborns.* Totowa, N.J.: Humana.

Capron, Alexander Morgan. 1987. "Alternative Birth Technologies: Legal Challenges." *University of California, Davis, Law Review* 20: 679-704.

Carbone, June. 1988. "The Limits of Contract Family Law: An Analysis of Surrogate Motherhood." *Logos* 9: 147-160.

Carson, Sandra Ann. 1988. "Sex Selection: The Ultimate in Family Planning." *Fertility and Sterility* 50 (1): 16-19.

Center for Reproductive Law and Policy. 1992a. *An Analysis of Planned Parenthood v. Casey.* New York.

___. 1992b. *Criminal Prosecutions of Women for Their Behavior during Pregnancy.* New York.

___. 1993a. *Ensuring Reproductive Freedom.* New York.

___. 1993b. *Legislative Responses to Violence and Harassment at Women's Health Clinics.* New York.

Center for Surrogate Parenting. 1993. "Surrogacy in the 1990's." *Newsletter* 1 (4): 1.

Chasnoff, Ira J. 1987. "Perinatal Effects of Cocaine." *Contemporary OB/GYN* 26 (5): 163-179.

___. 1988. "Newborn Infants with Drug Withdrawal Symptoms." *Pediatrics in Review* 9 (9): 273-277.

___. 1989. "Drug Use and Women: Establishing a Standard of Care." *Annals of the New York Academy of Sciences* 562: 208-210.

Chasnoff, Ira J., Kayreen A. Burns, William J. Burns, and Sidney H. Schnoll. 1986. "Prenatal Drug Exposure: Effects on Neonatal and Infant Growth and Development." *Neurobehavioral Toxicology and Teratology* 8: 357-362.

Chasnoff, Ira J., Dan R. Griffith, Catherine Freier, and James Murray. 1992. "Cocaine/Polydrug Use in Pregnancy: Two-Year Follow-up." *Pediatrics* 89 (2): 284-289.

Chasnoff, Ira J., Harvey J. Landress, and Mark E. Barrett. 1990. "The Prevalence of Illicit Drug or Alcohol Use during Pregnancy and Discrepancies in Mandatory Reporting in Pinellas County, Florida." *New England Journal of Medicine* 322 (17): 1202-1206.

Chavkin, Wendy, Cynthia R. Driver, and Pat Forman. 1989. "The Crisis in New York City's Perinatal Services." *New York State Journal of Medicine* 89 (12): 658-663.

Chi, I-Cheng, Deborah Gates, and Shyam Thapa. 1992. "Performing Tubal Sterilizations during Women's Postpartum Hospitalization: A Review of the United States and International Experiences." *Obstetrical and Gynecological Survey* 47 (2): 71-79.

Child Abuse Amendments of 1984. Pub. L. No. 98-457, sec. 121, 98 Stat. 1749.

"Child Abuse, 'Baby Doe' Legislation Cleared." 1985. *Congressional Quarterly Almanac, 1984.* Washington, D.C.: Congressional Quarterly, 482-484.

"Chipping Away at Roe." 1990. In National Issues Forum Staff, *The Battle over Abortion: Seeking Common Ground in a Divided Nation.* Dubuque, Iowa: Kendall/Hunt.

Clark, B. A., J. M. Bissonnette, S. B. Olson, and R. E. Magenis. 1989. "Pregnancy Loss in a Small Chorionic Villus Sampling Series." *American Journal of Obstetrics and Gynecology* 161 (2): 301-302.

Clayton, Ellen Wright. 1991. "Women and Advances in Medical Technologies: The Legal Issues." In *Women and New Reproductive Technologies: Medical, Psychosocial, Legal, and Ethical Dilemmas*, ed. Judith Rodin and Aila Collins. Hillsdale, N.J.: Lawrence Erlbaum Associates, 89-110.

Clement, Susan, Lori Goldstein, L. B. Krauss et al. 1987. "The Evolution of the Right to Privacy after *Roe v. Wade*." *American Journal of Law and Medicine* 13 (2-3): 368-525.

Cobb, Roger W., and Charles D. Elder. 1972. *Participation in American Politics: The Dynamics of Agenda-Building*. Boston: Allyn and Bacon.

Collins, M. S., and J. A. Bleyl. 1990. "Seventy-one Quadruplet Pregnancies: Management and Outcome." *American Journal of Obstetrics and Gynecology* 162: 1384-1392.

Committee to Defend Reproductive Rights. 1985. "Sterilization Abuse: Facts to Consider." *Newsnote* (August).

"Constitutional Limitations on State Intervention in Prenatal Care" (Note). 1981. *Virginia Law Review* 67 (3): 1051-1067.

Cook, Elizabeth Adell, Ted G. Jelen, and Clyde Wilcox. 1992. *Between Two Absolutes: Public Opinion and the Politics of Abortion*. Boulder, Colo.: Westview Press.

Corea, Gena. 1985. *The Mother Machine: Reproductive Technologies from Artificial Insemination to Artificial Wombs*. New York: Harper and Row.

Craig, Barbara Hinkson, and David M. O'Brien. 1993. *Abortion and American Politics*. Chatham, N.J.: Chatham House.

"Criminal Law and Procedure: Pregnant Defendant." 1989. *Daily Washington Law Reporter* 17: 441.

Crocetti, Annemarie F., Paul Mushak, and Joel Schwartz. 1990. "Determination of Numbers of Lead-Exposed Women of Childbearing Age and Pregnant Women." *Environmental Health Perspectives* 89 (2): 121-124.

Curie-Cohen, N., L. Luttrell, and S. Shapiro. 1979. "Current Practice of Artificial Insemination by Donor in the United States." *New England Journal of Medicine* 300: 585-590.

Curran, Maureen. 1984. "Silicone Plug Tubal Block May Achieve High Success Rate but Reversibility Questioned." *OB/GYN News* 14 (February): 1-14.

Cushner, Irvin M. 1986. "Reproductive Technologies: New Choices, New Hopes, New Dilemmas." *Family Planning Perspectives* 18 (3): 129-132.

D'Alton, Mary E., and Alan H. DeCherney. 1993. "Prenatal Diagnosis." *New England Journal of Medicine* 328 (2): 114-120.

Darney, Philip D., Cynthia M. Klaisle, Scott E. Monroe et al. 1992. "Evaluation of a One-Year Levonogestrel-Releasing Contraceptive Implant: Side Effects, Release Rates, and Biodegradability." *Fertility and Sterility* 58 (1): 137-143.

DiClemente, Ralph I. 1993. "Preventing AIDS among Adolescents: Schools as Agents of Behavior Change." *Journal of the American Medical Association* 270 (6): 760-762.

Diczfalusy, Egon. 1992. "Contraceptive Prevalence, Reproductive Health, and International Morality." *American Journal of Obstetrics and Gynecology* 166 (4): 1037-1043.

___. 1993. "Contraceptive Prevalence, Reproductive Health and Our Common Future." *Obstetrical and Gynecological Survey* 48 (5): 321-332.

Docksai, Mary Fiske. 1981. "Health Group Cites Multiple Violations of Medicaid Sterilization Rules." *Trial* 17 (10): 10.

Donovan, Patricia. 1990. "Funding Restrictions on Fetal Research: The Implications for Science and Health." *Family Planning Perspectives* 22 (5): 224-231.

Doyal, Lesley. 1988. "Women and the National Health Services." In *Reproductive Technologies: Gender, Motherhood, and Medicine*, ed. Michelle Stanworth. Minneapolis: University of Minnesota Press, 174-190.

Druzin, Maurice L., Frank Chervenak, Laurence B. McCullough et al. 1993. "Should All Pregnant Patients Be Offered Prenatal Diagnosis Regardless of Age?" *Obstetrics and Gynecology* 81 (4): 615-618.

Duff, Raymond, and A. G. M. Campbell. 1973. "Moral and Ethical Dilemmas in the Special-Care Nursery." *New England Journal of Medicine* 289 (17) (October 25): 890-894.

Edwards, Mary G. 1990. Teenage Childbearing: Redefining the Problem for Public Policy. Paper delivered to the annual meeting of the American Political Science Association, San Francisco, August 30.

Elias, Sherman, and George J. Annas. 1983. "Perspectives on Fetal Surgery." *American Journal of Obstetrics and Gynecology* 145 (4): 807-812.

Elias, Sherman, and George J. Annas, eds. 1992. *Gene Mapping: Using Law and Ethics as Guides*. New York: Oxford University Press.

Emergency Medical Treatment and Active Labor Act 42 U.S.C.A. 1395dd.

Ewigman, Bernard G., James P. Crane, and Frederic D. Frigoletto. 1993. "Effect of Prenatal Ultrasound Screening on Perinatal Outcome." *New England Journal of Medicine* 329 (12): 821-827.

Family Planning Services and Population Research Act, Pub. L. No. 91-572, 84 Stat. 1504 (1970).

Faux, Marian. 1989. *Roe v. Wade: The Untold Story of the Landmark Supreme Court Decision that Made Abortion Legal*. New York: New American Library.

Feinberg, Joel. 1973. *Social Philosophy*. Englewood Cliffs, N.J.: Prentice-Hall.

___. 1980. *Rights, Justice, and the Bounds of Liberty*. Princeton, N.J.: Princeton University Press.

Field, Martha A. 1987. "Surrogate Motherhood—The Legal Issues." *New York Law School Human Rights Annual* 4: 481-553.

___. 1988. *Surrogate Motherhood*. Cambridge, Mass.: Harvard University Press.

___. 1989. "Controlling the Woman to Protect the Fetus." *Law, Medicine, and Health Care* 17 (2): 114-129.

___. 1993. "Abortion Law Today." *Journal of Legal Medicine* 14: 3-24.

Fine, Alan. 1988. "The Ethics of Fetal Tissue Transplants." *Hastings Center Report* 18 (3): 5-8.

Fleming, Gretchen, et. al. 1990. "Infant Care Review Committees." *American Journal of the Diseases of Children* 144: 778-781.

Fletcher, John C. 1981. "The Fetus as a Patient: Ethical Issues." *Journal of the American Medical Association* 246 (77): 772-773.

___. 1983. "Emerging Ethical Issues in Fetal Therapy." In Kare Berg and Knut E. Tranoy, eds., *Research Ethics*. New York: Alan R. Liss.

___. 1993. "Human Fetal and Embryo Research: Lysenkoism in Reverse—How and Why?" In *Emerging Issues in Biomedical Policy, vol. 2*, ed. Robert H. Blank and Andrea L. Bonnicksen. New York: Columbia University Press, 200-231.

Fletcher, John C., and W. French Anderson. 1992. "Germ-line Gene Therapy: A New Stage of Debate." *Law, Medicine, and Health Care* 20 (1-2): 26-39.

Forrest, Jacqueline Darroch, and Susheela Singh. 1990. "Public-Sector Savings Resulting from Expenditures for Contraceptive Services." *Family Planning Perspectives* 22 (1): 6-15.

Fost, Norman. 1982. "Passive Euthanasia of Patients with Down's Syndrome." *Archives of Internal Medicine* 142 (5): 2295.

___. 1986. "Treatment of Seriously Ill and Handicapped Newborns." *Critical Care Clinics* 42 (2): 149-159.

___. 1989. "Maternal-Fetal Conflicts: Ethical and Legal Considerations." *Annals of the New York Academy of Sciences* 562: 248-254.

Franks, Darrell. 1981. "Psychiatric Evaluation of Women in a Surrogate Mother Program." *American Journal of Psychiatry* 138 (10) (October): 1378-1379.

Frederick, Winston, et al. 1987. "HIV Testing of Surrogate Mothers." *New England Journal of Medicine* 317 (21): 1351-1352.

Freed, Curt R., Robert E. Breeze, Neil L. Rosenberg et al. 1990. "Transplantation of Human Fetal Dopamine Cells for Parkinson's Disease: Results at One Year." *Archives of Neurology* 47: 505-512.

Freed, Curt R., Robert E. Breeze, and Neil L. Rosenberg. 1992. "Survival of Implanted Fetal Dopamine Cells and Neurologic Improvement 12 to 46 Months after Transplantation for Parkinson's Disease." *New England Journal of Medicine* 327 (22): 1549-1555.

Gallagher, Janet. 1987. "Prenatal Invasions and Interventions: What's Wrong with Fetal Rights?" *Harvard Women's Law Journal* 10: 9-58.

___. 1988. "Anxiety and the Law." In *Reproductive Technologies: Gender, Motherhood, and Medicine*, ed. Michelle Stanworth. Minneapolis: University of Minnesota Press, 139-150.

Galvan, Mary Elizabeth, attorney for Diane Pfannenstiel. Correspondence to the authors, March 12, 1990.

Garry, Daniel J., Arthur L. Caplan, Dorothy E. Vawter, and Warren Kearney. 1992. "Are There Really Alternatives to Use of Fetal Tissue from Elective Abortions in Transplantation Research?" *New England Journal of Medicine* 327 (22): 1592-1595.

Gash, Don M., and John R. Sladek. 1989. "Neural Transplantation: Problems and Prospects—Where Do We Go from Here?" *Mayo Clinic Proceedings* 64 (3): 363-367.

Ghidini, Alessandro, Waldo Sepulveda, Charles J. Lockwood, and Roberto Romero. 1993. "Complications of Fetal Blood Sampling." *American Journal of Obstetrics and Gynecology* 168 (5): 1339-1344.

Ginsburg, Faye D. 1989. *Contested Lives: The Abortion Debate in an American Community*. Berkeley: University of California Press.

Glass, Bentley. 1975. "Ethical Problems Raised by Genetics." In *Genetics and the Quality of Life*, ed. Charles Birch and Peter Albrecht. Sydney: Pergamon Press.

Goetz, Christopher G., C. Warren Olanow, and William C. Koller. 1989. "Multicenter Study of Autologous Adrenal Medullary Transplantation to the Corpus Striatum in Patients with Advanced Parkinson's Disease." *New England Journal of Medicine* 320 (6): 337-341.

Golbus, Mitchell S., Michael Harrison, Roy A. Filly et al. 1982. "In Utero Treatment of Urinary Tract Obstruction." *American Journal of Obstetrics and Gynecology* 142 (4): 383-386.

Gold, Michael. 1985. "The Baby Makers." *Science* 85 (April): 26-38.

Gold, Rachel B. 1990. *Abortion and Women's Health: A Turning Point for America?* New York: Alan Guttmacher Institute.

Gold, Rachel B., and Sandra Guardado. 1988. "Public Funding of Family Planning, Sterilization, and Abortion Services, 1987." *Family Planning Perspectives* 20 (5): 228-233.

Gold, Rachel B., and Dorothy Lehrman. 1989. "Fetal Research under Fire: The Influence of Abortion Politics." *Family Planning Perspectives* 21 (1): 6-11, 38.

Goodwin, Anne. 1992. "Determination of Legal Parentage in Egg Donation, Embryo Transplantation, and Gestational Surrogacy Arrangements." *Family Law Quarterly* 26 (3): 275-291.

Gordus, Enoch, Boris Tabakoff, David Goldman, and Kate Berg. 1990. "Finding the Gene(s) for Alcoholism." *Journal of the American Medical Association* 263 (15): 2094-2095.

Granberg, Donald, and James Burlison. 1983. "The Abortion Issue in the 1980 Elections." *Family Planning Perspectives* 15 (5): 231-238.

Green, Harold P. "Law and Genetic Control: Public Policy Questions." *Annals of the New York Academy of Sciences* 265 (1): 170-177.

Grimes, David A. 1986. "Reversible Contraception for the 1980s." *Journal of the American Medical Association* 255 (1): 69-74.

Grobstein, Clifford. 1981. *From Chance to Purpose: An Appraisal of External Human Fertilization.* Reading, Mass.: Addison-Wesley.

Gross, Richard, et al. 1983. "Early Management and Decision-making for the Treatment of Myelomeningocele." *Pediatrics* 72 (October): 450-458.

Guillemin, Jeanne Harley, and Lynda Lytle Holmstrom. 1986. *Mixed Blessings: Intensive Care for Newborns.* New York: Oxford University Press.

Haan, Ger. 1991. "Effects and Costs of In-Vitro Fertilization." *International Journal of Technology Assessment in Health Care* 7 (4): 585-593.

Hack, Maureen, and Avroy A. Fanaroff. 1989. "Outcomes of Extremely Low Birth-Weight Infants between 1982 and 1988." *New England Journal of Medicine* 321 (24): 1642-1647.

Haddow, James E., Glenn E. Palomaki, and George J. Knight. 1992. "Prenatal Screening for Down's Syndrome with Use of Maternal Serum Markers." *New England Journal of Medicine* 327 (9): 588-592.

Hanafin, Hilary. 1987. Surrogate Parenting: Reassessing Human Bonding. Paper delivered at a meeting of the American Psychological Association, New York City.

"Handicapped Groups Back 'Baby Doe' Rule." 1983. *Washington Post* (March 30).

Handyside, Alan H., John G. Lesko, Juan J. Tarin et al. 1992. "Birth of a Normal Girl after In Vitro Fertilization and Preimplantation Diagnostic Testing for Cystic Fibrosis." *New England Journal of Medicine* 327 (13): 905-909.

Hanna, Kathi E., Robert M. Cook-Deegan, and Robyn Y. Nishimi. 1993. "Finding a Forum for Bioethics in U.S. Public Policy." *Politics and the Life Sciences* 12 (2): 205-220.

Hanson, Frederick W., Frances Tennant, Stacy Hune, and Karen Brookhyser. 1992. "Early Amniocentesis: Outcome, Risks, and Technical Problems at $\leq$ 12.8 Weeks." *American Journal of Obstetrics and Gynecology* 166 (6): 1707-1711.

Hanson, Gayte. 1993. "Norplant Joins War on Teen Pregnancy." *Insight* (March 8): 96-101.

Harris, John. 1985. *The Value of Life: An Introduction to Medical Ethics.* New York: Routledge.

Harrison, M. R., N. S. Adzick, M. T. Longaker et al. 1990. "Successful Repair in Utero of a Fetal Diaphragmatic Hernia after Removal of Herniated Viscera from the Left Thorax." *New England Journal of Medicine* 322 (22): 1582-1584.

Harrison, Michael R., Mitchell S. Golbus, Roy A. Filly et al. 1982. "Fetal Surgery for Congenital Hydronephrosis." *New England Journal of Medicine* 306 (10): 591-593.

Hartz, Stuart C., Jane B. Porter, and Alan H. DeCherney. 1992. "National Documentation and Quality Assurance of Medically Assisted Conception: The Experience of the U.S. IVF Registry." In *Emerging Issues in Biomedical Policy, vol. 1,* ed. Robert H. Blank and Andrea L. Bonnicksen. New York: Columbia University Press, 252-261.

Hastings Center. 1976. "Treating the Defective Newborn." *Hastings Center Report* 6 (2): 2.

Hayes, C. V. 1992. "Genetic Testing for Huntington's Disease: A Family Issue." *New England Journal of Medicine* 327 (20): 1449-1451.

Healy, Bernadine. 1993. "The Pace of Human Gene Transfer Research Quickens." *Journal of the American Medical Association* 269 (5): 567.

Henshaw, Stanley K., and Jennifer Van Vort. 1989. "Teenage Abortion, Birth, and Pregnancy Statistics: An Update." *Family Planning Perspectives* 21 (2): 85-88.

___. 1994. "Abortion Services in the United States, 1991-1992." *Family Planning Perspectives* 26 (3): 100-112.

Hepburn, Lorraine. 1992. *Ova-Dose? Australian Women and the New Reproductive Technology.* Sydney: Allen and Unwin.

Hershey, Marjorie Randon, and Darrell M. West. 1983. "Single-Issue Politics: Prolife Groups and the 1980 Senate Campaign." In *Interest Group Politics,* ed. Allan J. Cigler and Burdett A. Loomis. Washington, D.C.: CQ Press, 31-59.

Hershlag, Avner, E. H. Kaplan, R. A. Loy, A. H. DeCherney, and G. Lavy. 1992. "Selection Bias in In Vitro Fertilization Programs." *American Journal of Obstetrics and Gynecology* 166 (1): 1-3.

Heyl, Barbara. 1988. "Commercial Contracts and Human Connectedness." *Society* 25 (3): 11-16.

"HHS to Publish Compromise 'Baby Doe' Rule." 1984. *Washington Post* (January 6).

Holden, Constance. 1991. "Probing the Complex Genetics of Alcoholism." *Science* 251 (4990): 163-164.

Holmes, Helen Bequaert. 1992. "Preface." In *Issues in Reproductive Technology I: An Anthology,* ed. Holmes. New York: Garland, ix-xii.

Houlgate, Laurence D. 1988. "Whose Child? *In re Baby M* and the Biological Preference Principle." *Logos* 9: 161-177.

Hubbard, Ruth. 1982. "Some Legal and Policy Implications of Recent Advances in Prenatal Diagnosis and Fetal Therapy." *Women's Rights Law Reporter* 7 (3): 201-218.

___. 1985. "Prenatal Diagnosis and Eugenic Ideology." *Women's Studies International Forum* 8 (6): 567-576.

___. 1990. *The Politics of Women's Biology.* New Brunswick, N.J.: Rutgers University Press.

Hunt, Vilma R. 1975. *Occupational Health Problems of Pregnant Women.* Washington, D.C.: Department of Health, Education, and Welfare.

Ingram, John Dwight. 1993. "Should In Vitro Fertilization Be Covered by Medical Expense Reimbursement Plans?" *American Journal of Family Law* 7 (2): 103-108.

Institute of Medicine. 1985. *Preventing Low Birthweight.* Washington D.C.: National Academy Press.

Isaacs, Stephen L., and Renee J. Holt. 1987. "Redefining Procreation: Facing the Issues." *Population Bulletin* 42 (3): 24-35.

Jackson, Laird G., Julia M. Zachary, Susan E. Fowler et al. 1992. "A Randomized Comparison of Transcervical and Transabdominal Chorionic-Villus Sampling." *New England Journal of Medicine* 327 (4): 594-598.

Johnsen, Dawn. 1986. "The Creation of Fetal Rights: Conflicts with Women's Constitutional Rights to Liberty, Privacy, and Equal Protection." *Yale Law Journal* 95 (3): 599-625.

Johnson, A. M., G. E. Palomaki, and J. E. Haddow. 1990. "Maternal Serum-α-Fetoprotein Levels in Pregnancies among Black and White Women with Fetal Open Spina Bifida: A United States Collaborative Study." *American Journal of Obstetrics and Gynecology* 162 (2): 328-331.

Joint Policy Statement. 1984. "Principles of Treatment of Disabled Infants." *Pediatrics* 73: 559-560.

"Judge to Decide on Triplets' Custody." 1994. *Arizona Republic* (January 4), A8.

"Judge Turns from Anger, Hoping to Help Addicted Mother." 1989. *Minneapolis Star Tribune.* (November 10), 1B, 4B.

Kaeser, Lisa. 1990. "Contraceptive Development: Why the Snail's Pace?" *Family Planning Perspectives* 22 (3): 131-134.

Kane, Elizabeth. 1988. *Birth Mother: America's First Legal Surrogate Mother Tells the Story of Her Change of Heart.* New York: Harcourt Brace Jovanovich.

Kaplan, Lawrence J., and Rosemarie Tong. 1994. *Controlling Our Reproductive Destiny: A Technological and Philosophical Perspective.* Cambridge, Mass.: MIT Press.

Kass, Leon R. 1979. "Implications of Prenatal Diagnosis for the Human Right to Life." In *Biomedical Ethics and the Law*, ed. J. M. Humber and R. F. Almeder. 2d ed. New York: Plenum, 335-350.

Kass, Nancy E. 1992. "Insurance for the Insurers: The Use of Genetic Tests." *Hastings Center Report* 22 (6): 6-11.

Kassirer, Jerome P., and Marcia Angel. 1992. "The Use of Fetal Tissue in Research on Parkinson's Disease." *New England Journal of Medicine* 327 (22): 1591-1592.

Katz, Zvi, Moshe Lancet, and Shmuel Shiber. 1986. "New Intracervical Contraceptive Device." *British Journal of Sexual Medicine* (May), 153-154.

Keane, Noel. 1989. "Perspectives on Surrogacy: Risks, Rewards, and Personal Choices." *Nova Law Review* 13 (2): 487-490.

Kern, Patricia A., and Kathleen M. Ridolfi. 1982. "The Fourteenth Amendment's Protection of a Woman's Right to Be a Single Parent through Artificial Insemination by Donor." *Women's Rights Law Reporter* 7 (3): 251-284.

Kerr, Kathleen. 1985. "Negotiating the Compromise." *Hastings Center Report* 15 (3): 6-7.

Kessler, David A., Jay P. Siegel, Philip D. Noguchi et al. 1993. "Regulation of Somatic-Cell Therapy and Gene Therapy by the Food and Drug Administration." *New England Journal of Medicine* 329 (16): 1169-1173.

Ketchum, Sara Ann. 1992. "Selling Babies and Selling Bodies." In *Feminist Perspectives in Medical Ethics*, ed. Helen B. Holmes and Laura M. Purdy. Bloomington: Indiana University Press, 284-294.

Kevles, Daniel J. 1986. *In the Name of Eugenics: Genetics and the Uses of Human Heredity.* Berkeley: University of California Press.

Kickler, T. S., K. Blakemore, R. S. Shirley et al. 1992. "Chorionic Villus Sampling for Fetal Rh Typing: Clinical Implications." *American Journal of Obstetrics and Gynecology* 166 (5): 1407-1411.

Klass, Perri. 1989. "The Perfect Baby?" *New York Times Magazine* (January 29), 45-46.

Klein, Renate Duelli. 1987. "What's 'New' about the 'New' Reproductive Technologies?" in *Man-Made Women: How New Reproductive Technologies Affect Women*, ed. Gena Corea. Bloomington: Indiana University Press, 64-73.

Klitsch, Michael. 1988. "FDA Approval Ends Cervical Cap's Marathon." *Family Planning Perspectives* 20 (3): 137-138.

Kolata, Gina. 1989. "More U.S. Curbs Urged in the Use of Fetal Tissue." *New York Times* (November 19), 1.

Kolbert, Kathryn. 1990. "A Reproductive Rights Agenda for the 1990s." In *From Abortion to Reproductive Freedom: Transforming a Movement*, ed. Marlene Gerber Fried. Boston: South End Press, 297-306.

Kolder, Veronika, Janet Gallagher, and Michael T. Parsons. 1987. "Court-Ordered Obstetrical Interventions." *New England Journal of Medicine* 316 (19): 1192-1196.

"Koop Acted as Midwife for New 'Baby Doe' Rule." 1984. *Washington Post* (January 10).

Kopelman, Loretta M., Thomas G. Irons, and Arthur Kopelman. 1988. "Neonatologists Judge the 'Baby Doe' Regulations." *New England Journal of Medicine* 318 (March 17): 677-683.

Krimmel, Herbert T. 1988. "Surrogate Mother Arrangements from the Perspective of the Child." *Logos* 9: 97-112.

Krimsky, Sheldon, Ruth Hubbard, and Colin Gracey. 1988. "Fetal Research in the United States: A Historical and Ethical Perspective." *Gene Watch* 5 (4-5): 1-3, 8-10.

Kuhse, Helga, and Peter Singer. 1985. *Should the Baby Live?* New York: Oxford University Press.

Ladd, Everett Carll. 1989. "Abortion—The Partisan Consequences—Trouble for Both Parties." *Public Opinion* 12 (1): 3-8.

Langfelder, Elinor J., and Eric T. Juengst. 1993. "Ethical, Legal and Social Implications (ELSI) Program." *Politics and the Life Sciences* 12 (2): 273-275.

Lantos, John D., Steven H. Miles, Marc D. Silverstein, and Carol B. Stocking. 1988. "Survival after Cardiopulmonary Resuscitation in Babies of Very Low Birth Weight." *New England Journal of Medicine* 318 (2): 91-95.

Laurikka-Routte, Marjut, and Maija Haukkamaa. 1992. "A Contraceptive Subdermal Implant Releasing the Progestin ST-1435: Ovarian Function, Bleeding Patterns, and Side Effects." *Fertility and Sterility* 58 (6): 1142-1147.

LeHew, Willette, L. 1992. "Teenage Pregnancy Prevention: The Vital Importance of the Medical Community's Involvement." *American Journal of Obstetrics and Gynecology* 167 (2): 299-302.

Lewis, Neil A. "Selection of Conservative Judges Insures a President's Legacy." *New York Times* (July 1, 1992), A13.

Lindvall, Olle, Patrik Brundin, Hakan Widner et al. 1990. "Grafts of Fetal Dopamine Neurons Survive and Improve Motor Function in Parkinson's Disease." *Science* 247 (4942): 574-577.

Lindvall, Olle, Stig Rehncrona, and Bjorn Gustavii. 1988. "Fetal Dopamine-Rich Mesencephalic Grafts in Parkinson's Disease" (letter). *Lancet* 2 (8626): 1483-1484.

Liskin, Laurie, and Richard Blackman. 1987. "Hormonal Contraception: New Long-acting Methods." *Population Reports*, Series K, no. 3, 57-87.

Lockwood, Charles J., Lauren Lynch and Richard I. Berkowitz. 1991. "Ultrasonographic Screening for the Down Syndrome Fetus." *American Journal of Obstetrics and Gynecology* 165 (2): 349-352.

Logli, Paul. 1990. "Drugs in the Womb: The Newest Battlefield in the War on Drugs." *Criminal Justice Ethics* 9 (1): 23-29.

London, Robert S. 1992. "The New Era in Oral Contraception: Pills Containing Gestodene, Norgestimate, and Desogestrel." *Obstetrical and Gynecological Survey* 47 (11): 777-782.

Luke, Barbara. 1994. "The Changing Patterns of Multiple Births in the United States: Maternal and Infant Characteristics, 1973 and 1990." *Obstetrics and Gynecology* 84 (1): 101-106.

Luker, Kristin. 1984. *Abortion and the Politics of Motherhood*. Berkeley: University of California Press.

Lyon, Jeff. 1986. *Playing God in the Nursery*. New York: W. W. Norton.

McCauley, A. P., and J. S. Geller. 1992. "Decisions for Norplant Programs." *Population Reports*, Series K, no. 4, 1-31.

Macklin, Ruth, and Willard Gaylin. 1981. *Mental Retardation and Sterilization: A Problem of Competency and Paternalism*. New York: Plenum.

McNulty, Molly. 1988. "Pregnancy Policy: The Health Policy and Legal Implications of Punishing Pregnant Women for Harm to Their Fetuses." *Review of Law and Social Change* 16: 277-319.

Madrazo, Ignacio, V. Léon, César Torres et al. 1988. "Transplantation of Fetal Substantia Nigra and Adrenal Medulla to the Caudate Nucleus in Two Patients with Parkinson's Disease" (letter). *New England Journal of Medicine* 318 (1): 51.

Mahowald, Mary B., Jerry Silver, and Robert A. Ratcheson. 1987. "The Ethical Options in Transplanting Fetal Tissue." *Hastings Center Report* 17 (1): 9-15.

Mains, Shelley, and Stephanie Poggi. 1990. "United We Are Going to Get Somewhere: Working Together for Lesbian/Gay Liberation and Reproductive Freedom." In *From Abortion to Reproductive Freedom: Transforming a Movement*, ed. Marlene Gerber Fried. Boston: South End Press.

Marshall, Allison B. 1992. "1992 Legislative Review." *Perinatal Addiction Research and Education Update* (October).

Martinez-Manautou, J., D. Hernandez, F. Alarcon, and S. Corren. 1991. "Introduction of Non-scalpel Vasectomy at the Mexican Social Security Institute." *Advances in Contraception* 7 (2-3): 193-197.

Merrick, Janna C. 1990. "In the Matter of Baby M: Implications for Surrogacy in the U.S." In *Beyond Baby M: Ethical Issues in New Reproductive Techniques*, ed. Dianne Bartels et al. Clifton, N.J.: Humana.

———. 1994. "Christian Science Healing of Minor Children: Spiritual Exemption Statutes, First Amendment Rights, and Fair Notice." *Issues in Law and Medicine* 10 (3): 321-342.

Merz, Beverly. 1989. "Gene Therapy Enters 'Second Generation.'" *American Medical News* (December 22-29), 3, 11.

Mies, Maria. 1987. "Sexist and Racist Implications of New Reproductive Technologies." *Alternatives* 12: 323-342.

Milbrath, Lester W. 1989. *Envisioning a Sustainable Society: Learning Our Way Out*. Albany: State University of New York Press.

Miringoff, Marque. 1989. "Genetic Intervention and the Problem of Stigma." *Policy Studies Review* 8 (2): 389-404.

Mohr, James C. 1978. *Abortion in America: The Origins and Evolution of National Policy, 1800-1900*. New York: Oxford University Press.

Morris, Leo, Charles W. Warren, and Sevgi O. Aral. 1993. "Measuring Adolescent Sexual Behaviors and Related Health Outcomes." *Public Health Reports* 108 (Supp. 1): 31-36.

Moskop, John C., and Rita L. Saldanha. 1986. "The Baby Doe Rule: Still a Threat." *Hastings Center Report* 16 (2): 8-14.

"MRI, SART, and AFS." 1990. *Fertility and Sterility* 55 (1): 14-23.

Mullen, Michelle A. 1992. *The Use of Human Embryos and Fetal Tissues: A Research Architecture.* Ottawa: Royal Commission on New Reproductive Technologies.

Mumford, Stephen D., and Elton Kessel. 1992a. "Sterilization Needs in the 1990s: The Case for Guinacrine Nonsurgical Female Sterilization." *American Journal of Obstetrics and Gynecology* 167 (5): 1203-1207.

___. 1992b. "Was the Dalkon Shield a Safe and Effective Intrauterine Device?" *Fertility and Sterility* 57 (6): 1151-1176.

Murphy, E. A., G. Chase, and A. Rodriguez. 1978. "Genetic Intervention: Some Social, Psychological, and Philosophical Aspects." In *Genetic Issues in Public Health and Medicine*, ed. B. H. Cohen, A. Lilienfeld, and P. C. Haung. Springfield, Ill.: Charles C. Thomas, 358-398.

Murray, Thomas H. 1985. "The Final, Anticlimactic Rule of Baby Doe." *Hastings Center Report* 15 (3): 5-9.

Murray, Thomas, and Arthur Caplan., eds. 1985. *Which Babies Shall Live?* Clifton, N.J.: Humana.

Nakamura, Robert T., and Frank Smallwood. 1980. *The Politics of Policy Implementation.* New York: St. Martin's Press.

National Abortion Rights Action League Foundation. 1993. *Who Decides? A State-by-State Review of Abortion Rights.*

National Center for Human Genome Research. 1990. *Understanding Our Genetic Heritage: The U.S. Human Genome Project.* Springfield, Va.: National Technical Information Service.

National Coalition Against Surrogacy. "Abuses in Surrogacy" (information sheet).

National Commission for the Protection of Human Subjects. 1975. *Research on the Fetus.* Washington, D.C.: U.S. Government Printing Office.

National Committee for Adoption. 1987. "Surrogate Parenting Issue and NCFA's Activities." *National Adoption Reports* 8 (1): 1-6.

National Conference of State Legislatures. 1989. "Bill Introductions in 1989 Legislative Sessions Relating to Surrogacy Contracts" (April 12).

___. 1993. "States with Surrogacy Laws" (December 1).

National Institute for Occupational Safety and Health. 1988. *Proposed National Strategies for the Prevention of Leading Work-Related Diseases and Injuries,* part 2. Washington, D.C.: Association of Schools of Public Health.

National Institutes of Health. 1988a. *Human Fetal Tissue Transplantation Research.* Report of the Advisory Committee to the Director. Bethesda, Md.: NIH (December 14).

___. 1988b. *Report of the Human Fetal Transplantation Research Panel.* Bethesda, Md.: NIH (September).

___. 1992. "National Institutes of Health Workshop Statement. Reproductive Genetic Testing: Impact on Women." *American Journal of Human Genetics* 51 (5): 1161.

National Issues Forum Staff. 1990. *The Battle over Abortion: Seeking Common Ground in a Divided Nation.* Dubuque, Iowa: Kendall/Hunt.

Nelkin, Dorothy. 1977. "Technology and Public Policy." In *Science, Technology, and Society,* ed. I. Spiegal-Rosing and D. DeSolla Price. Beverly Hills: Sage.

Nelkin, Dorothy, and Lawrence Tancredi. 1989. *Dangerous Diagnostics: The Social Power of Biological Information.* New York: Basic Books.

Nelson, Barbara J. 1984. *Making an Issue of Child Abuse: Political Agenda Setting for Social Problems.* Chicago: University of Chicago Press.

Nelson, Jeffrey R., Stephen L. Corson, Frances R. Batzer et al. 1993. "Predicting Success of Gamete Intrafallopian Transfer." *Fertility and Sterility* 60 (1): 116-122.

Nelson, Lawrence J., and Nancy Milliken. 1988. "Compelled Medical Treatment of Pregnant Women: Life, Liberty, and Law in Conflict." *Journal of the American Medical Association* 259 (7): 1060-1066.

Neumann, Peter J., and Magnus Johannesson. 1994. "The Willingness to Pay for In Vitro Fertilization: A Pilot Study Using Contingent Valuation." *Medical Care* 32 (7): 686-699.

Neumann, Peter J., Soheyla D. Gharib, and Milton C. Weinstein. 1994. "The Cost of a Successful Delivery with In Vitro Fertilization." *New England Journal of Medicine* 331 (4): 239-243.

Nevitte, Neil, William P. Brandon, and Lori Davis. 1993. "The American Abortion Controversy: Lessons from Cross-National Evidence." *Politics and the Life Sciences* 12 (1): 19-30.

New York State Task Force on Life and the Law. 1988. *Surrogate Parenting: Analysis and Recommendations for Public Policy.*

Nijs, Marine, Lieve Geerts, Elidé van Roosendaal et al. 1993. "Prevention of Multiple Pregnancies in an In Vitro Fertilization Program." *Fertility and Sterility* 59 (6): 1245-1250.

Nishimi, Robyn Y. 1993. "Cystic Fibrosis and DNA Tests—The Implications of Carrier Screening." *Journal of the American Medical Association* 269 (15): 1921.

Nolan, Kathleen. 1988. "Genug Ist Genug: A Fetus Is Not a Kidney." *Hastings Center Report* 18 (6): 13-19.

———. 1990. "Protecting Fetuses from Prenatal Hazards: Whose Crimes? What Punishment?" *Criminal Justice Ethics* 9: 13-23.

Nsiah-Jefferson, Laurie. 1989. "Reproductive Laws, Women of Color, and Low-Income Women." *Women's Rights Law Reporter* 11 (1): 15-38.

Oakley, Ann. 1988. "From Walking Wombs to Test-Tube Babies." In *Reproductive Technologies: Gender, Motherhood, and Medicine*, ed. Michelle Stanworth. Minneapolis: University of Minnesota Press, 36-56.

Office of Medical Applications of Research. National Institutes of Health. 1984. "The Use of Diagnostic Ultrasound Imaging during Pregnancy." *Journal of the American Medical Association* 252 (5): 669-672.

Office of Technology Assessment. U.S. Congress. 1985. *Reproductive Health Hazards in the Workplace.* Washington, D.C.: Government Printing Office.

———. 1988a. *Artificial Insemination: Practice in the United States.* Washington, D.C.: Government Printing Office.

———. 1988b. *Infertility: Medical and Social Choices.* Washington, D.C.: Government Printing Office.

———. 1990. *Neural Grafting: Repairing the Brain and Spinal Cord.* Washington, D.C.: Government Printing Office.

Overall, Christine. 1987. *Ethics and Human Reproduction: A Feminist Analysis.* New York: Routledge, Chapman and Hall.

———. 1992. "Selective Termination in Pregnancy and Women's Reproductive Autonomy." In *Issues in Reproductive Technology I: An Anthology*, ed. Helen Bequaert Holmes. New York: Garland, 145-160.

Overvold, Amy Zuckerman. 1988. *Surrogate Parenting.* New York: Pharos.

Paige, Constance, and Elisa B. Karnofsky. 1986. "The Antiabortion Movement and Baby Jane Doe." *Journal of Health Politics, Policy, and Law* 11 (Summer): 255-269.

Parker, Philip J. 1983. "Motivation of Surrogate Mothers: Initial Findings." *American Journal of Psychiatry* 140 (1): 117-118.

Penticuff, Joy Hinson. 1992. "The Impact of the Child Abuse Amendments on Nursing Staff and Their Care of Handicapped Newborns." In *Compelled Compassion: Government Intervention in the Treatment of Critically Ill Newborns*, ed. Arthur L. Caplan, Robert H. Blank, and Janna C. Merrick. Totowa, N.J.: Humana, 276-284.

Pergament, Eugene. 1993. "In Utero Treatment: Fetal Surgery." In *Emerging Issues in Biomedical Policy, vol. 2*, ed. Robert H. Blank and Andrea L. Bonnicksen. New York: Columbia University Press, 136-146.

Petchesky, Rosalind P. 1979. "Reproduction, Ethics, and Public Policy: The Federal Sterilization Regulations." *Hastings Center Report* 9 (5): 29-41.

___. 1980. "Reproductive Freedom: Beyond a Woman's Right to Choose." *Signs: Journal of Women in Culture and Society* 5: 661-685.

___. 1988. "Foetal Images: The Power of Visual Culture in the Politics of Reproduction." In *Reproductive Technologies: Gender, Motherhood, and Medicine*, ed. Michelle Stanworth. Minneapolis: University of Minnesota Press, 57-80.

___. 1990. *Abortion and Woman's Choice: The State, Sexuality, and Reproductive Freedom*. Rev. ed. Boston: Northeastern University Press.

Pierce, William. President, National Committee for Adoption. 1986. Social Services Professionals: Traffic Cops at the Intersection of Law and Medicine. Paper presented to the annual meeting of the American Society of Law and Medicine, Cambridge, Mass., October 18.

Platt, Lawrence D., and Dru E. Carlson. 1992. "Prenatal Diagnosis: When and How?" *New England Journal of Medicine* 327 (9): 636-638.

Platt, Lawrence D., Lisa Feuchtbaum, Roy Filly et al. 1992. "The California Maternal Serum and Fetoprotein Screening Program: The Role of Ultrasonography in the Detection of Spina Bifida." *American Journal of Obstetrics and Gynecology* 166 (5): 1328-1329.

Pomerance, Jeffrey, Teresita C. Yu, and Sharyn J. Brown. 1988. "Changing Attitudes of Neonatologists toward Ventilator Support." *Journal of Perinatology* 8 (3): 232-241.

President's Commission for the Study of Ethical Problems in Medicine and Biomedical and Behavioral Research. 1983. *Deciding to Forego Life-sustaining Treatment: A Report on the Ethical, Medical, and Legal Issues in Treatment Decisions* (March).

Pritchard, Jack A., Paul C. MacDonald, and Norman Gant. 1985. *William's Obstetrics*. Norwalk, Conn.: Appleton-Century-Crofts.

Ratsula, Kari. 1988. "Clinical Performance of a Levonorgestrel-releasing Intracervical Device during the First Year of Use." *Contraception* 36 (6): 659-664.

Rawlins, Richard G., Zvi Binor, Ewa Radwanska, and W. Paul Dmowski. 1988. "Microsurgical Enucleation of Tripronuclear Human Zygotes." *Fertility and Sterility* 50 (2): 266-272.

Raymond, Chris Anne. 1988. "In Vitro Fertilization Enters Stormy Adolescence as Experts Debate Odds." *Journal of the American Medical Association* 259 (4): 464-466.

Reagan, Michael D. 1992. *Curing the Crisis: Options for America's Health Care*. Boulder, Colo.: Westview Press.

Rehabilitation Act of 1973, 504, 29 U.S.C. 794 (1984).

Renfrow, Julia F. 1984. "The Child Abuse Amendments of 1984: Congress Is Calling North Carolina to Respond to the Baby Doe Dilemma." *Wake Forest Law Review* 20 (Winter): 975-1000.

"Reproductive Technology and the Procreation Rights of the Unmarried" (Note). 1985. *Harvard Law Review* 98 (3): 669-685.

"Respecting Differences: Private Lives and the Public Interest." 1990. In National Issues Forum Staff, *The Battle over Abortion: Seeking Common Ground in a Divided Nation*. Dubuque, Iowa: Kendall/Hunt.

"Rethinking Abortion: America's Most Divisive Issue." 1990. In National Issues Forum Staff, *The Battle over Abortion: Seeking Common Ground in a Divided Nation*. Dubuque, Iowa: Kendall/Hunt.

Rhoden, Nancy K. 1986a. "The Judge in the Delivery Room: The Emergence of Court Ordered Cesareans." *California Law Review* 74 (6): 1951-2030.

___. 1986b. "Treating Baby Doe: The Ethics of Uncertainty." *Hastings Center Report* 16 (4): 34-42.

Rhoden, Nancy K., and John D. Arras. 1985. "Withholding Treatment from Baby Doe: From Discrimination to Child Abuse." *Milbank Memorial Fund Quarterly* 63 (1): 18-51.

Robertson, John A. 1983a. "Medicolegal Implications of a Human Life Amendment." In *Defining Human Life*, ed. Margery W. Shaw and A. Edward Doudera. Ann Arbor: Health Administration Press, 161-173.

___. 1983b. "Procreative Liberty and the Control of Conception, Pregnancy, and Childbirth." *Virginia Law Review* 69 (3): 405-464.

___. 1988. "Rights, Symbolism, and Public Policy in Fetal Tissue Transplants." *Hastings Center Report* 18 (6): 5-12.

___. 1992. "Ethical and Legal Issues in Preimplantation Genetic Screening." *Fertility and Sterility* 57 (1): 1-11.

Robinson, Cherylon. 1993. "Surrogate Motherhood: Implications for the Mother-Fetus Relationship." *Women and Politics* 13 (3-4): 203-224.

Rose, Hilary. 1988. "Victorian Values in the Test Tube: The Politics of Reproductive Science and Technology." In *Reproductive Technologies: Gender, Motherhood, and Medicine*, ed. Michelle Stanworth. Minneapolis: University of Minnesota Press, 151-174.

Ross, John A. 1989. "Contraception: Short-Term vs. Long-Term Failure Rates." *Family Planning Perspectives* 21 (6): 275-277.

Rothman, Barbara Katz. 1986. *The Tentative Pregnancy: Prenatal Diagnosis and the Future of Motherhood*. New York: Viking.

___. 1987a. "Reproductive Technology and the Commodification of Life." *Women and Health* 13 (1) and 13 (2): 95-100.

___. 1987b. "Surrogacy: A Question of Values." *Conscience* 8 (3): 1-4.

Rowland, Robin. 1985. Quoted in *New Birth Technologies*, Wellington, New Zealand: Law Reform Commission, Department of Justice, 39.

Rubin, Alissa. 1991. "Interest Groups and Abortion Politics in the Post-*Webster* Era." In *Interest Group Politics*, ed. Allan J. Cigler and Burdett A. Loomis. Washington, D.C.: CQ Press, 239-256.

Ruzek, Sheryl. 1991. "Women's Reproductive Rights: The Impact of Technology." In *Women and New Reproductive Technologies: Medical, Psychosocial, Legal, and Ethical Dilemmas*, ed. Judith Rodin and Aila Collins. Hillsdale, N.J.: Lawrence Erlbaum Associates, 65-88.

Schenker, Joseph G., and Yossef Ezra. 1994. "Complications of Assisted Reproduction Techniques." *Fertility and Sterility* 61 (3): 411-422.

Schneider, William. 1989. "A Debate on Abortion—The Partisan Consequences—Trouble for the GOP." *Public Opinion* 12 (1): 2, 59-60.

Scriver, Charles R. 1985. "Population Screening: Report of a Workshop." *Progress in Clinical and Biological Research* 163B: 89-152.

Sellors, John W., James B. Mahony, Max A. Chernesky, and Darlyne J. Rath. 1988. "Tubal Factor Infertility: An Association with Prior Chlamydial Infection and Asymptomatic Salpingitis." *Fertility and Sterility* 49 (3): 451-456.

"Senate Passes Bill to Require Care of Deformed Babies." 1984. *Washington Post* (July 27).

Seoud, Muhieddine A. F., James P. Toner, Catherine Kruithoff, and Suheil J. Muasher. 1992. "Outcome of Twin, Triplet, and Quadruplet In Vitro Fertilization Pregnancies: The Norfolk Experience." *Fertility and Sterility* 57 (4): 825-834.

Shankaran, Seetha, Sanford N. Cohen, Marsha Linver, and Susan Zonia. 1988. "Medical Care Costs of High-Risk Infants after Neonatal Intensive Care: A Controlled Study." *Pediatrics* 81 (3): 372-378.

Shapiro, Donald L., and Paul Rosenberg. 1984. "The Effect of Federal Regulations Regarding Handicapped Newborns." *Journal of the American Medical Association* 252 (October 19): 2031-2033.

Shaw, Anthony. 1973. "Dilemmas of 'Informed Consent' in Children." *New England Journal of Medicine* 289: 885-890.

___. 1977. "Defining the Quality of Life." *Hastings Center Report* 7 (5): 11.

___. 1992. "Baby Doe and Me: A Personal Journey." In *Compelled Compassion: Government Intervention in the Treatment of Critically Ill Newborns*, ed. Arthur L. Caplan, Robert H. Blank, and Janna C. Merrick. Totowa, N.J.: Humana, 185-206.

Shaw, Anthony, Judson G. Randolph, and Barbara Manard. 1977. "Ethical Issues in Pediatric Surgery: A National Survey of Pediatricians and Pediatric Surgeons." *Pediatrics* 60 (October): 588-599.

Shaw, Margery W. 1984. "Conditional Prospective Rights of the Fetus." *Journal of Legal Medicine* 5 (1): 63-116.

Shevory, Thomas C. 1992. "Through a Glass Darkly: Law, Politics, and Frozen Human Embryos." In *Issues in Reproductive Technology I: An Anthology*, ed. Helen Bequaert Holmes. New York: Garland, 231-249.

Shihata, Alfred A., and Erica Gollub. 1992. "Acceptability of a New Intravaginal Barrier Contraceptive Device (Femcap)." *Contraception* 46: 511-517.

Shulman, L. P., and Sherman Elias. 1990. "Percutaneous Umbilical Blood Sampling, Fetal Skin Sampling, and Fetal Liver Biopsy." *Seminars in Perinatology* 14: 456-464.

Shy, Kirk K., Andy Stergachis, Louis G. Grothaus et al. 1992. "Tubal Sterilization and Risk of Subsequent Hospital Admission for Menstrual Disorders." *American Journal of Obstetrics and Gynecology* 166 (6): 1696-1706.

Simpson, Joe Leigh, and Sandra Ann Carson. 1992. "Preimplantation Genetic Diagnosis." *New England Journal of Medicine* 327 (13): 951-953.

Singer, Peter. 1993. *Practical Ethics*. 2d ed. New York: Cambridge University Press.

Singer, Peter, and Deane Wells. 1985. *Making Babies: The New Science and Ethics of Conception.* New York: Charles Scribner's Sons.

Singh, Kuldip, O. A. C. Viegas, and S. S. Ratnam. 1992. "Acceptability of Norplant-2 Rods as a Method of Family Planning." *Contraception* 45: 453-461.

Siperstein, Gary, Mark L. Wolraich, David Reed, and Paul O'Keefe. 1988. *Journal of Pediatrics* 113: 835-840.

Sivin, Irving, Janet Stern, and Soledad Diaz. 1992. "Rates and Outcomes of Planned Pregnancy after Use of Norplant Capsules, Norplant-2 Rods, or Levonorgestrel-releasing or Copper TCU 380 Ag Intrauterine Contraceptive Devices." *American Journal of Obstetrics and Gynecology* 166 (4): 1208-1213.

Skolnick, Andrew. 1990. "Religious Exemptions to Child Neglect Laws Still Being Passed Despite Convictions of Parents." *Journal of the American Medical Association* 264 (10): 1226-1233.

Smith, Lee. 1994. "The New Wave of Illegitimacy." *Fortune* (April 19): 81-90.

Smith, Ramada S., and Sidney F. Bottoms. 1993. "Ultrasonographic Prediction of Neonatal Survival in Extremely Low Birth-Weight Infants." *American Journal of Obstetrics and Gynecology* 169 (3): 490-493.

Snowden, Robert, G. D. Mitchell, and E. M. Snowden. 1983. *Artificial Reproduction.* London: George Allen and Unwin.

Society for Assisted Reproductive Technology. 1992. "In Vitro Fertilization-Embryo Transfer (IVF-ET) in the United States: 1990 Results from the IVF-ET Registry." *Fertility and Sterility* 57 (1): 15-25.

___. 1993. "Assisted Reproductive Technology in the United States and Canada: 1991 Results from the Society for Assisted Reproductive Technology Generated from the American Fertility Society Registry." *Fertility and Sterility* 59 (5): 956-962.

Soliman, Samuel, Salim Daya, John Collins, and John Jarrell. 1993. "A Randomized Trial of In Vitro Fertilization versus Conventional Treatment for Infertility." *Fertility and Sterility* 59 (6): 1239-1244.

Sor, Yvonne. 1986-1987. "Fertility or Unemployment: Should You Have to Choose?" *Journal of Law and Health* 1 (2): 141-228.

Spencer, Dennis D., Richard J. Robbins, Frederick Naftolin et al. 1992. "Unilateral Transplantation of Human Fetal Mesencephalic Tissue into the Caudate Nucleus of Patients with Parkinson's Disease." *New England Journal of Medicine* 327 (22): 1541-1548.

Stanford University Medical Center Committee on Ethics. 1989. "Special Report: The Ethical Use of Human Fetal Tissue in Medicine." *New England Journal of Medicine* 320 (16): 1093-1096.

Stanworth, Michelle. 1988. "Reproductive Technologies and the Deconstruction of Motherhood." In *Reproductive Technologies: Gender, Motherhood, and Medicine,* ed. Michelle Stanworth. Minneapolis: University of Minnesota Press, 10-35.

Staver, Sari. 1981. "Siamese Twins' Case 'Devastates' MDs." *American Medical News* 1 (October 9): 47-48.

Steel, Michael. 1993. "Cancer Genes: Complexes and Complexities." *Lancet* 342 (8874): 754-755.

Steinbrook, Robert. 1986. "In California, Voluntary Mass Prenatal Screening." *Hastings Center Report* 16 (5): 5-7.

Stinson, Peggy, and Robert Stinson. 1983. *The Long Dying of Baby Andrew.* Boston: Little, Brown.

Street, John. 1992. *Politics and Technology.* New York: Guilford Press.

Subak, Leslee L., G. David Adamson, and Nancy L. Boltz. 1992. "Therapeutic Donor Insemination: A Prospective Randomized Trial of Fresh versus Frozen Sperm." *American Journal of Obstetrics and Gynecology* 166 (6): 1597-1606.

Sulak, Patricia J., and Arthur F. Haney. 1993. "Unwanted Pregnancies: Understanding Contraceptive Use and Benefits in Adolescents and Older Women." *American Journal of Obstetrics and Gynecology* 168 (6): 2042-2048.

"Surrogate Mother Needed." 1988. *USA Today* (September 2), 5D.

"Take the Baby and Run." 1986. *Economist* (September 6), 27.

Tarin, Juan J., and Alan H. Handyside. 1993. "Embryo Biopsy Strategies for Preimplantation Diagnosis." *Fertility and Sterility* 59 (5): 943-952.

Todres, David, et al. 1977. "Pediatricians' Attitudes Affecting Decision-Making in Defective Newborns." *Pediatrics* 60 (2): 197-201.

Todres, David, et al. 1988. "Life-Saving Therapy for Newborns: A Questionnaire Survey in the State of Massachusetts." *Pediatrics* 81 (5): 643-649.

Tooley, William H., and Roderic Phibbs. 1976. "Neonatal Intensive Care: The State of the Art." In *Ethics of Newborn Intensive Care*, ed. Albert R. Jonsen and Michael J. Garland. San Francisco: Regents of the University of California.

Torres, Aida, and Asta M. Kenney. 1989. "Expanding Medicaid Coverage for Pregnant Women: Estimates of the Impact and Cost." *Family Planning Perspectives* 21 (1): 19-24.

Traugott, M., and M. Vinovskis. 1980. "Abortion and the Congressional Elections." *Family Planning Perspectives* 12 (5): 238-246

"Treating the Defective Newborn." 1976. *Hastings Center Report* 6 (2): 2.

Tribe, Laurence H. 1990. *Abortion: The Clash of Absolutes.* New York: W. W. Norton.

Trussell, James, and Barbara Vaughan. 1992. "Contraceptive Use Projections: 1990 to 2010." *American Journal of Obstetrics and Gynecology* 167 (4): 1160-1164.

Tushnet, Mark. 1984. "An Essay on Rights." *Texas Law Review* 62 (8): 1363-1403.

United States Commission on Civil Rights. 1989. *Medical Discrimination against Children with Disabilities* (September).

United States Congress. House of Representatives. 1982. Subcommittee on Select Education. *Hearings on Treatment of Infants Born with Handicapping Conditions* (September 16).

___. 1983. Subcommittee on Select Education. *Hearings on H.R. 1904* (March 9).

___. 1987a. Committee on Energy and Commerce. Subcommittee on Transportation, Tourism, and Hazardous Materials. *Hearing on the Surrogacy Arrangements Act of 1987* (October 15).

___. 1987b. Committee on Post Office and Civil Service. Subcommittee on Civil Service. *Hearing on Federal Employee Family-Building Act of 1987.* 100th Cong., 1st sess.

___. 1987c. Select Committee on Children, Youth, and Families. *Hearing on Alternative Reproductive Technologies: Implications for Children and Families.* 100th Cong., 1st sess.

___. 1988. Committee on Small Business. Subcommittee on Regulation and Business Opportunities. *Hearing on Consumer Protection Issues Involving In Vitro Fertilization Centers.* 100th Cong., 2d sess.

___. 1990. Committee on Education and Labor. *A Report on the EEOC, Title VII, and Workplace Fetal Protection Policies in the 1980s.* 101st Cong., 2d sess.

United States Congress. Senate. 1983. Subcommittee on Family and Human Services. *Hearings on Child Abuse Prevention and Treatment and Adoption Reform Act Amendments of 1983* (April 6, 11, 14).

United States. Department of Health and Human Services. 1982. Notice to Health Care Providers (May 18). 47 Fed. Reg. 26,027 (June 15).

___. 1983. Nondiscrimination on the Basis of Handicap. Interim Final Rule. 48 Fed. Reg. 9630 (modifying 45 C.F.R. 84.61).

___. 1984. Nondiscrimination on the Basis of Handicap. Procedures and Guidelines Relating to Health Care of Handicapped Infants. Final Rule. 49 Fed. Reg. 1622 (codified at 45 C.F.R. 84.55).

___. 1985. Child Abuse and Neglect Prevention and Treatment Program (April 15). Final Rule. 50 Fed. Reg. 14,878 (codified at 45 C.F.R. pt. 1340).

___. 1987a. *Infant Care Review Committees under the Baby Doe Program* (September).

___. 1987b. *Survey of State Baby Doe Programs* (September).

___. National Institute on Drug Abuse. 1989. "NIDA Capsules: Drug Abuse and Pregnancy" (June).

United States. Department of Justice. 1991. Bureau of Justice Statistics. "National Update 10."

Vanderveen, Ernestine. 1989. "Public Health Policy: Maternal Substance Use and Child Health." *Annals of the New York Academy of Sciences* 562: 255-259.

Vawter, Dorothy E. 1993. "Fetal Tissue Transplantation Policy in the United States." *Politics and the Life Sciences* 12 (1): 79-85.

Vawter, Dorothy E., Warren Kearney, Karen G. Gervais et al. 1990. *The Use of Human Fetal Tissue: Scientific, Ethical, and Policy Concerns.* Minneapolis: Center for Biomedical Ethics.

Veit, Christina R., and Raphael Jewelawicz. 1988. "Gender Preselection: Facts and Myths." *Fertility and Sterility* 49 (6): 937-940.

Wagner, Marsden G., and Patricia A. St. Clair. 1989. "Are In-Vitro Fertilization and Embryo Transfer of Benefit to All?" *Lancet* 1989 (October 28): 1027-1030.

Walther, Deborah Kay. 1992. " 'Ownership' of the Fertilized Ovum In Vitro." *Family Law Quarterly* 26 (3): 235-256.

Warren, Kenneth. 1985. "Alcohol-Related Birth Defects: Current Trends in Research." *Alcohol Health and Research World* 10: 4-5.

Warsof, Steven L., Derek J. Cooper, David Little, and Stuart Campbell. 1986. "Routine Ultrasound Screening for Antenatal Detection of Intrauterine Growth Retardation." *Obstetrics and Gynecology* 67 (1): 33-38.

Wasserstrom, Richard. 1964. "Rights, Human Rights, and Racial Discrimination." *The Journal of Philosophy* 61 (20): 628-641.

Watson, James D. 1990. "The Human Genome Project: Past, Present and Future." *Science* 248: 44-48.

Weir, Robert. 1984. *Selective Nontreatment of Handicapped Newborns: Moral Dilemmas in Neonatal Medicine.* New York: Oxford University Press.

___. 1987. "Pediatric Ethics Committees: Ethical Advisers or Legal Watchdogs?" *Law, Medicine, and Health Care* 15 (3): 99-109.

Weiss, Rick. 1989. "Bypassing the Ban." *Science News* 136 (November 5): 378-379.

Wilcox, Lynne S., and William D. Mosher. 1993. "Use of Infertility Services in the United States." *Obstetrics and Gynecology* 82 (1): 122-127.

Wilcox, Lynne S., Herbert S. Peterson, Florence P. Haseltine, and Mary C. Martin. 1993. "Defining and Interpreting Pregnancy Success Rates for In Vitro Fertilization." *Fertility and Sterility* 60 (1): 18-25.

Will, George. 1982. "The Killing Will Not Stop." *Washington Post* (April 22).

Williams, John III, Boris B. T. Wang, Cathi H. Rubin, and Dawn Aiken-Hunting. 1992. "Chorionic Villus Sampling: Experience with 3016 Cases Performed by a Single Operator." *Obstetrics and Gynecology* 89 (6): 1023-1029.

Williamson, R. A., C. P. Weiner, W. T. C. Yuh, and M. M. Abu-Yousef. 1989. "Magnetic Resonance Imaging of Anomalous Fetuses." *Obstetrics and Gynecology* 73 (6): 952-957.

Woliver, Laura R. 1989. "New Reproductive Technologies: Challenges to Women's Control of Gestation and Birth." In *Biomedical Technology and Public Policy,* ed. Robert H. Blank and Miriam K. Mills. Westport, Conn.: Greenwood Press, 43-46.

Yazigi, Ricardo A., Randall R. Odem, and Kenneth L. Polakoski. 1991. "Demonstration of Specific Binding of Cocaine to Human Spermatozoa." *Journal of the American Medical Association* 266 (14): 1956-1959.

Zaner, Richard M., and Mark D. Fox. 1993. "Selective Termination and Moral Risk: Choices and Responsibility." In *Emerging Issues in Biomedical Policy, vol. 2,* ed. Robert H. Blank and Andrea L. Bonnicksen. New York: Columbia University Press.

Zaneveld, Lourens J. D., James W. Burns, Stan Beyler, William Depel, and Seymour Shapiro. 1988. "Development of a Potentially Reversible Vas Deferens Occlusion Device and Evaluation in Primates." *Fertility and Sterility* 49 (3): 527-533.

Zatuchni, Gerald I., Alfredo Goldsmith, Jeffrey M. Spieler, and John J. Sciarra, eds. 1986. *Male Contraception: Advances and Future Prospects.* New York: Harper and Row.

Zelizer, Viviana A. 1988. "From Baby Farms to Baby M." *Society* 25 (3): 23-28.

Zimmerman, Burke K. 1991. "Human Germ-Line Therapy: The Case for Its Development and Use." *Journal of Medicine and Philosophy* 16 (6): 593-612.

Zohar, Noam J. 1991. "Prospects for 'Genetic Therapy'—Can a Person Benefit from Being Altered?" *Bioethics* 5 (4): 275-288.

Table of Court Cases

Index

About the Authors

Robert Blank holds the Chair of Political Science at the University of Canterbury, Christchurch, New Zealand. He received his Ph.D. from the University of Maryland. Among his numerous books and articles on biomedical policy are *Rationing Medicine* (1988), *Regulating Reproduction* (1990), *Fertility Control* (1991), *Mother and Fetus* (1992), *Fetal Protection in the Workplace* (1993), and *Biomedical Policy* (1995).

Janna C. Merrick is associate dean and professor of government and international affairs at the University of South Florida. She received her Ph.D. from the University of Washington. She is the coeditor of *Compelled Compassion: Government Intervention in the Treatment of Critically Ill Newborns* (1992), *The Politics of Pregnancy: Policy Dilemmas in the Maternal-Fetal Relationship* (1993), and *Encyclopedia of Biomedical Policy* (1994).